Cohabitation

An Alternative Form
of Family Living

Zheng Wu

OXFORD
UNIVERSITY PRESS

OXFORD
UNIVERSITY PRESS

70 Wynford Drive, Don Mills, Ontario M3C 1J9
www.oupcan.com

Oxford University Press is a department of the University of Oxford.
It furthers the University's objective of excellence in research, scholarship,
and education by publishing worldwide in

Oxford New York

Athens Auckland Bangkok Bogotá Buenos Aires Calcutta
Cape Town Chennai Dar es Salaam Delhi Florence Hong Kong Istanbul
Karachi Kuala Lumpur Madrid Melbourne Mexico City Mumbai
Nairobi Paris São Paulo Singapore Taipei Tokyo Toronto Warsaw

with associated companies in Berlin Ibadan

Oxford is a trade mark of Oxford University Press
in the UK and in certain other countries

Published in Canada
by Oxford University Press

Copyright © Oxford University Press Canada 2000

The moral rights of the author have been asserted

Database right Oxford University Press (maker)

First published 2000

Canadian Cataloguing in Publication Data

Wu, Zheng, 1960-
Cohabitation : an alternative form of living
(Studies in Canadian Population)
Includes bibliographical references and index.
ISBN 0-19-541378-4
1. Unmarried couples - Canada. I. Title. II. Series.

HQ560.W82 2000   306.84   C00-931049-5

Cover & Text Design: Tearney McMurtry
1 2 3 4 - 03 02 01 00

This book is printed on permanent (acid-free) paper ∞
Printed in Canada

Contents

Preface

Not so long ago, when Harry met Sally, so goes the romance in the movie, they fell in love. He proposed to her. She accepted. Although the movie ends here, movie-goers would not have much trouble imagining the rest of the story: they would marry, then start a family, and probably remain married 'till death do them part'. For centuries, the Western family had centred on the institution of marriage. The only other acceptable alternative to marriage was to remain single. For many people, living together without being legally married was unthinkable, unethical, and immoral.

All that has changed since early 1970s. The number of unmarried people who choose to live together has increased dramatically. Between 1981 and 1996 in Canada, the number of heterosexual cohabiting couples more than doubled, from 356,000 to over 920,000. During the same period, heterosexual cohabiting unions, which are known as common-law unions in Canada, increased from 6 per cent to 14 per cent of all (heterosexual) unions. Cohabitation as a lifestyle choice is particularly popular in the largely Francophone province of Quebec. Currently, nearly one out of four heterosexual couples in Quebec is not married, compared to one out of nine elsewhere in Canada. In fact, almost one-half (43.4 per cent) of all heterosexual cohabiting couples in Canada are now residing in the province of Quebec.

The principal purpose of this book is to provide a social-demographic perspective on heterosexual unmarried cohabitation. It documents the trends in cohabitation, explores the explanations of these trends, and discusses their consequences for individuals and society. It provides a detailed individual-level analysis of unmarried cohabitation using the most recent national data available. It covers such topics as attitudes towards non-marital sexual behaviour and marriage, the transition into and out of cohabitation, child-bearing in cohabitations, and the division of household labour in cohabiting families. It is my observation that unmarried heterosexual cohabitation has become not just a prelude to legal marriage, but increasingly an alternative form of family living. All indicators seem to suggest that, for at least the coming decade, the trends in cohabitation will continue. While readers may not agree with all of my conclusions, it is my hope that they will benefit from these analyses and be able to draw their own conclusions.

Many people have contributed to this book. First, I wish to thank Frank Trovato of the University of Alberta for inviting me to contribute to Oxford's Studies in Canadian Population Series. As series editor, he provided support and direction at all stages of this study. His suggestions concerning the organization, style, and content of the manuscript are greatly appreciated.

I would like to thank Daniel J. Koenig, who introduced me to the field of demography and who continues to share his insights and wisdom on population issues. I also wish to thank many former teachers at the University of Western Ontario, particularly Thomas K. Burch, Roderic Beaujot, Rajulton Fernando, Kevin McQuillan, Eddie Ebanks, Carl Grindstaff, Douglas Baer, and Paul Maxim, who have taught me and influenced, in small and large ways, what I know, how I think, and what I can do. In particular, I wish to extend my special appreciation to T.R. Balakrishnan of the University of Western Ontario. As my teacher, supervisor, mentor, and colleague, T.R. Balakrishnan has had more influence on my approach to demographic problems than anyone else in my academic career. His work on fertility, family planning, marriage, and urban sociology have stimulated much of my own research in these and other areas. I am grateful for his wisdom, guidance, and friendship over the last decade. As a longtime collaborator, T.R. Balakrishnan contributed directly to the writing of this book—portions of the research reported in Chapters 6 and 8 are based on our past work together. He is a co-author of these chapters.

Much of this project was conducted while I was on study leave from the University of Victoria. I wish to thank the university and the Department of Sociology for its support. I would also like to thank my colleagues in the department, particularly R. Alan Hedley, Cecilia Benoit, Mikael Jansson, Morgan Baker, and Bill McCarthy, for sharing their ideas and insights with me and for providing support and encouragement. Special thanks are due to Michael Pollard, my research assistant, former student, and colleague, who carefully produced the figures and tables and studiously read and edited many drafts of this manuscript. Thanks are also due to Randy Hart for proofreading the manuscript, and to the staff in the department, Carole Rains and Catherine Sanden, for sharing the administrative responsibilities for this project.

I am also grateful to several federal and provincial agencies that funded parts of this project: the Social Science and Humanities Research Council of Canada, the British Columbia Health Research Foundation, and Statistics Canada. Particularly, I would like to acknowledge my gratitude to Statistics Canada for making the General Social Survey data available to me, and to the Population Studies Centre at the University of Western Ontario for permission to access data from the Canadian Fertility Survey.

Portions of Chapter 6 are based on Zheng Wu and T.R. Balakrishnan, 'Cohabitation after marital dissolution in Canada', *Journal of Marriage and the*

Family 56, 3 (1994): 723–34, used with the permission of the National Council on Family Relations. Portions of Chapter 7 are based on Zheng Wu, 'Childbearing in cohabitation relationships', *Journal of Marriage and the Family* 58, 2 (1996): 281–92, used with the permission of the National Council on Family Relations. Parts of Chapter 8 are based on Zheng Wu and T.R. Balakrishnan, 'Dissolution of premarital cohabitation in Canada', *Demography* 32, 4 (1995): 521–32, used with the permission of the Population Association of America. Finally, portions of Chapter 9 are based on Zheng Wu, 'Premarital cohabitation and the timing of first marriage', *Canadian Review of Sociology and Anthropology* 36, 1 (1999): 109–27, used with permission of the Canadian Sociology and Anthropology Association.

Several individuals at Oxford University Press Canada helped me from the beginning to the completion of this book. I am indebted to Euan White, Laura Macleod, Len Husband, and Phyllis Wilson for their encouragement and support. I am particularly grateful to Richard Tallman, who carefully copy-edited the entire manuscript.

Numerous people have read all or portions of the manuscript and provided generous comments concerning organization, analysis, and presentation. In particular, I would like to thank two anonymous reviewers, who provided invaluable suggestions. The final version of the book has benefited greatly from their input.

Finally, I wish to express my deep appreciation of my wife, Lanjing Li, for her patience, support, encouragement, and love, despite the burden of her own demanding work and studies.

1 | Introduction

This is a book about an emerging form of family living—cohabitation or common-law union. These unions consist of opposite-sex couples who choose to live together in a family setting without being legally married. In this book I detail its incidence, trends, and patterns. I also explain its process by describing how it begins and ends. Finally, I discuss the consequences of cohabitation for individuals and society.

Since 1981, when the Canadian census first began to collect data on cohabitation, the demographics of this new family form have changed dramatically. For example, the number of cohabiting-couple families increased from 356,600 in 1981 to over 920,640 in 1996. One in every seven families currently involves unmarried couples, compared to one in 17 only 15 years ago.

About half of cohabiting couples' families also include children, either born to the cohabiting couple or brought into the family from previous relationships. Over two-thirds of cohabiting persons have never been married, and over a quarter are divorced.

Cohabitation is a particularly popular lifestyle in the province of Quebec. Cohabitation is also common among young Canadians. The 1996 Canadian census shows that 37 per cent of the women and 28 per cent of the men that cohabited were under age 30. Indeed, 40 per cent of all Canadians aged 15–29 living in couple relationships are unmarried.

Cohabitations are often short-lived. Over half of cohabiting unions end within three years (Burch and Madan, 1986; Wu and Balakrishnan, 1995). However, these unions are more likely to end in marriage than in separation: about one-third of cohabiting couples marry each other within three years of cohabitation, while another quarter dissolve their relationships through separation.

What do these statistics mean? Why are more people choosing non-marital cohabitation as an alternative form of family living these days? It may be that the dramatic increase in cohabitation reflects the changing norms regarding sexual behaviour outside of marriage. Studies have shown that since the turn of the century there has been a gradual increase in the rate of premarital sex, and the rate of this increase has been accelerating since the 1960s (Hobart, 1984; McLaughlin et al., 1988; Modell, 1989; Shorter, 1975). Along with these changes, there has been a shift in public attitudes regarding premarital sex; men and women are increasingly accepting the notion of 'sex for fun'. Sexual activities have been accepted not only for reproductive purposes, but also for physical pleasure and as an expression of love, affection, and intimacy. Family scholars and demographers have interpreted this shift in sexual attitudes as an indication of the growth of individualism in the Western world. Belgian demographer Ron Lesthaeghe characterizes the rise in individualistic ideology as 'an ideational change' that emphasizes individual autonomy, the importance of self-fulfilment, and the rejection of external institutional authority (Lesthaeghe, 1983; Lesthaeghe and Surkyn, 1988). From this perspective the upward trend in cohabitation is a result of a gradual erosion of societal norms concerning family life, in general, and sexuality, in particular.

The rise in cohabitation may also be a response to changing sex roles, particularly the role of women in our society. Since World War II, women's participation in the paid labour force has steadily increased. Today women make up nearly one-half of all employed Canadians (45 per cent), with two-thirds of mothers with children under age 16 working outside the home.[1] The rise in women's labour force participation, particularly among married women with young children, is attributable to the increase in women's wage rates, women's education, the growth of service industries, the rising demand for clerical jobs, and the deteriorating position of young men in the labour market (Espenshade, 1985; Oppenheimer, 1994). It is not difficult to see that the rise in women's wage rates and the availability of employment opportunities make staying at home a very expensive proposition for married women. The deterioration in young men's economic position in recent years also makes it difficult for a young man alone to support a two-parent family.

Economist Gary Becker (1981) argued that men and women marry only if both will gain from marriage. The primary gains from marriage come from their comparative advantages at home and in the labour market. Implicit in this argument is that women have a greater comparative advantage over men in home production, whereas men have a greater advantage over women in the workplace. As women become more like men in terms of their labour market activities, the incentive for people to marry will decline. If non-marital cohabitation provides young people with an alternative form of family living and a way of avoiding singlehood, while still retaining the freedom to pursue their careers, many may choose to cohabit. Cohabiting also provides other benefits of the single state, such as requiring less commitment to the relationship and fewer legal responsibilities, as well as benefits of the married state, such as sharing residence and pooling resources (Oppenheimer, 1994). In short, the rise in cohabitation may also be a result of changing external circumstances, particularly structural changes in our economy, that make cohabitation a viable lifestyle choice.

Demographic trends are interrelated. The recent trend in cohabitation has important implications for the changing patterns of marriage and the family. As in many other Western countries, young Canadians today are increasingly reluctant to marry, and the likelihood that they never will marry has probably reached an all-time high. Cohabiting may well be a major factor in recent marriage patterns for two reasons. The first is the intuitive notion that cohabitation delays marriage simply because it takes time to experience cohabitation. This may be particularly true when cohabitations do not later become marriages (Oppenheimer, 1994). The second reason is that cohabitation is selective. Not everyone chooses to cohabit. Research suggests that people who cohabit tend to have less conventional views towards marriage or see themselves as poor risks in terms of a long-term relationship (Axinn and Thornton, 1992; Thomson and Colella, 1992; also see Chapter 9). In accordance with its definition, cohabitation does not imply a long-term relationship and commitment for many people. Therefore, it is reasonable to expect that people who choose to cohabit are less likely to make a long-term commitment to their partner or to the institution of marriage than those who choose not to cohabit. To these people, cohabitation may be seen as an institutional form of family living alternative to traditional marriage. Many may indeed opt out of marriage altogether.

Surely not every cohabiting couple chooses to avoid marriage completely. Indeed, many cohabiting couples eventually marry each other. From this point of view, cohabitation seems to perform the function of a 'trial marriage', weeding out the 'bad matches' from the assortative mating process and keeping the good ones. The good matches tend to turn into marriages. Intuitively, we would expect that these marriages should be more stable and last longer than marriages that were not preceded by cohabitation. However, evidence is clearly not in favour of our intuition. Premarital cohabitation raises the risk of subsequent divorce (Balakrishnan et al., 1987; Bennett et al., 1988; Burch and Madan, 1986; also see Chapter 8).

Why do cohabitors have a higher risk of divorce? Again, it may be the self-selective process of cohabitation. Because people who cohabited prior to marriage are generally less religious and conventional, they are probably less hesitant to end their marriages when they encounter marital problems than people who did not cohabit before marriage. Moreover, the experience of living together may itself also be a factor. Living together without marriage can change a couple's views of marriage and divorce, and foster less conventional attitudes regarding marriage and family life. There is evidence that the experience of cohabitation increases young people's acceptance of divorce in the United States (Axinn and Thornton, 1992).

The dramatic rise in cohabitation also has important consequences for marriage and the family as social institutions. The recent changes in family patterns have attracted not only scholarly attention, but that of the media and public as well. For example, according to a 1994 Angus Reid survey featured in *Maclean's*, 63 per cent of Canadians believed that the family is in crisis (Nemeth, 1994).

'Family in Crisis' also was the theme of the 1986 conference of the Federation of Canadian Demographers.

However, the notion that the family is in crisis is not new. As sociologist William Goode (1976: 513) wrote, 'According to eyewitnesses, the family has been in a state of constant decline for several hundred years.' For generations, observers predicted that the family as known to their grandparents' generation would not survive much longer. But, as we now know, the institutions of marriage and the family have been changing and always adapting to the new environment, and they show no signs of disappearing in the immediate future. Most young people still wish to get married, and most eventually do.

Perhaps the most disturbing news is that the chance a marriage will end in divorce has been rising steadily, while the rate of remarriage has been declining. These trends may suggest a growing disillusionment with the institution of marriage. Do divorced people prefer the single state? The answer appears to be 'no'. It is becoming clear that cohabitation is now a popular alternative union choice among divorced people (Blanc, 1987; Bumpass and Sweet, 1989; Wu and Balakrishnan, 1994). A significant number of these people will eventually marry their partners.

Demographer Robert Schoen (1989) argued that non-marital cohabitation poses a greater challenge to the institution of marriage than does divorce. This is because, although both undermine the permanence of marriage, only cohabitation can substitute for marriage as an alternative form of family living. The rising delays in marriage and the increasing chance of never marrying both provide evidence for the view that cohabitation has increasingly become an alternative to traditional marriage. In fact, evidence shows that the upward trend in cohabitation has compensated for much (but not all) of the decline in marriage rates for young people. The overall rates of union formation in North America have declined less in recent decades than might be imagined (Bumpass et al., 1991; Burch and Madan, 1986; Wu, 1999a).

The Study and Its Goals

Although non-marital cohabitation has been practised for centuries in Western and other civilizations, the rapid increase in cohabitation in recent years caught most of us, academe and public alike, by surprise. The rising popularity of cohabitation raises important concerns about its implications for the members of this new family form and for the future of marriage. It is important now to take a close look at the trends and patterns of cohabitation and identify the forces underlying these patterns. So far there has been no Canadian national study that systematically examines the process of non-marital cohabitation as an alternative institutional form. This book intends to use national census and survey data to document the trends and patterns of cohabitation, examine the formation and dissolution of cohabiting unions, explain what has been going on, and talk about the implications of this 'new' phenomenon. It is my view that the rapid increase in cohabitation has fundamentally changed the institutions of marriage and the family, and that 'the family', formerly defined in traditional terms, should be redefined to include cohabiting families that may or may not involve children belonging to one or both partners.

The reliance here on a social-demographic perspective and methodology partly reflects the nature of the subject in question and partly reflects my training as a social demographer. There is little dispute that cohabitation is now as important a demographic process as are marriage or divorce, owing partly to the sheer number of Canadians who are choosing to live in this alternative family form. While I approach the problem from a social-demographic point of view, I do not negate the importance of the advances made by social scientists in other disciplines, notably economics and psychology. In fact, the economic theory of family, particularly the work of Gary Becker, has influenced and shaped much of my own thinking and understanding of the changing family patterns in recent decades. As the reader will see in the following chapter, my theoretical analysis of cohabitation comprehends economic, sociological, and demographic considerations. It seems to me that no single theory alone can encompass and explain the phenomenon of cohabitation.

Like many books with a demographic focus, this book involves numbers. However, the numbers are used only to the extent that they facilitate the understanding of the arguments being made. In presenting the demographics of this new family form, I draw on the findings of many first-hand analyses carried out exclusively for the writing of this book. I also draw on the results of my earlier studies, as well as those of my Canadian colleagues and those in the United States and Western Europe. In carrying out the empirical analyses, I rely on national data collected by Statistics Canada. Specifically, the study relies on two data sources. The first of these, the Canadian census from 1981 onward, is used to examine the trends and patterns of cohabitation. The second data source includes primarily two cycles of the General Social Survey conducted by Statistics Canada in 1990 and 1995 as well as the 1984 Canadian Fertility Survey. These survey data are used to investigate the factors that may affect the changing trends and patterns of cohabitation.

Given the scope of this study, certain topics have had to be excluded. Because the focus is on the demographic aspect of cohabitation, the study does not have much to say about its psychological dimension or its economic consequences. For example, personality, sexual promiscuity, self-esteem, attitudes, and economic hardships may all have some bearing on the decision to cohabit. Similarly, the experience of cohabitation may have an impact on the quality of subsequent marital relationships, power relationships between the partners, and the economics of the partnership (see, e.g., Macklin, 1983; Newcomb, 1979; Tanfer, 1987).

My reliance on census data and national surveys also limits the focus of the study to heterosexual couples. This decision does not mean that studies on other alternative lifestyles, such as same-sex relationships, communal living, and group cohabitation, are not important, but simply that the number of people involved in these lifestyles is relatively small at the national level. For example, while a few recent national surveys have begun collecting information on same-sex relationships, the incidence of same-sex union is invariably uncommon, making any generalization questionable.[2] For this and other reasons, the Canadian census has yet to collect information on people living in these and other alternative lifestyles. The numbers of Canadians living in many of these unconventional lifestyles remain largely unknown statistics. The same can be said for the incidence of cohabitation before 1981, when the Canadian census first began to collect information on unmarried heterosexual cohabitation.

The use of census and national survey data also makes it necessary to rely on the census and survey definitions of cohabitation, which may differ from the definitions adopted by provincial legislatures. Although its legal, social, and economic implications demand a simple and unambiguous definition of the relationship, there is no consensus among legislators, social scientists, and social workers on what constitutes a cohabiting relationship. For example, how long and/or how many days a week must a couple live together to be called a cohabiting union? In British Columbia, the Family Relations Act states that an unmarried couple must live together for at least two years before they are eligible for financial support from their ex-partners. The Canadian federal government recognizes cohabitation (common-law union) as equivalent to marriage for tax purposes after a one-year period. However, no provincial family law grants unmarried couples rights to share in family property, irrespective of how long the couple have lived together. It is somewhat fortunate, however, that most recent national surveys, including the Canadian census, use similar questions to identify cohabitation. Thus, to be consistent with census and survey definitions, in this study cohabitation refers to an intimate relationship involving two persons of the opposite sex living together as husband and wife but without being legally married.[3] Throughout the study, the term 'cohabitation' is used as a synonym for 'common-law relationship/union'.

Overview of the Study

Unmarried cohabitation as a widespread lifestyle choice is only a recent phenomenon. This book provides a comprehensive analysis of this phenomenon. The main conclusion is that unmarried heterosexual cohabitation has become not simply a prelude to legal marriage, but increasingly is an alternative family form in Canadian society. The conventional definition of the family must be expanded to include unmarried heterosexual couples, whether or not they are together the biological parents of one or more children.

To understand what has happened to the Canadian family, my first task will be to provide in Chapter 2 a theoretical analysis of recent change in family patterns. The analysis draws on three principal theories in social demography, namely the economic perspective, the sociological perspective, and the demographic perspective. These theories are important not only for understanding family change, particularly the rise in cohabitation, but also for guiding the empirical analyses throughout the book.

Chapter 3 reviews the data sources. As noted, the empirical analyses of Canadian cohabitation are based on the data from two primary sources: censuses and surveys. I trace the genesis of the Canadian census and discuss the cohabitation data contained within it. This review is followed by a discussion of survey data. Data from three national surveys are used in the primary analyses. While the Canadian Fertility Survey (CFS) is used only in Chapter 5, two cycles of the Canadian General Social Survey (GSS–90 and GSS–95) are used extensively in the analyses of various aspects of cohabitation throughout the book. Since we do not want to 'compare apples with oranges', differences in the definitions of cohabitation are also discussed and evaluated.

My empirical analysis begins in Chapter 4, which documents the demographic trends in cohabitation since the 1980s. Aggregate (macro-level) data from Canadian censuses constitute the primary data source for the analyses. Changing patterns of cohabitation are presented from a period as well as a cohort perspective. To look at Canadian cohabitation in an international perspective, the chapter ends with a comparative analysis of cohabitation in selected industrial societies, such as Britain, France, Sweden, and the United States.

Individual-level data analysis begins in Chapter 5. The chapter examines the issues of the changing attitudes towards family issues, partly because the trends in cohabitation may well reflect the changing societal attitudes towards premarital sexual behaviour and marriage. It looks at the patterns of these attitudes and focuses on the changes in these patterns over time. It also examines the socio-economic and demographic determinants of these attitudes using multivariate analytical techniques.

Chapter 6 examines the transition into cohabitation. Using traditional life table techniques, it analyses the timing of cohabitation, both prior to marriage (pre-marital cohabitation) and after marital disruption (post-marital cohabitation). Using survival model techniques, individual-level 'risk' factors influencing the individual's decision to cohabit are identified. Throughout the analyses, marriage is treated as a competing 'risk' of union formation because conceptually (re)marriage and cohabitation are two competing union choices that people consider when they decide to begin an intimate co-residential relationship. The chapter answers such key questions as: How many people choose cohabitation over marriage? At what age do people cohabit? What are the characteristics of cohabitors?

Child-bearing is an important aspect of family life in every society. The replacement of its members is a requisite for the continuation of a family as well as of a society. What are the fertility patterns of cohabiting women? What influences a cohabiting couple to have a mutual child? Chapter 7 begins with an examination of child-bearing intentions among cohabiting couples. It then examines the child-bearing experiences of cohabiting women. Using survival model techniques, the analysis of child-bearing experience focuses on the timing and determinants of first births in the relationship.

Chapter 8 examines the transition out of cohabitation. A cohabitation can be terminated in one of three ways: union separation, marriage, and the death of a partner. Because death in cohabitations is extremely rare and usually beyond human control, our analyses focus on the two other types of exit. Separation and marriage are modelled as two competing outcomes. The hazard rates of separation and marriage are estimated, and the 'risk' factors are identified. The analyses provide answers to such questions as: How long does a typical cohabitation last? How many cohabitations end in separation, and how many end in marriage? Why do some cohabiting couples marry each other, but others do not, and what went wrong to cause a couple to break up?

Chapter 9 discusses the consequences of cohabitation for individuals. The empirical analyses focus on three specific aspects of the phenomenon: (1) cohabitation and the timing of first marriage; (2) premarital cohabitation and subsequent marital instability; and (3) cohabitational status and the division of household labour. The primary goal of this chapter is to evaluate three research hypotheses: (1) cohabitational experience prior to marriage has a delaying effect on marriage timing; (2) couples who cohabited prior to marriage have greater risks of marital disruption than couples who did not cohabit premaritally; and (3) cohabiting-couple families have a more egalitarian division of household labour than married-couple families.

Chapter 10 summarizes the major findings and discusses their repercussions for broader society. The discussion concentrates on three issues: (1) the future of marriage as a social institution; (2) implications for fertility; and (3) the need for a new definition of the family. Using the main theories reviewed in Chapter 2, I consider the future trends in unmarried cohabitation on the basis of the current trends. What will the future be? A look at the Swedish experience in this area may prove valuable, as what is happening to the Swedish family today may well be what will happen to the Canadian family in the coming decades. The chapter ends with a discussion of policy issues, including the legal aspects of cohabitation. I highlight the rights and responsibilities of Canadian cohabitors, present arguments for family law reform, and make policy recommendations.

2 | Theoretical Perspectives

The rise in non-marital cohabitation has been unprecedented in the history of the Canadian family. Although some Canadians still may consider unmarried couples living together to be unthinkable, wrong, and even immoral, more and more Canadians appear to accept it as an alternative form of family life, and more are likely to experiment with it. Perhaps by now, most adult Canadians, if not currently living in cohabitation, have either lived in cohabitation at one time in their lives or have known someone who has. Evidence seems to suggest that the trend in cohabitation that we have observed over the last two decades likely will continue, and there is no sign of a reversal of the trend in sight.

The rising incidence of cohabitation has led many Canadians to wonder what is happening to our union life. How many Canadians are living in cohabitations? Why do people choose to cohabit without first being married? Who are the people who opt for this lifestyle? Are they mostly young people, or are they mainly divorced people? How long do their relationships last, and how do they end? To understand what has happened to the Canadian family, and to anticipate future trends, we need a theoretical perspective. A sound theoretical perspective is also important and necessary in guiding our empirical analysis of cohabitation. Theory will help us make sense of the data we have collected, identify potential factors that may have influenced the process of cohabitation, and provide insights into the modelling of this process. Analysing data without a theoretical framework would be like sailing on the ocean without a compass. The purpose of this chapter is to review recent theories proposed by economists, sociologists, and demographers to account for the recent changes in union life.

While several theories have been proposed to explain the changing marital patterns, to my knowledge, there have been no theories developed specifically for the understanding of the process of non-marital cohabitation. However, demographers Nancy Landale and Renata Forste (1991) once argued that the theoretical frameworks used to explain the process of marital union could be applied to the process of non-marital union. Given the paucity of theoretical work on cohabitation, this may be a useful proposition for several reasons. First, the two processes probably share more common characteristics than any other demographic processes. For example, marriage and cohabitation both involve an intimate (sexual) relationship. Both involve sharing the same living quarters and at least some level of economic consolidation (Davis, 1985c). Either or both can be chosen by people throughout their adult life. Most important of all, they both provide a safe family environment where children are born, cared for, and raised. Therefore, it is not unreasonable to use the theories of marital union as a point of departure to explore and examine the process of non-marital union. In the following sections we will do just that. In our discussion, we focus on the entry into and exit out of a cohabiting union, and we explore and identify factors that may influence the processes of union formation and dissolution.

Our analysis will begin with a review of the economic theory of marriage, placing particular emphasis on the changing roles of women and men in and outside of the home. Next, we will look at the sociological theory of marriage, focusing on how social norms and values may influence union behaviour, and how these norms and values may change over time. We will then turn to the influences of demographic and family characteristics on marriage, making distinctions between age, period (calendar time), and cohort effects. The effects of other demographic and family attributes that may also have a bearing on the cohabitation process will be similarly examined.

The Economic Perspective

The notion that economic factors affect demographic behaviour is hardly new. Over a century ago, Alfred Marshall (1898) discussed the relationships of economic factors to the timing of marriage in his *Principles of Economics*. He claimed that 'given the climate, the average age of marriage depends chiefly on the ease with which young people can establish themselves, and support a family according to the standard of comfort that prevails among their friends and acquaintances' (1898: 258). Explaining human behaviour is always of interest to economists. Indeed, the power of economics, as Fuchs (1983) observed, has come from its success in explaining human behaviour in the marketplace (e.g., labour and foreign exchange markets).

The economic approach begins with the assumption that individuals are faced constantly with the necessity to make choices; and in making choices, they try as best they can to 'maximize welfare as *they conceive it,* whether they be selfish, altruistic, loyal, spiteful, or masochistic' (Becker, 1993: 386). Choices are made in a forward-looking manner, in the sense that individuals make their best efforts to anticipate the uncertain consequences of their choices. The choices they do make, and the subsequent actions they take, are constrained by a host of factors, including time, money, energy, imperfect memory, information, as well as the opportunities available to them (Becker, 1993; Fuchs, 1983).[1]

One exemplary application of this market paradigm to social issues is Gary Becker's (1981) analysis of marital behaviour, the so-called theory of gain to marriage.[2] In essence, Becker's theory is an application of modern trade theory to marital behaviour. Individual women and men are seen as trading partners analogous to individual countries. A couple marries (trades) because each gains from the other party's specialized skills such that each benefits from this marriage (trade).[3] Traditionally, married women specialized in domestic activities, and married men in market activities. Consequently, married women directed much time and energy towards fulfilling their biological commitments because they wanted their biological investment (in reproduction) to be worthwhile. Married men, on the other hand, allocated most of their time and energy to growing crops, hunting, fishing, and other market activities. This partnership persists as long as both partners feel that they gain from this trade.

Becker believed that this distinct sexual division of labour between the market and household sectors prevailed throughout most of modern history. The primary reason for men and women to live in the same household is that they both gain from their specialized investments.[4] In effect, households with only women or only men would be less efficient than those with both, because they would not be able to gain from their biological differences in comparative advantage. Thus, if the theory were correct, in a traditional society an efficient household would be one in which a woman allocated her time and energy exclusively to domestic activities, while a man devoted his to market activities. These sexual differences in comparative advantage, Becker claimed, explain why in traditional societies virtually all households had both sexes and why the traditional sexual division of labour persisted in the past.

However, when a nation is advancing into modern society, forces of social change,[5] which have in turn been propelled by changes in the economic system,[6] radically change family life (Becker, 1981; Westoff, 1983). As evidence that the family has experienced unprecedented changes in recent decades, Becker (1981) cited American data indicating a descending trend in marital fertility but ascending trends in areas such as non-marital fertility, marital disruption, cohabitation, school enrolment, female labour force participation, and elderly persons living alone.

According to Becker, the single most important factor underlying these changes has been the rise in the earning power of women. Such a rise increases women's participation in the labour force and reduces the fertility rate, because an increase in the wage rate also increases the forgone value of women's time if spent at domestic production (Espenshade, 1985). This increases school enrolment, because now women are more willing than ever to invest more in market skills and experiences. The fraction of elderly adults living apart from their children increases because the ties between children and their parents are weakened, and more important, because the rise in the earning power of women has helped to expand the welfare system and raise social security payments. These changes in turn have reduced the gain from marriage, and consequently, marriage rates have declined.

The decline in the gain from marriage not only makes non-marriage more attractive, it also undermines the stability of ongoing marriages. According to

Becker, this is because an increase in married women's economic independence impairs the efficiency of the household and reduces the mutual dependence between marital partners. Further, as the cost of women's time increases, the incentive to stay at home and raise a large family declines. Consequently, marital fertility declines. Since children represent the primary source of marital-specific capital, declining fertility reduces the 'stock' of this capital and increases marital instability (Becker et al., 1977).[7] Certainly, the theory does not exclude the possibility that this causal relationship can run in the opposite direction. That is, the high rate of marital dissolution in society may discourage a couple from investing heavily in marital-specific capital, as it will be worth less if the marriage dissolves. This line of reasoning also suggests that the decline in the gain from marriage may also contribute to the growth of female-headed families and the rise in non-marital fertility.

The decline in the *expected* gains from marriage makes non-marital cohabitation an attractive alternative for several reasons. One is that the decline in the expected gains may have caused men and women to be more cautious and reluctant to enter into a marital union. This may have resulted in the delays in marriage timing that we have seen in recent decades. Whatever the reasons for delaying marriage, cohabiting offers young people an opportunity to live in a family environment, which allows them to avoid the penalties of sexual isolation or promiscuity (Oppenheimer, 1994: 308). There are economic benefits to cohabiting as well. Like married couples, cohabiting couples living together in the same household pool their resources and reduce the costs of living. At the same time, cohabiting offers some of the benefits of the single state. Since cohabitation is an informal relationship by its very nature, the transition into and out of a cohabiting union entails fewer social, financial, and legal obligations than does a marital union. Clearly, it makes good sense to many young couples to cohabit rather than marry.

The application of the economic perspective to non-marital cohabitation is readily evident. We assume that union behaviour is a conscious decision-making process, and that the avoidance of costs and the maximization of benefits are the primary motives behind union behaviour. Given constraints, individuals choose to enter into a union when the gains expected from the union exceed the gains expected from remaining single. Similarly, they dissolve a union when they feel that they will be better off if they return to the single state, given the costs (emotional and financial) of terminating the relationship.

While we assume that individuals seek to maximize the expected gains from cohabitation by deciding whether to enter, stay in, or terminate a cohabitation relationship, uncertainty presides over all union decisions. Uncertainty about the outcomes of union decisions arises because of constraints, such as imperfect market information, the cost of finding a desirable partner, or the cost of terminating an ongoing relationship. The economic theory assumes that uncertainty should have a negative impact on the gain from the union, as it induces couples to accept lower gains than they would receive if, for example, finding a perfect match were costless. In other words, an increase in uncertainty, such as around the marriage market and/or partners' long-term commitment to family and career responsibilities, should raise the cost of partner search and delay the entry into the union. An increase in search costs should also result in a larger deviation from the optimal sorting, which reduces the gain from the union (Becker et al., 1977: 1147). Similarly, union separation may not be fully anticipated but may result from unexpected events. Therefore, according to Becker, the optimal union decision at any moment is likely to be the one that maximizes the gain that one expects to receive over one's lifetime, given the realization up to that moment.

Women's Economic Independence

The core of Becker's theory is that the primary gain from marriage comes from mutual dependence between marital partners, where women specialize in home production and men in market work. An increase in women's wage rates may spur women's participation in the paid labour market. Consequently, women become less specialized in home-oriented activities and more economically independent, and the gain from marriage declines. The rising wage rate of women and the subsequent rise in women's labour force participation also contribute to the growth of the welfare state and raise welfare payments. In turn, this reduces women's economic dependence. If the theory is correct, given the constraints, we should expect that increases in women's earning power and participation in the labour market would discourage individuals, particularly women, from entering into marriage because of reduced economic gain from the union. Similarly, women's economic independence should also increase marital instability.

There are two competing hypotheses about the effects of women's economic independence on cohabitation. On one hand, Becker's theory suggests that women's economic independence reduces the benefits of a union relationship, whether marital or non-marital, because economic independence undermines the sexual division of labour and reduces interdependence between the partners. On the other hand, as noted earlier, declining gains from marital unions may encourage people to form non-marital cohabiting unions, as cohabiting offers the benefits of both marriage and being single. Underlying the latter hypothesis is the assumption that, all else being equal, people generally prefer living and/or sharing their households to living alone.[8] However, when it comes to union stability, the economic theory predicts that an increase in women's economic position within the family undermines the stability of both marital and non-marital unions.

While there is much emphasis on the effect of women's changing economic status on union behaviour, there has been very little work on the role of men's economic position. Sociologist Valerie Oppenheimer (1994) goes so far as to argue that the difficulties faced by young men in the labour market are making a significant, if not primary, contribution to the recent changes in marital behaviour (also Oppenheimer et al., 1997). For one thing, marriage timing traditionally depends on whether young men are able to establish independent households that meet socially acceptable standards. The recent retreat from marriage may reflect the deterioration in young men's labour market position, which makes marriage an increasingly unaffordable proposition. In addition, uncertainty about a young man's long-run prospects in the labour market (i.e., his career immaturity) and about his long-term lifestyle often makes him less attractive in the marriage market. The net result of all of this is that he spends more time searching for a match and possibly turns to cohabiting as 'an interim arrangement' (Oppenheimer et al., 1997: 313). Thus, for Oppenheimer, such factors related to men, *rather than* women's economic independence, may well be responsible for the delays in marriage and the rise in cohabitation, although they may not have much to say about the rate of non-marriage. Following this line of reasoning, an increase in a man's economic status should increase his chances of marrying but reduce those of cohabiting.

Educational Attainment and School Enrolment

Another important element in the economic theory is the role of education in union behaviour. Although there is little dispute over the importance of education in social relationships, social interaction, and individual lives, the effects of education on union behaviour are rather ambiguous. On one hand, the economic theory predicts that a union between highly educated partners should yield greater gains because the partners' market skills are highly valued (Becker et al., 1977: 1146). On the other hand, the theory also predicts that unions between highly educated partners gain less because they, particularly women, typically invest less in home production and more in market activities (ibid., 1146–7). As a result, education level may have little or no *net* effect on union behaviour.

Level of education, also referred to as educational attainment, should not be confused with school enrolment. The former refers to school accumulation, whereas the latter involves school attendance. Unlike school accumulation, there are reasons to believe that enrolment may impede union entry and impair union stability. For one thing, as Thornton, Axinn, and Teachman (1995) reason, the student role is usually associated with being a child, a teenager, or a young adult. There is often a sense of immaturity associated with being a student. For many people, intimate family living, such as marriage and cohabitation, is an adult status that is incompatible with being a student. For reasons such as lack of institutional support and/or financial means, it is difficult to combine the student role with an adult role(s), such as spouse, parent, and/or worker. It is no wonder, then, that not long ago the completion of schooling was seen as a marker in the transition to adulthood (Marini, 1978; Goldscheider and Waite, 1991).

Maturity aside, on the economics of scale, students generally are unable to support the independent household most often entailed by a union. While students could drop out of school to marry/cohabit, and some actually do, the decision to quit school is very costly, as it reduces the chances they will ever complete the educational program in which they enrol. More importantly, dropping out diminishes the accumulation of knowledge and skills necessary to pursue a career (Thornton et al., 1995). This line of reasoning should apply to ongoing relationships as well. Factors impeding the entry into cohabitation may facilitate union dissolution because of role conflicts.

A revised version of the economic theory, known as uncertainty reduction theory (Friedman et al., 1994), also speaks of the effects of schooling on marital behaviour. The theory rests on the assumption that people always seek to reduce uncertainty in their lives, including uncertainty about the outcome of union decisions and long-term career opportunities. The theory further assumes that behaviour is forward-looking and that people try as best they can to anticipate and reduce the uncertainty of consequences of their actions. People tend to pursue some sort of global strategy to reduce uncertainty because by doing so they can reduce uncertainty about 'whole strings of future courses of action' (ibid., 382).

What are the global strategies available to young people today? According to Friedman and her colleagues, the most common strategies include stable careers, marriage, and parenthood. Each of the three strategies may embed individuals in abiding social relations, which reduce uncertainty. Generally, when opportunities for one strategy are blocked, people will resort to the other two strategies. Although it is possible to combine marriage and parenthood as one joint strategy, it is more difficult, particularly for women, to combine a stable career with either marriage or parenthood. Since stable careers generally are built on prolonged schooling, the theory predicts that the better-educated, particularly among women, tend to delay marrying or forgo marriage altogether. Similarly, a committed student is unlikely to jeopardize his/her career goals by quitting school to marry.

Although the theory of uncertainty reduction focuses on marital unions, cohabitation may also be viewed as a global, perhaps an 'interim', strategy. It follows that when opportunities for marriage are blocked, for whatever reasons, people may turn to cohabitation as an alternative and, possibly, compromised solution. Partly because cohabitation generally entails fewer legal and familial obligations than marriage, and partly because an increasing number of people extend their schooling well into their late twenties or older, people who want to balance the student role and the role of a spouse may choose to cohabit. As noted earlier, living together may also help the economics of scale for students. This may explain why cohabitation in North America started largely as a college campus phenomenon in the early 1970s (Macklin, 1983). This line of reasoning suggests that (college) school enrolment may actually encourage cohabitation. In addition, if cohabitation is used as a global strategy for uncertainty reduction, an increase in school accumulation should reduce the incentive to cohabit because the opportunities for stable careers will increase.

In short, Becker's economic theory predicts that educational attainment has no net effect on cohabitation, whereas school enrolment deters its formation and undermines its stability. However, the theory of uncertainty reduction suggests that school enrolment may accelerate the formation of cohabiting unions, whereas school accumulation may deter it. Further, the theory of uncertainty reduction is generally salient to union stability. To assess the validity of these theoretical claims, we will have to wait for the results of our empirical analyses.

The Sociological Perspective

The sociological approach to family behaviour starts with the assumption that human societies regulate the behaviour of their members through some basic institutional arrangements, called social norms (Lesthaeghe, 1980; Ryder, 1980). A norm may be defined as a set of rules for human behaviours in a given situation (Freedman, 1963). The society regulates its members to conform to norms so that behaviours benefiting others are rewarded, while detrimental behaviours are punished. The complete set of norms in a society constitutes the value system, which is part of the culture (Preston, 1986).

Norms, however, do not go unchanged, although changes often occur slowly and over long periods of time (ibid.). Normative changes are likely to occur when a society is undergoing massive social and structural changes. This is because when social change occurs, many members of the society are affected; their established lifestyles and ways of thinking are affected and/or challenged in one way or another. To face this common problem, members of the society tend to develop a normative solution (Freedman, 1963). In many cases, this solution calls for replacing old norms with new attitudes and new values, which often encourage members of the society to break traditional behaviour patterns (van de Kaa, 1987). Therefore, within a society, competing norms surrounding one particular behaviour may coexist. When new norms become dominant in the society, the old value system is gradually deconstructed and a new one will emerge and prevail.

Marriage and cohabitation are social behaviours to which socially defined values are attached. Thus, the values and norms concerning union behaviour may vary across cultures and historical periods. The findings of the European Fertility Project (EFP) are particularly relevant here (Coale and Watkins, 1986). This project, led by Princeton demographer Ansley Coale, was designed to collect evidence on the decline in European fertility rates and determine the *economic* conditions under which voluntary fertility control started. However, to the surprise of the investigators, several cultural indicators, such as religion, language, and geographic region, served as the most important determinants of marriage and fertility patterns in Europe from around 1850 to 1960.[9] Contiguous provinces in Europe shared similar levels of marriage and fertility despite differing levels of economic development.

Why? One of the original investigators, Susan Watkins (1986), believed that marriage and fertility behaviours varied by language and region because people living in one region or adjacent regions often speak the same language and share a common culture and heritage. These people were most likely to act within some common norms for the appropriate age for marriage, the appropriate economic circumstances under which a marriage ought to take place, and the appropriate number of children a married couple should have. It could also be that regional boundaries serve as 'firebreaks which temporarily confine' a diffusion of new ideas and norms (Coale, 1973: 67). The result is that family and other social behaviours are more likely to be homogeneous within a geographic and/or linguistic region than across regions.

Results from the World Fertility Survey (WFS) provide further evidence for the cultural interpretation of family change. In the first-ever worldwide survey of human fertility and contraceptive practice, the WFS collected data from 41 less-industrialized countries across Asia, Africa, and Latin America.[10] Using the WFS data, Cleland and Wilson (1987) failed to find a linkage between economic development and fertility change, thus providing evidence for the cultural interpretation. Between the societies examined, the timing of fertility decline observed in some countries responded more to cultural boundaries and social indicators, such as literacy, than to the level of economic development. The same appeared to be true within the societies: literacy, ethnicity, religion, and other cultural variables best explained fertility variations. Economic factors such as familial control of economic life and women's employment outside the home had little influence on fertility variations.

The findings of the EFP and WFS give rise to a more culturally oriented interpretation of marriage and fertility changes, which became known as ideational theory. The theory was developed mainly by European demographers, particularly Ron Lesthaeghe (1980, 1983, 1998; Lesthaeghe and Surkyn, 1988). Ideational theory assumes, from a generally sociological perspective, that changes in our normative (value) system and the degree of institutional regulation have a direct impact on family change. While acknowledging the importance of economic conditions, changes in opportunity structures, and the role of human capital, the theory emphasizes the influence of changes in the ideational goals that prevail in the society. According to the theory, there has been a definite ideational change in Western societies over the last century or so that has gradually shifted the norms from family-centred orientations to relatively more self-oriented pursuits (Aries, 1980). This century-long ideational change is frequently referred to as the rise of *individualism*, which is characterized by an egoistic search for self-fulfilment, a growing demand for gender equality and independence on the part of women, and the emergence of the ideology of materialism (Lasch, 1975; Shorter, 1977; Westoff, 1983). In short, this ideational change is believed to be the driving force underlying the changes in family behaviour that we have observed over the last century.

In a series of papers published in *Population and Development Review*, Lesthaeghe (1980, 1983, 1998) and Lesthaeghe and Surkyn (1988) presented evidence demonstrating that historical variations in family behaviour were largely a result of differences in religious beliefs, individualism, and secularism. Particularly, the historical decline in European fertility that began in the second half of the last century was, by and large, a response to the growth of individualism and secularism. In terms of the recent family changes, Lesthaeghe believed that the increase in marriage and fertility rates through the late 1940s and 1950s (the post-World War II baby boom), which may appear to be evidence against his argument, reflects the material aspirations of the generations reared in pre-war environments.[11] However, the more recent 'baby bust' is again attributable to the long-term ideational shift in value orientations towards individualism and materialism.

Regional Patterns of Family Behaviour

The key to a sociological understanding of the recent changes in union behaviour is to focus on cultural variables. To sociologists, culture includes such elements as customs, beliefs, norms, values, habits, and preferences that are shared in common by the members of a social group and passed on to new group members. Culture is an attribute not just of an individual but of individuals as members of groups (Kottak, 1987). Culture is patterned in the sense that cultural elements are interrelated, integrated, and overlapped in such ways that if one changes, others may change as well. While shared by individual members of the cultural group, culture is more than a simple summation of individual preferences or overlapping values; it is the underlying framework for these individual characteristics (Taylor, 1985).

Until recently, many demographers resisted using values, norms, attitudes, and other cultural attributes in their research (Hirschman, 1994). Part of the reason was that the origins of many cultural values remain unknown to us; there are unresolved disputes over what some of them really mean (Preston, 1986). Consequently, it is difficult, although not necessarily impossible, to construct concrete measures for cultural variables. In addition, there are conceptual difficulties. For example, Davis (1963) dismisses all cultural explanations because they contain an inherent logical flaw; that is, behavioural variations are often explained as resulting from the same cultural preferences that also give rise to that behaviour. To avoid this 'circular' problem, demographers wishing to use cultural variables must explain them in terms of structural conditions and/or historical experiences that are unique to the cultural group (Hirschman, 1994).

Findings from European fertility and WFS studies provide valuable insights into what could be useful *proxy* indicators for cultural influences. In the Canadian context, there is little doubt that regionalism has been one of the most important cultural features characterizing the diversity of our society.[12] Past research shows persistent regional disparities in political ideologies, psychological orientations, and social and political behaviour (e.g., Brym, 1986a).

A 1979 government task force report on Canadian unity offers a good synopsis of the sources that may have caused these disparities (Pepin, Robarts, et al., 1979).[13] The report identifies five main sources: (1) geographic barriers separating the nation's territories; (2) historically tenuous connections between regions, arising from the geographic barriers; (3) uneven economic development owing in part to the uneven distribution of natural resources; (4) ethnic diversity, resulting from unequal distribution of new immigrants among the regions; and (5) the political system, which allows political inequality between provinces (Brym, 1986b: 4).[14]

While there are considerable behavioural variations within English provinces, the English-French dualism has been a predominant cultural characteristic of our nation's history. The persistence of this dualism has been attributed to the fact that Canada was founded by two nations: French Quebec and English Canada.[15] The ideological differences between the two regions have been consistently greater than the differences between the English provinces (Ornstein, 1986). Other research has demonstrated persistent differences in values, ideologies, and psychological orientations regarding a variety of social, economic, and political issues between Quebec and the rest of Canada (Baer et al., 1990; Beaujot and McQuillan, 1982; Lipset, 1990; Wu and Baer, 1996). Indeed, in his recent book on the values and institutions of the United States and Canada, Seymour Lipset (1990: 216) states that 'Quebec, once the most conservative part of Canada, has become the most liberal on social and welfare issues.'

The transition of Quebec from a religious and conservative society to a secular and modern one came during the era of the Quiet Revolution. Until the 1960s, Quebec remained a rural traditional society dominated by the Roman Catholic Church (Guindon, 1988; Rocher, 1987). The Church controlled the educational system, almost the entire hospital sector, and most of the welfare and charitable organizations. The provincial government was small and most of the senior positions in the private sector were occupied by Anglophone Quebecers. Among Francophone Quebecers there was little social mobility.

After World War II, the political, institutional, and ideological structures of Quebec became incompatible with the rapid social changes and industrial growth elsewhere in North America. The Quiet Revolution, which started with the election of the Liberal government of Jean Lesage in 1960, 'quietly' transformed the province. With a series of legislative changes, the Quebec government extended its powers and opened up the mobility channels to Francophone Quebecers. The government grew rapidly between 1960 and 1966, taking utter control over the province's educational, health, and welfare institutions. While the Quiet Revolution was viewed as a time of 'catching up', Quebec has clearly gone further than the rest of Canada and its southern neighbour on many social and welfare issues, as well as on some social and demographic behaviours.

The Canadian context provides an ideal setting for testing ideational theory (Pollard and Wu, 1998). Specifically, the above analysis leads to the testable hypothesis that cohabitational behaviour varies across Canadian regions. Further, in light of the recent social and attitudinal changes in the province of Quebec, I anticipate that cohabitation is more acceptable and a more established form of family living in Quebec than elsewhere in Canada. This implies not only that Quebecers are more likely to live in this family form, but that cohabiting unions also are more stable in Quebec than elsewhere in Canada.

Other Cultural Indicators

Aside from geographic region, three other cultural variables will be considered in the analysis of cohabitation: religious denomination, church attendance, and immigration status. The sociological perspective on the family emphasizes the role of norms, values, and beliefs in regulating family behaviour. Perhaps no other system of values and beliefs is more complete or has permeated social life more than the institution of religion. While secularization has been an important trend in Canada, as in other industrial countries, 87.5 per cent of Canadians identify themselves with a religious denomination (Canadian census). The vast majority (88 per cent) of Canadians believe in God, and more than two-thirds do not rule out the possibility that one can communicate with the dead (Bibby, 1983).

The history of religion in Canada has been dominated by three religious institutions: the Roman Catholic Church, the United Church, and the Anglican Church, with memberships of 45.2 per cent, 11.5 per cent, and 8.1 per cent, respectively, of the Canadian population in 1991.[16] Other Protestant denominations comprise 7.1 per cent of the population; and other religions, including Jewish, include 5.6 per cent of the population. In 1991, 12.5 per cent of Canadians claimed that they had no religious preferences. This percentage was up from 4.3 per cent in 1971, and 0.1 per cent in 1871 (Statistics Canada, 1976).

Largely because of the predominance of Catholics in the Canadian population, our analysis will focus on the role of Catholicism in union behaviour. However, in some analyses we will also make comparisons including Protestants as well as those with no religious affiliation. There are good reasons to believe that Catholics may differ in union behaviour from non-Catholics. First, because the Catholic Church discourages premarital sex, Catholics may be less apt to choose to cohabit than non-Catholics. Second, if Catholics are less likely to use contraception once married (Westoff and Ryder, 1977), they may delay entering a sexual union such as cohabitation until they are ready to have children. Third, if premarital cohabitation is viewed as an extended courtship leading to marriage, Catholics may experience a higher partner-search cost than non-Catholics, in part because they may have a greater preference to marry someone with a similar religious background. Again, this will delay the timing of cohabitation. Moreover, as the Catholic Church prohibits most of the common grounds for divorce, the cost of a poor match (divorce) would be higher for Catholics than for non-Catholics (Becker et al., 1977). An increase in the cost of a poor match should reduce union instability. Finally, while most traditional religious denominations have experienced some decline in membership, the Catholic Church has actually experienced a small gain in its membership in relation to the overall population, from 42.9 per cent of the total population in 1871 to 45.2 per cent in 1991. This indicates the resilience of the Church's influence on Canadian society. It also indicates that many non-practising Francophone Catholics still consider themselves to be or are considered to be Catholic, and that immigration from predominantly Catholic countries has had a significant impact.

However, we cannot simply equate church membership with commitment. For example, while most Canadians affiliate with one Christian denomination or another, less than half are *committed* Christians (Bibby, 1983; emphasis added). It is conceivable that the same may be true for non-Christian religions. In fact, the findings of the 1995 General Social Survey show that only one in five Canadians aged 15 and over attend services in churches and synagogues on a weekly basis (my own calculation).

Prior research has shown the importance of religious commitment in determining family values and behaviour. For example, research by Bibby (1982) shows that weaker religious commitment is associated with a greater acceptance of premarital or extramarital sex, abortion, and use of illicit drugs. The findings of the 1984 Canadian Fertility Survey (CFS) suggest that religious commitment, measured by church attendance, has a much stronger influence on fertility and contraceptive practice than religious denomination (Balakrishnan and Chen, 1990). In light of these findings, in this study we will examine the effects of both religious denomination and religious commitment (church attendance).

Finally, immigration status is also used as a cultural indicator. Like its southern neighbour, Canada is largely a country of immigrants. While Aboriginal Canadians (the Indians and Inuit) lived in this land long before it was known as Canada, the growth of the Canadian population and of Canada as a nation-state was largely a result of net immigration, as well as the reproduction of this immigrant population. The 1996 Canadian census shows that 17.4 per cent of Canadians were born outside Canada. The fraction of the foreign-born population has changed little since the turn of this century (between 13 per cent and 22 per cent).

Immigration status may affect union behaviour because international migration often involves a process of 'uprooting' in the sense that social networks in the home country are disrupted. A reduced social network may increase the costs of partner search and delay the union entry process. Moreover, from the economic perspective, place of birth and/or ethnic origin are complementary traits for which the assortative mating of 'likes' is optimized (Becker, 1981). This implies that optimal sorting (desirable mating) occurs when partners share similar characteristics, such as age, height, intelligence, physical attractiveness, and education. It follows that search costs will increase when a marriage (cohabitation) candidate has relatively unusual traits, such as being extremely tall or being an ethnic minority. Increased search costs should result in a longer search and encourage the candidate to accept a less desirable offer. The result is that the gain from a union will decline, the timing of the union will be delayed, and the stability of the union will be undermined. Further, Hirschman (1994) argues that traditional and cultural values may persist long after the environmental conditions in which they originated have changed. Immigrants may actively restore their social networks in the receiving country, and they also may retain their cultural values, which may differ considerably from those in the receiving country. This suggests that their union behaviour patterns (e.g., age at union) may more closely follow those in their home country than those in the receiving country.

The Demographic Perspective

Ever since John Graunt's groundbreaking analysis in *Observations Made Upon the Bills of Mortality* (1662, cited in Weeks, 1996: 19), which included a rough life table, demographers have searched for the regularities in human fertility, mortality, and migration. Nuptiality, which comprises the events of marriage, divorce, remarriage, and widowhood, was not a major concern to demographers (Newell, 1988). However, nuptiality was important because of its affinity with fertility. As exposure to the risk of child-bearing was generally confined to married women, nuptiality mattered because it was related to the time when sexual relations began and ended, and to the time when a family was formed and dissolved. For example, a woman's age at marriage and, to a lesser extent, her age at widowhood were important in the traditional demographic regime because they were the times when she first became exposed to the risk of child-bearing and when she ceased to be at that risk.[17] Obviously, what demographers really had in mind were fertility outcomes.[18]

While demographers may have been preoccupied with fertility patterns, there are two other reasons for their lack of attention to nuptiality and the family. One is the paucity of statistical data on families and the household, particularly information on marital/union histories (United Nations, 1963).[19] The other reason is the complexity of the subject matter. This complexity arises in two ways. First, from a technical point of view, nuptiality involves *renewable* events—that is, unlike the event of mortality, the events of marriage, divorce, remarriage, and widowhood can be repeated in one's life cycle. This requires the collection of an enormous amount of information on family/marital histories, and demands sophisticated statistical techniques, for example, to trace the marital histories of individual members of the family and to estimate the probabilities of marital transitions. Second, families and households are multi-dimensional: family and/or household members are related to each other in a variety of ways (Bongaarts, 1990). This web of relationships makes the family an important social, economic, and familial unit on which most of us anchor our lives. Thus it has been a formidable undertaking, both methodologically and behaviourally, for demographers to understand and determine how these interrelated groups of individuals evolve over time under the influence of vital processes (Bongaarts, 1990: 189).

In response to the emerging interest in the family and household, in February 1982 the Council of the International Union for the Scientific Study of Population (IUSSP), the foremost international organization of population specialists, established a Scientific Committee on Family Demography and the Life Cycle. Its mandate was to promote research in family demography and to publicize the subject matter within the scientific community (Bongaarts et al., 1990: v). Over the past two decades, as more data on families and households have been made available, the field of family demography has boomed.

Like many demographers in other fields, family demographers' interests are embedded in emerging demographic trends. The last few decades have witnessed unprecedented changes in the patterns of family formation and dissolution in much of the Western world. The changing marriage patterns, particularly the rising popularity of non-marital cohabitation, have caught many demographers, as well as the general public, by surprise. As would be anticipated, the field has seen a growing body of literature on cohabitation—its causes and its consequences as they pertain to children, other members of the family, and society at large. With the rising popularity of unmarried cohabitation, the concept of nuptiality must be expanded to include cohabitation as a separate and independent vital process.

Demographers work with numbers and are routinely referred to as 'number crunchers'. The numbers (data) they work with come from two primary sources: population censuses (see Chapter 3 for more on this topic) and vital statistics registration systems (continuous recordings of vital events such as births, deaths, marriages, and divorces). As John Weeks (1996: 23) notes, there are two inherent problems with using these data for demographic analysis. First, since the census and vital events data generally are collected for purposes other than demographic analysis (e.g., tax collection), the data may not reflect the relevant theoretical concerns of demographers. Second, census and vital statistics data generally are collected by different government agencies using different methodologies. Thus, it is not uncommon that the definitions of key concepts and the quality of data vary by source and time period.

For these reasons, on the one hand, demographers always question the data quality and studiously refine their estimation techniques. On the other hand, they routinely work with a small number of covariates (independent variables), such as age and sex, which are typically available from these data sources and generally involve fewer measurement errors and inconsistencies. Using these data, they set out to estimate the rate of vital events of interest and determine the factors (e.g., age and sex) that influence the rate at which these events occur. This practice has led demographic analysis to be seen as being more descriptive than analytical, and more empirical than theoretical. This may also explain why demographers are accused sometimes of being 'atheoretical' in their approach and of being overly 'fussy' about data quality.

Although demographers may be forced to rely on a few covariates as they are constrained by the data, in reality these variables may explain much of what is going on. For example, age-sex mortality patterns (life table analysis) probably account for much of the variation in human mortality statistics. The same can be said for the patterns of first marriage and fertility (e.g., Coale, 1971; Coale and McNeil, 1972; Coale and Trussell, 1974; Henry, 1961). In keeping with this tradition, the empirical part of this study starts with a descriptive analysis of cohabitation. We examine age-sex cohabitation patterns using Canadian census data (see Chapter 4). By taking advantage of recent national surveys of the family, we will extend this tradition by examining the relationship between cohabitation and a host of other demographic and family variables.

Age, Period, and Cohort Effects

Aside from convenience, there are theoretical and practical reasons why age effects are important in vital processes. First, because age is a reasonable proxy for physiological state, biological theories may be used to explain aging effects in vital processes (Hobcraft et al., 1982). For example, in the case of morbidity and mortality, biological and physiological theories may provide a more precise explanation than behavioural theories as to why morbidity and mortality rates increase with age. To be sure, we have long known that individuals age at different rates, and that the development of various age-related illnesses varies between individuals. Second, as noted above, prior research has demonstrated enormous regularities in the age-patterns of vital events between populations and over time (e.g., United Nations, 1982). Perhaps for this reason, age has been found to be the most important predictor of variations in virtually all vital processes (Hobcraft et al., 1982). Does age have a similar impact on cohabitation? Do we expect distinct age-patterns of cohabitation? For both questions, the answer appears to be 'yes' (see Chapter 4 for details).

Age effects sometimes are confused with the effects of calendar time, or *period* effects, although sometimes it is difficult to completely separate the two. Like age, *period* is used as a proxy variable, albeit a less satisfactory one, to reflect the influences of prevailing environmental and structural conditions in each successive period of time (e.g., calendar year). The underlying assumption for period effects is that the changes in vital processes reflect the changing social and structural conditions in the society. To examine the presence of period effects, demographers compute vital rates for one or more populations over time—so-called *period analysis* (see Wunsch and Termote, 1978: ch. 2). Empirically, especially over a long stretch of time, period effects emerge in all vital events, including cohabitation. From time to time, we observe fluctuations in the trends of fertility, mortality, marriage, and remarriage, which presumably are responses to social and structural changes. For example, the postwar baby boom during the late 1940s and 1950s is widely believed to have been a consequence of postwar prosperity, and the recent baby bust to be of changing value orientations towards individualism and materialism. Do we expect similar *period* effects for cohabitation? Again the answer is 'yes'. As mentioned in the previous chapter, we have already seen a sharp increase in cohabitation from the census data.

The word *cohort* refers to a group of individuals who experience the same significant life events together. Thus, a *birth cohort* refers to individuals who have the same birth year; a *marriage cohort* has the same marriage year.[20] As Hobcraft and his colleagues (1982: 6) noted, one primary motivation for demographers to study cohort influences is to investigate whether age patterns for individuals in the same cohort respond only to period effects, such that the variation of a vital event within a cohort can be completely captured by age and period influences. If not, they may also respond to additional cohort influences.

There are other reasons to study cohort effects. In his classic paper, demographer Norman Ryder argued effectively for the use of (birth) cohort as a temporal factor in the study of social change. He claimed that as the members of a birth cohort share a common historical location and live through similar experiences, each birth cohort has 'a distinct composition and character reflecting the circumstances of its unique origination and history' (Ryder, 1965: 845). According to Ryder (1965, 1969, 1983), social changes occur primarily through the new generations that are exposed to important historical events in their childhood and adolescence. In other words, *cohort* may be used as a proxy for the past history of the individuals in that cohort, reflecting the life experience of those who lived through a particular historical era together. Cohort changes in vital events (e.g., fertility) may reflect and capture social changes in the society.

Interest in cohort experiences has stimulated the development of cohort analysis, a method developed first by demographers for studying fertility and later extended to other social behaviour and attitudes (Glenn, 1977). In its most elementary form, *cohort analysis* involves a comparison of the measures of one or more characteristics of one cohort at two or more time points. In other words, it is a (panel) study of change in one cohort from one point in time to another. For example, if we wish to study the change in attitudes towards non-marital cohabitation, we can set out to measure the attitudes of a group of individuals aged 20–5 in 1998 (who were born between 1973–8). We recall these persons after a period of 10 years, when they are 30–5 years old, and collect the same measurements. We then compare the two aggregate measures and determine the change in attitudes. In Ryder's words, this is a 'study of *intracohort* development throughout the life cycle' (1965: 861). Another type of cohort analysis involves a comparison of characteristics from different cohorts at a given point in time. A simple example of this sort of analysis is to compare the cumulative marriage rates across birth cohorts. For instance, if marriage is suspected to be in decline, then we would estimate the cumulative marriage rates for the 1963–8 cohort and the 1953–8 cohort (they were, respectively, 30–5 and 40–5 years of age in 1998). If our initial conjecture is correct, we should see that the cumulative marriage rate by, say, age 25 is higher for the older cohort than the younger cohort. Ryder (1965) calls this latter type of analysis an *intercohort* study.

According to Hobcraft et al. (1982: 10), cohort influences emerge only when the past history of individuals in the cohort affects their current behaviour in ways not fully captured by aging effects. Cohort effects can be measured only when the historical events occurred before the initial observation. However, since cohorts continue to expose themselves to the social world, it becomes difficult to separate cohort effects from age and period effects, especially when period effects variously affect individuals in the cohort as they progress through the life cycle. There is a simple reason for this. The three sources of temporal variations (age, period, and cohort) are not independent, in the sense that each variable can be fully explained by the other two (Knoke and Burke, 1980: 57):

Cohort = Period – Age.

It is obvious that, algebraically, we have an identification problem if we try to estimate all three parameters simultaneously. The parameters in such models cannot be uniquely estimated.

There appears to be no easy solution to this problem. One strategy is to set one demographic attribute as a constant, then estimate the effects of the other two. This strategy works well in multivariate models such as log-linear models (e.g., Knoke and Burke, 1980). It is also appealing for our analysis of cohabitation, as we rely primarily on two cross-sectional surveys (i.e., GSS–90 and GSS–95). Since these surveys were conducted within five years of each other, period effects are likely minimal. As Glenn (1977: 54) observed, when using cross-sectional data (i.e., when period effects are constant), a cohort analysis is motivated by the knowledge of age patterns of a vital event. A cohort analysis would help determine whether an observed difference (e.g., in cohabitation rate) between groups (e.g., age groups) is due to aging effects, cohort effects, or a combination of the two. However, wherever possible, attempts are made to disentangle the age-period-cohort effects.[21]

Other Demographic and Family Determinants

Although cohabitation responds to age, period, and cohort effects, it may also be influenced by other demographic and family attributes. In this study we consider some of the individual-level attributes known to be important in the marital process. These include, for example, gender, union, and child-bearing histories, spousal characteristics, childhood experiences, and parental characteristics. Here again, the underlying assumption is that the cohabitation and marital processes may respond to the same fundamental forces and that attributes important to marriage may also be pertinent to cohabitation.

Among demographic attributes, there is no dispute over the importance of sex to vital processes.[22] Sex differences are found in mortality, marriage, and remarriage across historical time and space. Because of this, demographers routinely separate women and men in their research, based on the assumption that the vital process in question and its determinants may operate differently between the sexes. While biological and physiological differences between women and men may cause some of the differences, for example in mortality, there are also social and economic explanations. For example, the economic theory suggests that women and men may marry for different reasons. Differences in the traditional sexual division of labour between home production and market activities may explain why men with more resources are more likely to marry than men with less, and why the opposite appears to be true for women. Sociological theory, on the other hand, suggests that in most human societies there are prevailing norms for age differences between marital spouses. With few exceptions, men marry women who are one or more years younger than themselves. Above all, whatever the reasons, men seem to have a greater preference for marriage than women (Goldscheider and Waite, 1986). Do men also have a greater preference for cohabitation than do women? Do the determinants of cohabitation vary between the sexes? To address these questions, I conduct analyses separately for women and men in most of the substantive studies throughout this book.

Union histories, such as age at union, age at union dissolution, and duration of union, are important determinants in union formation and dissolution. For example, prior research suggests that age at first marriage affects marital stability. Becker's economic theory predicts that a decrease in age at marriage raises the likelihood of divorce because people marrying at younger ages tend to experience greater search costs and are less informed about themselves and the marriage market (Becker et al., 1977). For the same reason, we would anticipate that a decrease in age at entry into a cohabiting union might increase the probability of union disruption. Further, the economic theory also predicts that the risk of marital disruption decreases with the duration of marriage. This is because the gain from marriage increases with duration (Becker et al., 1977). Obviously poor marriages (marriages with lower gains) would end sooner than later. This line of reasoning suggests that an increase in non-marital union duration should also reduce the risk of union disruption, but increase the probability of formalizing the relationship through marriage.

Child-bearing histories, such as the timing of birth, age, and number of children, have important consequences for union formation and dissolution. For example, the economic theory argues that children are the most valuable marriage-specific capital that a couple invests in during their marriage. As with all other marriage-specific investments, because of reduced access and a number of other reasons, children would be worth considerably less in the event of marital breakdown or remarriage (Becker et al., 1977). This implies that an increase in the number of children in the marriage should improve marital stability, but reduce the probability of remarriage. This same reasoning should apply to cohabitation—that is, an increase in the number of children born in the cohabitation may enhance union stability and discourage (cohabiting) union formation after divorce. Similarly, children born outside the union should deter the entry into the union and undermine union stability if a union is formed.

The sociological perspective predicts similar effects of children. For example, a Durkheimian view on marital exchanges suggests that child-bearing and child-rearing increase role specialization and the interdependence between spouses, or, in Durkheim's terms, *marital solidarity* (1984). Espenshade (1985: 193) argues that the institution of marriage is a social invention that has survived because it performs important functions needed by society. Perhaps no other marital functions are more important than the procreation and socialization of children (see also Parsons, 1951). For these reasons, children, particularly young children, should enhance the stability of marriage and, by extension, cohabitation.

Spousal characteristics are important attributes in the process of union dissolution. The economic theory suggests that discrepancies between spousal characteristics, such as age, education, and religious background, are likely the result of a shorter marital search. People sacrifice the benefits associated with an ideal match in order to reduce search costs, such as time and money expended on the search (Becker et al., 1977). Thus, the gain from marriage should be lower and the probability of union disruption higher in heterogamous unions than in homogeneous unions. Moreover, from a more sociological perspective, Udry (1974) believes that heterogamy in union status increases social differences between union partners, which, in turn, constitute a source of conflict not only between the couple and other social groups, but also between the partners themselves. This conflict within the partnership should lower the gains from the union and undermine its stability.

Childhood experiences and parental characteristics may influence the union process as well. Individual attributes, such as having a happy childhood, growing up in a broken family, and parents' socio-economic status, are relevant because they bear on the family environment in which a child grows up. For years, lifespan and developmental psychologists have shown us the importance of a stable family structure and family environments in the development of the individual (e.g., Vander Zanden, 1985). Life-course theorists also emphasize the consequences of early life transitions and unanticipated life events as they pertain to later life chances (e.g., Elder, 1985; George, 1993).

Empirical evidence is remarkably consistent in that children who grow up with greater financial hardships, more familial disruption, less supervision, and less contact with adult role models are more likely to develop problems later in life. These problems may range from leaving home at young ages, low school achievement, high chances of dropping out of school, early sexual activity, teenage pregnancy, and premarital birth, to emotional distress and deviant behaviour (e.g., Hogan and Kitagawa, 1985; Holden and Smock, 1991; McLanahan and Sandefur, 1994; Seltzer, 1994; Wallerstein and Kelly, 1980; Wu and Martinson, 1993). If non-marital cohabitation tends to attract individuals who are unconventional in attitude and behaviour (Axinn and Thornton, 1993), then we would anticipate that an unstable family structure and unfavourable family environment experienced by an individual while growing up may increase the probability that he or she will form a non-marital cohabitation and raise the risk of union instability.

Summary

We have discussed three theoretical perspectives relevant to union behaviour and have identified several important determinants of union formation and dissolution. The economic perspective assumes that people choose to enter a union relationship because they expect to gain from the union. They choose to dissolve their relationship because they expect that they would be better off being 'single', given the costs of terminating the relationship. The theory argues that the primary gain from the union comes from the traditional sexual division of labour between the home sphere and the marketplace—that is, men engage in market activities and women in domestic activities. The theory focuses on women's economic independence and women's education as two key elements in the union process, both of which may undermine the division of labour.

The sociological perspective is based on the assumption that union behaviour is regulated by social norms. Because norms tend to be confined within geographic and/or linguistic boundaries (regions), union behaviour is expected to be more homogeneous within regions than between regions. This theory focuses on changing norms and values as a key determinant of union changes. The recent changes in union behaviour, particularly the decline in marriage and the rise in cohabitation, are interpreted as responses to the long-term ideational shift towards greater individualism and materialism.

Finally, the demographic perspective highlights the importance of age-period-cohort effects on union behaviour. Cohabitation is age-dependent because cohabitation is particularly common among young people, although questions regarding biologically based reasons for this phenomenon remain unresolved. Cohabitation is period-dependent because the social and structural conditions of the period, such as changes in economic structures and legal systems within a specific interval of time, influence the decision to cohabit or dissolve a cohabitation. Cohabitation is cohort-dependent because the members of a (birth) cohort experiencing similarly significant life events together may manifest distinct patterns of union behaviour reflecting the circumstances of their unique historical location.

3 | Data Sources

As demographers, we collect, manipulate, and present numerical data in attempts to probe into the *external* world and look for clues to the origins and changing patterns of demographic events. While numbers do not necessarily speak for themselves, they 'serve to discipline rhetoric. Without them it is too easy for a writer—or a reader—to follow flights of fancy, to ignore the world as it is, and to "remold it nearer to the heart's desire"' (Fuchs, 1983: 5).[1] Thus, it should come as no surprise that this book involves numbers.

In this chapter I describe the data sources on which the analyses of cohabitation are based. The data are drawn from two main sources: censuses and surveys. As this book focuses on Canada, I limit the primary analyses to Canadian data. I use Canadian population census data from 1981 onward for the aggregate analyses presented in Chapter 4. For analytical and substantive studies of various aspects of cohabitation, I draw on three recent national surveys: the 1984 Canadian Fertility Survey (CFS), and the 1990 and 1995 cycles of the General Social Survey (GSS–90, GSS–95). In the following sections I provide some brief background information on population censuses and describe each of the data sources, beginning with census data.

Census Data

A population census is a statistical portrait of its people. According to the United Nations Department of International Economic and Social Affairs, an agency that prescribes standards for the taking of censuses, the population census is 'the total process of collecting, compiling, evaluating, analysing and publishing or otherwise disseminating demographic, economic and social data pertaining, at a specified time, to all persons in a country or in a well-delimited part of a country' (United Nations, 1980, cited in Nam, 1994: 96). Today most countries in the world carry out a census to enumerate their population and collect important information about them.[2]

The taking of a population census has a long history. The first censuses were carried out in the ancient civilizations of Egypt, Babylonia, China, Palestine, and Rome (Shryock et al., 1971). For example, for about 800 years in ancient Rome, counts of the citizens and evaluations of their property were conducted every five years for taxation and military purposes. After conquering England, William the Conqueror ordered an enumeration of all English landed wealth in 1086 to determine the revenue that landowners owed (Weeks, 1996: 8). For the next six centuries there were a few occasional censuses conducted in Europe, but it was not until the mid-eighteenth century that regular censuses were resumed. For example, Sweden started its regular censuses in 1749, and Norway and Denmark in 1760 (Weeks, 1996: 8). The United States began its decennial census in 1790.

Canadian Censuses

The first Canadian census was carried out in the colony of New France in 1666.[3] The census was conducted under the guidance of Intendant Jean Talon, who was sent to the new colony by King Louis XIV. Talon ordered a door-to-door enumeration of the colony's 3,215 inhabitants, who were settled primarily in Montreal, Trois-Rivières, Cap-de-la-Madeleine, and Quebec. His first census was based on the principle of *de jure* (by right), whereby persons are enumerated according to the place of their regular residence, not where they happen to be on census day, a tradition that remains in place today. The census recorded the names of inhabitants and collected information on age, sex, marital status, trade, and occupation. In the following year, additional information was obtained on cattle, sheep, and farmland under cultivation. Under French rule (1608–1763), there were a total of 36 censuses taken in the colony, the last in 1739. During the later years of the French regime, there were some 51 censuses undertaken in Nova Scotia, Cape Breton Island, Newfoundland, New Brunswick, and Prince Edward Island.

Under British rule, censuses were taken in Lower Canada in the years of 1765, 1784, and 1790. After 1817 the census became more frequent, albeit less regular, in New Brunswick and Nova Scotia, with an annual census in Upper and Lower Canada. However, it was not until the second half of the nineteenth century that censuses were conducted on a regular basis. A landmark event in the history of the Canadian census was the passage of the Statistics Act of 1848, which provided for the censuses of 1851, 1861, and thereafter one in every tenth year. In response to rapid socio-economic changes in the postwar periods, the first national quinquennial census was introduced in 1956, which generally included fewer questions than the decennial census. Under the Statistics Act of 1971, it became a statutory requirement to carry out a census every five years.

The British North America Act of 1867 stipulated that censuses must be held on a fixed date and the Census Act of 1870 further required that the census take place no later than 1 May. The census day remained in April until 1911, when it was moved forward to the first day of June, primarily because of the poor weather and road conditions that often hampered the enumeration during early spring. The June date was again moved forward to the first Tuesday in June in 1981, as many people change residence on the first day of the month and some people may be away when 1 June falls on a weekend. For the 1996 census, the date was moved back to the second Tuesday in May (14 May). One reason for this last change was to ensure that the completed census forms (questionnaires) could be returned during the same month, reducing the probability that forms could become lost due to a residential move.

The method of data collection for the census has changed over time. Before 1971, the census data were collected by face-to-face interviews. Census enumerators went door to door collecting information and writing down the answers on census forms. The 1971 census introduced the method of self-enumeration. For the first time, respondents were asked to complete questionnaires themselves. This method has been used ever since for approximately 98 per cent of the Canadian population, with the personal interview method used for the remainder.

With advances in statistical knowledge, the sampling method was first introduced in the 1941 census. In that year, in order to provide information about postwar housing problems, additional housing data were collected from 10 per cent of Canadian households. In order to reduce sampling errors, the sample fraction was increased to 20 per cent in 1951 and has remained unchanged except for 1971 and 1976, when the fraction was 33 per cent. In 1996, 80 per cent of households received the short census questionnaire (including 7 questions), while 20 per cent received the long one (including 48 *additional* questions).

It should not be surprising that the content of the census has also changed over time, reflecting changing socio-economic and political conditions in the society. It has become increasingly difficult to maintain historical continuity in the content of the census questionnaire. For example, questions about household facilities and amenities have changed continuously to reflect the changing standards of living and lifestyles. Questions relating to dwelling characteristics (e.g., garage, use of flush toilet, method of sewage disposal, source of water supply) were dropped in the 1976 census due to their decreasing importance. Questions such as household activities (unpaid housework, child care, and care for seniors) were first introduced in the 1996 census to reflect the increasing awareness of the importance of unpaid work. However, questions about basic demographic characteristics have been retained from the first census and some questions, such as dwelling type, have remained on the census questionnaire for over a hundred years.

Cohabitation Data from the Census

Although indirect reference was made to common-law (cohabitation) relationships in both the 1971 and 1976 census forms, no explicit attempts were made to solicit or retain information on common-law (CL) unions.[4] In effect, the only direct reference to CL status was made in the Census Guide, where respondents living in CL relationships were instructed to report their marital status as 'now married'.[5] Although neither census intended to collect information on CL status, no fewer than 73,000 respondents in the 1976 census provided a write-in response indicating that they were living in a CL type of arrangement (e.g., 'common-law', 'fiancé', and 'future husband/wife'). These and other respondents deemed to live in a common-law relationship were treated as husbands and wives in all census publications.

Information on CL status was first retained in the 1981 census. The term 'common-law' appears in several places on the census form, although no definition of a 'common-law' relationship is provided either on the census form or in the Guide. The CL status of the respondent and/or the members of the household was determined based on his or her response to Question 2 (Person 2 in relation to Person 1; see Appendix) in one of the two ways: (1) the respondent checked the pre-coded answer box for the CL partner of Person 1; or (2) the respondent provided a 'write-in' answer indicating a CL partner(s) in the household. In the data processing stage, several 'edit rules' were followed to verify the CL status. Specifically, a CL partnership was only established if it involved two persons of opposite sex who were not legally married to each other but lived together as husband and wife in the same dwelling. The 'edit rules' further required that both partners be 15 years of age or older. The 1986 census retained the practice of the 1981 census on common-law issues.

Using the 'editing' method, over one-third of a million CL partnerships were identified in the 1981 census and nearly half a million in the 1986 census. These figures comprised 5.6 per cent and 7.2 per cent of all Canadian families identified in 1981 and 1986, respectively. While these numbers are by no means trivial in either absolute or relative terms, the rate of CL union in these censuses could be underestimated for several reasons. First, since no explicit effort was made to collect the information on CL status, information on a CL partnership was not captured if the respondent chose not to volunteer this information. Thus, a CL partner could be erroneously classified as a relative, a friend, a roommate, or a lodger living in the household. Second, in the data processing, attempts were made to avoid 'the *a priori* identification of common-law partnerships because two persons were living together' (Statistics Canada, 1989: 42). This may have encouraged census staff to leave out CL partnerships when such partnerships were not explicitly expressed. Third, it was also possible that many CL partners may have chosen to report themselves as husbands and wives, partly because the CL relationship was not defined in the census. However, this does not imply that CL partners would not have chosen to do the same if the relationship had been defined in the census, as in the subsequent Canadian censuses.

In response to the rising popularity of cohabitation in Canadian society, a question on CL status was first introduced in the 1991 census. While the pre-coded answer circle for CL partner in Question 2 remained the same as in 1986, Question 6 was created to identify the CL status. As Question 6 is directed to all members of the household, the respondent was asked, 'Is this person currently living with a common-law partner?' with 'yes' and 'no' as possible responses. A note that follows the questions states, 'We ask this question to better understand the growth and structure of this important change in living arrangements.' The 1996 census retained the wording for Question 6. However, a note was added to provide an explicit definition of *common-law*—that is, '*Common-law refers to two people who live together as husband and wife but who are not legally married to each other.*'

Based on the responses to Question 6, nearly three-quarters of a million common-law families (719,275) were identified in the 1991 census and nearly a million (920,635) in the 1996 census. These figures represent 9.8 per cent and 11.7 per cent of all Canadian families in 1991 and 1996, respectively. In this study, I use census data to examine the trends in cohabitation between 1981 and 1996. I also examine age and regional patterns of cohabitation over the census years.

Survey Data

With the development of statistical science, demographers increasingly rely on survey data to monitor and study population changes. As noted above, sampling has been used in the Canadian census since 1941. While a sample survey involves selecting only a small fraction of the population, sample results generally are representative, accurate, and reliable when good (scientific) sampling procedures are followed.[6] In addition to their use in censuses, government agencies and research organizations routinely conduct surveys to obtain current information. In Canada, perhaps the best-known survey is the monthly Labour Force Survey (LFS).[7] The Canadian Fertility Survey (1984) and two cycles of the General Social Survey (1990, 1995) provide the most recent and detailed information on cohabitation in Canada.

Canadian Fertility Survey (CFS)

The Canadian Fertility Survey was the first and only in-depth national fertility survey ever conducted in Canada.[8] The survey was funded by the Social Sciences and Humanities Research Council of Canada (SSHRC) and directed by three prominent Canadian demographers: T.R. Balakrishnan of the University of Western Ontario, Evelyne Lapierre-Adamcyk of the University of Montreal, and Karol Krótki of the University of Alberta. The fieldwork was carried out primarily by the Survey Research Centre at the University of Montreal and the Institute for Behavioural Research at York University in April-May 1984.

The target population for the survey was all women of reproductive ages 18 to 49. Because the sampling strategy involved random digit dialing (RDD), only households that could be reached by direct dialing were included in the sampling frame. Thus, the target population excluded those households without telephones. However, it was estimated that only about 2 per cent of private households did not have a telephone in 1984 (Statistics Canada, 1997a). Further, to improve efficiency and reduce cost, the target population did not include people living in the Yukon and Northwest Territories or people in institutions.

Telephone survey methods were used exclusively to collect data. To determine the feasibility of using telephone interviews to collect data on fertility and contraceptive practices, a pilot study of 150 women was conducted in the summer of 1982. In the pilot study, half of the respondents were interviewed by telephone and the other half in person (face-to-face interview). The study suggested no substantial differences in the responses from the two types of methods, which indicates that telephone survey methods are feasible and acceptable techniques in fertility surveys. However, as expected, telephone methods yielded a slightly lower response rate than personal interview methods in the pilot study. Respondents were interviewed for an average of 36 minutes in the official language of their choice (English or French). A total of 5,315 women aged 18–49 completed CFS interviews, for an overall response rate of 70 per cent.

The CFS survey questionnaire is comprised of nine sections: (1) respondent's family and socio-economic background; (2) values and attitudes on family issues; (3) union history; (4) pregnancy and child-bearing history; (5) contraceptive use and sterilization; (6) child-bearing intentions and sterilization expectations; (7) employment history and attitudes towards work and child care; (8) economic resources and old age expectations; and (9) partner's socio-economic characteristics.

One important innovation of the CFS was to include an extensive sequence of questions on attitudes towards cohabitation, marriage, abortion, divorce, child-bearing, and other family issues not commonly found in fertility surveys. It is these questions that are used in the present study. Particularly relevant here are the items on premarital sex, cohabitation, and marriage. I am aware of no other national surveys containing information on people's views of non-marital cohabitation. Together with the attitudinal items included in the GSS–95 (discussed below), we are able to examine the changes in attitudes towards marriage, particularly people's views on the importance of marriage in their life (Chapter 5). As noted in Chapter 2, social norms, attitudes, and values play a crucial role in the union process. Our examination of changes in family values and attitudes will help us to understand the changes in union behaviour that we observe in recent years.

While the CFS also asked respondents to report their cohabitational history, I chose not to analyse union history data from the CFS for several reasons. One is that the target population of the CFS was limited to women in their reproductive years. Second, the CFS data are somewhat dated given the rapid change in cohabitational behaviour. Third, as some preliminary (descriptive) analysis of cohabitation using the CFS data was completed by Balakrishnan and his colleagues (Balakrishnan et al., 1993), research efforts and resources should be directed to analyse more recent data in order to confirm and update earlier studies.

General Social Survey (GSS)

The General Social Survey is a national household survey conducted annually by Statistics Canada.[9] Since its inception in 1985, eleven survey cycles have been released for public use at the time of writing. The GSS has two principle objectives: (1) to gather information on social trends in order to monitor changes in Canadian society; and (2) to provide information relevant to specific policy issues of current and/or emerging interests.

The content of the survey for each year (cycle) consists of three principal segments: core, focus, and classification. The core section is designed to meet the first objective and is selected from five theme areas on a rotating basis: health, time use, personal risk, work and education, and the family. The focus section is designed to meet the second objective and collects information on specific policy issues and social problems. The last section (classification) contains conventional socio-economic and demographic characteristics that commonly appear in the social survey. The GSS is designed and carried out by the Housing, Family, and Social Statistics Division at Statistics Canada.

1990 General Social Survey (GSS–90)

The core content for the 1990 GSS (Cycle 5) was family and friends. There was no focal content for the GSS–90. While the GSS–90 repeated the section on social support used in the GSS–85, it was the first in the GSS series to focus on the family and friends. Fieldwork was completed from January through March 1990.

The target population of the GSS–90 consisted of all persons aged 15 and older in Canada, excluding residents in the Yukon and Northwest Territories and full-time institutionalized residents. The population was sampled through telephone interviews using random digit dialing. The target population excluded households without telephones, which were estimated at 1.5 per cent of all Canadian households in 1990 (Statistics Canada, 1997a). Sample size was allocated to the square root of the size of their populations and to strata or geographic areas within provinces in proportion to their populations. To gather information on social support among the elderly, Health Canada sponsored a supplementary sample of the elderly population (aged 65 and over). The province of Ontario also sponsored an increased sample in Ontario. The combined effect was to roughly double the size of the sample of elderly persons outside Ontario, double the sample size of persons aged 15–64 in Ontario, and quadruple the sample size of elderly Ontario residents.

The sample consisted of about 18,300 households. Once a household was contacted by telephone, GSS staff recorded all household members and collected basic demographic information such as age, sex, marital status, and relation to reference person for each of them. A respondent 15 years of age or over was then randomly selected from each household to complete the entire questionnaire. A total of 13,495 respondents completed interviews, yielding an overall response rate of 73.7 per cent.

Telephone interviews were the sole means of data collection. Respondents were given the choice of being interviewed in either official language. To test the validity of the questionnaire and data collection procedure, a pilot study of about 800 households was conducted in August 1989.

The survey questionnaire included 10 sections: (1) parents and grandparents (e.g., frequency of contact and their living arrangements); (2) siblings (including step-, adopted, and half-brothers and sisters); (3) children (child-bearing/parenting history); (4) fertility intentions; (5) friends; (6) household help; (7) social support; (8) marriage (union history); (9) satisfaction (e.g., life, family, friends, and health); and (10) classification (various conventional measures of socio-economic and demographic attributes).

As our focus is on cohabitation, the questions on union history are used extensively in this study. In this segment of the questionnaire, respondents were asked to provide a detailed history of their marriages, cohabitation relationships, separations, divorces, and widowhood. By obtaining information on when each event started, ended, or whether the event was ongoing (i.e., the year and month of each event), we are able to reconstruct respondents' union histories. Using demographic and statistical tools appropriate for these event history (survival) data, we are able to estimate the transition rate of each marital event and to determine how this rate may vary with individuals' socio-economic and demographic characteristics. The GSS–90 data are used in most of the substantive chapters (Chapters 6–9). Unfortunately, the GSS–90 did not ask any questions about values and attitudes towards family issues.

1995 General Social Survey (GSS–95)

The GSS–95 (Cycle 10) was the first replication of the family core content used in the GSS–90. The GSS–95 had a focal content, which the GSS–90 lacked. As noted, a focal content is intended to gather information relevant to specific policy issues. The focal content for the GSS–95 covers two separate issues: environmental tobacco smoke (e.g., tobacco use and second-hand smoking) and wartime service (for persons aged 55 and over). Health Canada and Veterans Affairs Canada sponsored the two focal areas, respectively.

As in the GSS–90, the GSS–95 target population was all persons 15 years of age and older in Canada, excluding residents of the Yukon and Northwest Territories and full-time residents of institutions. Similar RDD sampling techniques were used in the sample selection. Over 98.5 per cent of Canadian households had telephones in 1995 (Statistics Canada, 1997a). However, unlike the GSS–90, the sample selection (survey) was carried out evenly over the 12 months of the year in order to correct for seasonal variability in the data. The sample was allocated in a similar fashion as in the GSS–90. The province of Quebec sponsored an additional sample of 1,250 respondents in the province. Since 1993 (Cycle 8), data for the GSS have been collected using computer-assisted telephone interview (CATI) technology, greatly improving efficiency and reducing errors at the data collection stage. A total of 10,749 respondents aged 15 and over completed the full questionnaire following the same procedures as in the GSS–90. The overall response rate was 81 per cent.

The GSS–95 questionnaire had a total of 11 topical areas: (1) family origin (e.g., parental characteristics); (2) siblings (including step-, adopted, and half-brothers and sisters); (3) values and attitudes; (4) children (child-bearing/parenting history); (5) fertility intentions; (6) marriage; (7) common-law partnerships; (8) paid and unpaid work; (9) work interruptions; (10) environmental tobacco smoke; and (11) classification (conventional measures of socio-economic and demographic attributes).

Union histories and topical areas in values and attitudes are used extensively in this study. The section on values and attitudes includes a series of questions on attitudes towards marriage, union separation, children, paid and unpaid work, and gender equality, many of which were used also in the CFS. Although the GSS–95 did not collect respondents' attitudes towards premarital sex or non-marital cohabitation, which the CFS did, both surveys included items on the importance of marriage and a long-term relationship. These attitudinal items are analysed in Chapter 5. Also, as in the GSS–90, the GSS–95 collected detailed information on union histories, which are analysed in Chapters 5 through 9.

While both cycles of the GSS have comparable union history data, I chose not to combine them in the analyses for several reasons. First, both surveys involve large and nationally representative samples. Even the subsample of cohabitors in either survey is sufficiently large to supply meaningful analyses. Second, one primary reason for combining data from cross-sectional surveys is to study the trends in an event. Demographic trends are best studied and presented with census (and vital statistics) data if they are available. Since cohabitation in Canada is a fairly recent phenomenon, and the census began collecting data on cohabitation in 1981, Canadian census data on cohabitation should be analysed and presented in the study (Chapter 4). Third, on a practical level, this book combines the efforts of my continuous studies on non-marital cohabitation over the past several years. In doing so, several of my earlier analyses of various aspects of cohabitation are incorporated here. These previous studies were invariably based on the 1990 GSS data. Since the two cycles of the GSS are only five years apart and are comparable in many other ways, it seems somewhat redundant to replicate analyses based on the 1990 data.[10] However, whenever feasible, new analyses conducted for this book *all* are based on the 1995 data.

Definition of Cohabitation

As noted in Chapter 1, the use of census and national survey data makes it necessary to depend on the definition of cohabitation used in these sources. Since different data sources are used in this study, it is important to compare the ways in which cohabitation is defined in each of the sources. Because the union history data in the CFS are not analysed in this study, my focus is on the *Census of Canada* and GSS definitions.[11]

Although no formal definition of cohabitation was provided in the 1981, 1986, or 1991 censuses, the term 'common-law' was used in the census questionnaire and/or the guide to the questionnaire. A working definition of cohabitation was employed in the process of editing and cleaning the data on cohabitation, which is not much different from the one provided on the 1996 census form:

'Common-law refers to two people who live together as husband and wife but who are not legally married to each other.' However, as argued earlier, there are reasons to believe that the rate of cohabitation may be underestimated in the 1981 and 1986 censuses. While we may never know the *true* rate of cohabitation from 1981 and 1986 census data, I do not believe that the problem of underestimation is serious enough to cast doubt about the overall trend of cohabitation that we observe from the census data.

In a similar fashion, the GSS–90 defined cohabitation as '(two) partners living together as husband and wife without being legally married'. However, the GSS–95 definition is somewhat different. It defines cohabitation as 'two persons having a sexual relationship while sharing the same usual address'. Clearly, the GSS–95 has a less restrictive definition of cohabitation than either the census or the GSS–90. Consequently, the rate of cohabitation could be higher (overestimated) in the GSS–95, or lower (underestimated) in the GSS–90 and the census, depending on how cohabitation is defined. Indeed, there is some evidence to support this view. For example, the 1996 census reports that 7.7 per cent of Canadians aged 15 and over were cohabiting at the time of the census (May 1996),[12] compared to 8.6 per cent *estimated* by the GSS–95 (recall that the data collection in the GSS–95 was evenly distributed over the year). The higher rate *estimated* by the GSS–95 runs against our intuition, since the incidence of cohabitation is believed to be rising over time. However, the difference in the rate of cohabitation between the 1996 census and the GSS–95 is small and probably negligible when sampling errors/biases involved in the survey and under-reporting problems in the census are taken into account. Nonetheless, it is important to exercise caution when comparing cohabitation rates across the surveys or when comparing the findings reported in this study to those reported elsewhere in and outside the country.

Summary

In this chapter we reviewed the data sources used in this study. The data come from two primary sources: Canadian censuses and surveys. The Canadian census began collecting information on cohabitation in 1981. Census data from the four quinquennial censuses (1981, 1986, 1991, and 1996) are used primarily to show cohabitation trends, as well as age and regional patterns of cohabitation, between 1981 and 1996 (Chapter 4). The substantive chapters (Chapters 5–9) use survey data. The survey data come from three sources: the 1984 Canadian Fertility Survey and the 1990 and 1995 General Social Surveys. All three surveys employed nationally representative samples and collected information on union histories. However, not all survey data are used to analyse union behaviour in the study. The CFS data are used only in the analyses of values and attitudes towards premarital sex, cohabitation, and marriage. The GSS–90 and GSS–95 data are used to analyse various aspects of cohabitation, such as its formation and dissolution. Because various data sources are used in the study, it is important to identify whether the definition of cohabitation varies between the data sources. While the census definition is similar to the definition provided in the GSS–90, the GSS–95 defines cohabitation in a slightly different manner. Nevertheless, there is no reason to believe that this difference would lead to different conclusions in any substantive way. It is my view that there is a fairly widespread consensus of what constitutes a cohabitational relationship in Canadian society. In other words, most Canadians have some idea of what a cohabitation (common-law) relationship is, whether we make the reference to 'common-law', 'husband and wife' (as in the census), or simply to 'having a sexual relationship while sharing the same usual address' (as in the GSS–95). Most Canadians share the sentiment that a cohabitation relationship involves two people of opposite sex who live together intimately and share the same household.

4 | Cohabitation Trends Since the 1980s

In its variant forms, cohabitation has been practised in many, if not all, human societies. From a historical perspective, perhaps the most common and widespread form of extramarital relationship was concubinage (Sarantakos, 1984). For example, in China concubinage was practised by wealthy people, particularly well-to-do landlords in the rural areas. It was not until the People's Republic was founded in 1949 that concubinage was obliterated. In Islamic societies, polygamy is permitted; a man can marry up to four wives and have as many concubines as he wishes. In ancient Rome, concubinage was practised among both rich and poor, although it was generally considered to be morally repugnant and socially undesirable. In France, people in all social strata also practised concubinage. Concubinage, *union libre*, and triangular relationships were common among the French aristocrats (ibid., 12). In Great Britain, 'living tally' in Wales and 'living over t'brush' in northern England were permanent and even respectable sexual unions outside marriage in the eighteenth and nineteenth centuries (Kiernan and Estaugh, 1993). Indeed, John Gillis, an English historian, went as far as suggesting that between the mid-eighteenth and mid-nineteenth centuries, as many as one-fifth of the adult population in England and Wales may have cohabited unlawfully at some time in their lives (1985: 219).

While there are no statistical records on the incidence of cohabitation in Canada in the early periods of its history, non-marital cohabitation may have been far from non-existent. Some indirect evidence supports this view. First, throughout the nation's history, premarital sexual activities and premarital pregnancy were more rampant than commonly believed. For example, according to one estimate, up to 10 per cent of all first live births delivered in Canada between 1700 and 1730 may have been conceived premaritally (Henripin, 1972: 8). Since women who conceived premaritally tended to marry before the child was delivered, the high incidence of premarital conception was not reflected in the rate of illegitimate birth, which remained low at under 1 per cent between 1700 and 1850 (except for the period 1741–60, when the rate rose to 1.2 per cent).

Figure 4.1: Number of Persons 15+ in Cohabitations

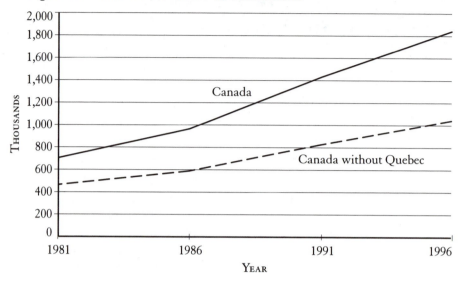

Source: *Census of Canada*, various years.

Given the high incidence of premarital sex and premarital conception, it is conceivable that many couples may have lived together prior to marriage.

Second, birth control was a widespread practice among women in their reproductive years. Although it was illegal to disseminate information on contraception, discussion of family planning was readily available in the mass-produced medical and self-help literature by the end of the nineteenth century (McLaren, 1978). During the same period, the total fertility rate declined from 6.8 (children per woman) in 1871 to 4.0 in 1921, which could well reflect the practice of birth control and induced abortion (Henripin, 1972: 30). Indeed, according to one estimate, as many as one-seventh of all pregnancies around the turn of the century may have been aborted (Cannon, 1922, cited in McLaren, 1978: 338). Thus, it would not be surprising if a significant number of these aborted pregnancies occurred to unwed women.

While non-marital cohabitation is not a new social invention, the recent increase in cohabitation is most likely unprecedented in any historical period in Canada. The objective of this chapter is to document the trends in cohabitation since the 1980s, when national data on cohabitation first became available. While a description of the trends is important in its own right, it also sets the stage for subsequent analysis in the remainder of the book. Our discussion begins with the overall Canadian trends in cohabitation: the number of cohabitors and the rate of cohabitation. We then examine the age, gender, and regional patterns of cohabitation. To find out whether cohabitation is primarily a phenomenon among young and never-married people, we will look at the 1996 census data on

Figure 4.2: **Percentage of Persons 15+ in Cohabitations**

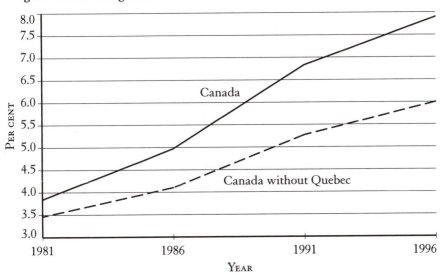

Source: *Census of Canada*, various years.

cohabitation by legal marital status. Finally, I assemble published data on cohabitation from selected industrial countries, looking at Canadian cohabitation from a comparative perspective.

Aggregate Trends

As noted, the Canadian census began collecting information on non-marital cohabitation in 1981. Figure 4.1 presents census data on the number of persons in cohabitation relationships since 1981. Given the distinctiveness of Quebec society, we examine data in and outside Quebec separately. The rising trend in cohabitation is evident. The 1981 census recorded 356,605 cohabiting couples, or 713,210 cohabiting persons. The number of cohabiting persons rose to nearly a million (973,880) in 1986, 1.5 million (1,438,550) in 1991, and 1.84 million in 1996. In relative terms, between 1981 and 1996 the number of cohabiting persons increased by 158 per cent. Moreover, a regional pattern is unmistakable. In fact, the number of cohabitors in Quebec rose by 231 per cent during this period. When Quebec is not included, the number of cohabitors increased by only 121 per cent.

   While the number of cohabiting individuals has increased over time, the rise in the number may reflect the change in the age structure of the population. Since the cohabiting question was asked only to people who were 15 years of age and older, the rising number of cohabitors could simply reflect growth in that age segment of the population. To correct for a potential age bias, Figure 4.2

Table 4.1: Percentage of Persons in Cohabitations by Age Group, 1981–1996

Year	15–19	20–4	25–9	Age 30–4	35–9	40–4	45–9	50–4
1981	1.7	8.2	7.6	5.7	4.2	3.2	2.4	1.9
1986	1.6	9.5	10.4	7.8	5.9	4.8	3.7	2.1
1991	1.8	11.6	14.0	10.9	8.5	6.8	5.8	4.4
1996	1.6	11.8	16.9	14.1	11.2	9.0	7.3	6.1

Source: *Census of Canada*, various years.

presents the percentage of cohabitors among Canadians who were aged 15 and over in the four census years. The resemblance of the graphs is obvious, suggesting that the increasing trend in cohabitation has little to do with the changes in age structure.[1] The percentage of the population aged 15 and over that was cohabiting increased from 3.8 per cent in 1981 to 7.9 per cent in 1996, or a 108 per cent increase within the 15-year period. When the province of Quebec is excluded from the calculation, the comparable increase in cohabitation was 73 per cent.

Overall, the census data indicate a rising trend in Canadian cohabitation since 1981, particularly in Quebec. In 1981, about one-third (34 per cent) of all Canadian cohabiting couples were residing in the province of Quebec. In 1996, this percentage rose to 43 per cent. During the same period, Quebec's share of the total national population aged 15 and over changed from 25 per cent to 24 per cent.

Age, Gender, and Regional Patterns

Age Patterns

While the increase in cohabitation is evident among Canadians, not every adult Canadian is equally likely to cohabit. Past research has demonstrated that cohabitation is more common among young people than older people (e.g., Bumpass and Sweet, 1989; Burch and Madan, 1986). Thus, it is important to examine cohabitation patterns by age and see whether these patterns have changed over time.

Table 4.1 presents census data on cohabitation patterns by age between 1981 and 1996. Because cohabitation is a relatively rare event among the elderly, we limit the discussion to the population aged 15–54. Patterns of cohabitation by age are clearly visible. For example, in 1981, 1.7 per cent of the population aged 15–19 were cohabiting at the time of the census. This percentage rose to 8.2 per cent for people of ages 20–4. It then declined to 7.6 per cent for people of ages 25–9 and continued to decline as age increased. Similar age patterns are observed for the years of 1986, 1991, and 1996 with one important exception. That is, the modal age group shifted up to ages 25–9 after 1981.

Table 4.1 also shows distinct *period* cohabitation patterns. Period effects emerge when we examine cohabitation rates within age groups. Clearly, for each age group shown in the table, the rate of cohabitation increases over time. For example, for ages 20–4, the percentage of the population cohabiting increased from 8.2 per cent in 1981 to 9.5 per cent in 1986 and to 11.6 per cent in 1996. Interestingly, the greatest increase occurred in the oldest age group (50–4), which experienced a 221 per cent increase within the 15-year period. The smallest increase occurred to the 20–4 age group (44 per cent). These data demonstrate that the incidence of cohabitation has increased across all age groups considered here.

Since the quinquennial census data are used and age is broken down into five-year groups, we may follow the (five-year) age group (cohort) over time and look for clues regarding cohort changes.[2] For example, assuming that the influences of international migration and mortality are minimal, people who were aged 15–19 in 1981 should progress to the 20–4 age group in 1986, to 25–9 in 1991, and to 30–4 in 1996. To examine cohort effects, we may follow this age cohort to see whether the rate of cohabitation changes over time. The data provide some indication of a rising cohort rate of cohabitation. The percentage of the population cohabiting for this cohort rose from 1.7 per cent when they were at age 15–19 (in 1981), to 9.5 per cent at age 20–4 (in 1986), to 14 per cent at age 25–9 (in 1991), and to 14.1 per cent at age 30–4 (in 1996). Similar patterns are observed for age cohorts of 15–19 in 1986 and 1991.[3] Obviously, the census series is not long enough to provide a more meaningful discussion of cohort changes. It is also important to bear in mind that the rate of cohabitation is the rate of prevalence, which only tells us the percentage of people who were *currently* cohabiting at the time of the census. People who had dissolved their unions are not reflected in this rate.[4] Further, as we discussed in Chapter 2, these cohort effects cannot be separated entirely from aging and period effects.

In short, census data show distinct patterns of cohabitation by age. Cohabitation is a common union form among young people, particularly those aged 20–9. Period effects of cohabitation are also evident, confirming the earlier findings on the overall cohabitation trend. While far from definitive, evidence suggests a cohort change as well. All these data appear to indicate that some fundamental changes have taken place in union behaviour over the last two decades. Cohabitation has become a more common lifestyle choice than ever before.

Gender Patterns

Research has shown important gender differences in the timing and entrance into marriage (e.g., Davis, 1985a). Vital statistics data tell us that men tend to marry women who are younger than themselves. Goldscheider and Waite (1986) argued that, other things being equal, men may have a greater preference for marriage than women. Do men also have a greater preference for cohabitation as well?

Figure 4.3 shows the rate of cohabitation for women and men between 1981 and 1996. While earlier we used the proportion of the population aged 15 and over cohabiting as a prevalence measure of cohabitation, Figure 4.3 uses a

Figure 4.3: Cohabitation Rates

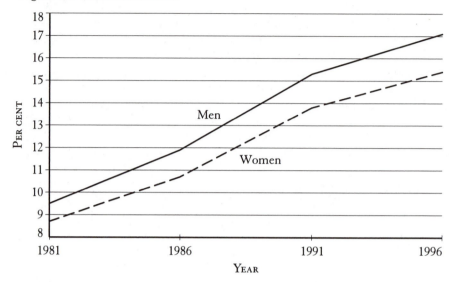

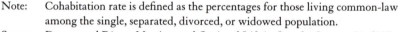

Note: Cohabitation rate is defined as the percentages for those living common-law among the single, separated, divorced, or widowed population.

Source: Dumas and Péron, *Marriage and Conjugal Life in Canada*. Cat. no. 91–534E (Ottawa: Statistics Canada, 1992), 97. Calculations by author.

refined measure of prevalence that removes the married population from the calculation (denominator). The reason for this is that the married population is generally not 'at risk' of cohabitation. Figure 4.3 shows distinct gender patterns of cohabitation. In 1981, the rate of cohabitation was 8.7 for women and 9.5 for men, reflecting the fact that there are more adult women than men in the total population. The gender difference prevails for the subsequent three censuses. There is also evidence suggesting the gender difference is widening over time, with men increasingly more likely to cohabit than women. Indeed, the gender difference in the rate of cohabitation increased from 0.8 to 1.7, an increase of 113 per cent. However, with census data we cannot separate cohabitations that occur prior to marriage (premarital cohabitations) from those occurring after marital disruption (post-marital cohabitations). As shown in Chapter 6, (never-married) women enter premarital cohabitation at a faster pace than men do. However, the converse seems to be true for post-marital cohabitation.

Regional Patterns

Regional patterns in marriage and fertility have been documented in Canada (e.g., Beaujot and McQuillan, 1982; Balakrishnan and Wu, 1992). We have already seen that there has been a divergence in cohabitation patterns between the

Figure 4.4: Cohabitations as a Percentage of All Unions by Province or Territory

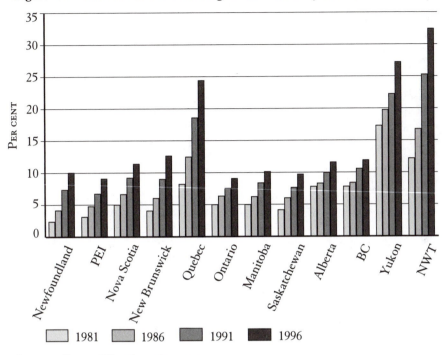

Source: *Census of Canada*, various years.

province of Quebec and elsewhere in Canada. It would be interesting to know whether there are also differences in cohabitation patterns between the English provinces, and if there are, whether these differences have changed over time.

Figure 4.4 presents regional cohabitation patterns between 1981 and 1996. It is clear that the rate of cohabitation, as measured by cohabitation as a proportion of all unions, is considerably higher in the two northern territories than in the other provinces, including Quebec. Since most of the residents in the two territories are Native Canadians, it appears that non-marital cohabitation is a popular lifestyle choice among Canada's indigenous populations. This tendency has increased over time. However, caution must be exercised when we interpret these data, as the population base in the territories is relatively small.[5]

Among the 10 provinces, Quebec clearly stands out as the home of Canadian cohabiting families. In each census year, the rate of cohabitation was highest in Quebec. In 1996, the rate in Quebec stood at 24 per cent, compared to 13 per cent in New Brunswick (the second highest) and 9 per cent in PEI (the lowest). Overall, we see relatively less variation between the English provinces, ranging from 2 per cent to 8 per cent in 1981 and from 9 per cent to 13 per cent in 1996. There is some evidence of convergence in the rates among English provinces over time,

Table 4.2: Non-marital Cohabiting Unions by Legal Marital Status, Selected
Age Groups, and Sex, Quebec and Outside Quebec, 1996 (%)

Legal Marital Status	Total	Women			Men		
		15–34	35–59	60+	15–34	35–59	60+
QUEBEC							
Never-married (single)	71.1	92.6	49.2	16.5	94.8	51.8	13.8
Separated	3.1	1.1	4.4	5.6	0.9	5.3	10.9
Divorced	22.9	6.1	41.3	30.1	4.2	41.0	49.5
Widowed	2.9	0.2	5.0	47.8	0.1	1.9	25.8
Total*	100	100	100	100	100	100	100
NON-QUEBEC							
Never-married (single)	60.1	83.9	30.2	11.2	88.6	36.2	14.6
Separated	8.0	4.4	11.7	6.9	3.2	13.6	15.4
Divorced	28.7	11.4	52.2	36.9	8.2	48.2	47.5
Widowed	3.2	0.4	5.8	45.0	0.1	2.0	22.5
Total*	100	100	100	100	100	100	100

* May not total to 100 per cent due to rounding.
Source: *Census of Canada*, 1996.

which is consistent with the general trends of convergence in marriage and fertil-ity observed in the last several decades (Balakrishnan and Wu, 1992).

While regional patterns within English Canada are less salient than the dif-ferences between English Canada and Quebec, period effects are evident in all provinces and territories. In fact, it may come as a surprise that the most rapid increase in *the rate of cohabitation* did not occur in Quebec, but in Newfound-land, the most eastward province (from 2.3 per cent to 9.9 per cent, or a 330 per cent increase). Comparing the data from 1981 with the 1996 data, the rate of increase is rank-ordered as follows: Newfoundland (330 per cent), New Brunswick (207 per cent), PEI (200 per cent), Quebec (194 per cent), the North-west Territories (161 per cent), Nova Scotia (131 per cent), Saskatchewan (128 per cent), Manitoba (98 per cent), Ontario (82 per cent), Yukon (56 per cent), British Columbia (51 per cent), and Alberta (47 per cent). Overall, excluding the two northern territories, we observe great changes in the rate of cohabitation in the Atlantic provinces and moderate changes in Ontario and the West.

Cohabitation by Legal Marital Status

Are Canadian cohabitors mainly single (never married) or primarily previously married persons? Table 4.2 presents the 1996 census data on cohabitation patterns by *legal* marital status. We observe that in Quebec (the top panel) 71 per cent of *current* cohabitors are single, 23 per cent are divorced, and the remaining 6 per cent are divided equally between the separated and the widowed. A similar pattern is also observed outside Quebec, with the exception that the share of 'never-married' cohabitors is reduced but the share of separated and divorced is somewhat greater.

When age is held constant, different cohabitation patterns are observed. For the 15–34 age group, we see the share of never-married cohabitors increases, particularly in Quebec. For the 35–59 age group, while the never-married share remains predominant in Quebec, the dominant position shifts to the divorced outside Quebec. For the 60+ age group, regional differences abate, while gender patterns emerge. For women, 'widowed' cohabitors become predominant, whereas for men the divorced do. In short, as common sense tells us, the legal marital status of cohabitors changes with age; 'never-married' is predominant among young people, and 'previously married' is common among middle-aged and older people.

The larger share of widowed women among elderly cohabitors may reflect the relatively short supply of eligible male partners in older ages. Because women generally live longer than men, and because women tend to marry men older than themselves, unmarried women face a shortage of eligible (marriageable) men in older ages. This explains why the remarriage rate has always been lower among widows than widowers (Wu, 1995). The implication is that some widows may opt for cohabitation as an alternative to widowhood.

Another explanation also is possible. For the same reasons as noted (sex differences in mortality and remarriage), there are always more widows than widowers around. In fact, the 1996 census reports over 1.2 million widows but only a little over one-quarter million widowers (261,785) in Canada. Over three-quarters (77.5 per cent) of the widowed population were aged 65 and over. Nearly one-half (47 per cent) of all Canadian women 65 and over were widows, compared to only 14 per cent of men. This distribution is quite comparable to the distribution of legal marital status for older cohabiting women. Older women cohabitors are more likely to be widows because the most common marital status for older women is widowhood. In relative terms, there may be no more widows cohabiting than women in other marital groups.[6]

The most conspicuous regional difference is probably in the 35–59 age group. Obviously, Quebec cohabitors in this age group are more likely to be single (never married) than non-Quebec cohabitors. This pattern holds for both women and men. Put differently, there are more older never-married people cohabiting in Quebec than outside Quebec. This age pattern suggests that cohabitation may not merely be a transitory living arrangement but a more established lifestyle choice in Quebec than elsewhere in Canada. The implication is that many Quebecers may not see cohabitation as a prelude to legal marriage but as an alternative to it. As time will tell, many Quebecers in this age group may forgo marriage altogether.

Table 4.3: Cohabitations as a Percentage of All Unions in Selected Countries

Country	Early 1980s	Mid-1980s	Early 1990s	Mid-1990s
Canada	6.3	8.3	11.1	13.7
United States	3.1	4.0	5.1	6.3
Denmark	—	2.1	—	27.0
Finland	—	—	16.0	21.8
Iceland	—	—	—	25.4
Italy	—	1.0	—	—
Netherlands	—	5.0	—	—
Norway	5.0*	—	—	8.6**
Portugal	—	—	3.8	—
Sweden	15.5	—	22.7	—
West Germany	—	10.0	—	—
Australia	4.7	5.7	—	—

*   Women ages 18–44.
** Unmarried cohabiting couples with at least one biological child.
Sources: H. Brunborg, *Cohabitation without Marriage in Norway*. Artikler no. 116 (Oslo: Central Bureau of Statistics, 1979); *Census of Canada*, 1981–96; G.A. Carmichael, 'A Cohort Analysis of Marriage and Informal Cohabitation Among Australian Men', *Australian and New Zealand Journal of Sociology* 27 (1990): 53–72; Nordic Statistical Secretariat, *Yearbook of Nordic Statistics 1996*, vol. 34 (Stockholm: Nordic Council, 1996): 53; G. Spanier, 'Living Together in the Eighties', *American Demographics* 4 (1982): 17–19; J. Trost, *Unmarried Cohabitation* (Vasteras: International Library, 1979); United Nations, *1995 Demographic Yearbook* (New York: UN, 1997); US Bureau of the Census, *Statistical Abstract of the United States, 1997* (Washington, 1997).

Canada in International Perspective

Census data provide clear evidence that cohabitation is now a popular lifestyle choice in Canada, and its popularity is increasing over time. But is Canada alone? Are similar cohabitation patterns observed in other industrial societies? In this section, we take a look at this phenomenon from a comparative perspective.[7] While comparative studies can provide valuable insights on the evolution of cohabitation and its long-term consequences, it is important to point out that it is often difficult, though not impossible, to make comparisons across countries because the definition of cohabitation and representativeness of the studies may vary across countries and historical time. Moreover, to provide a meaningful comparison, we limit our discussion to Western industrial countries around the same time periods. Bearing these points in mind, let us look at what has happened in other countries.

    Table 4.3 presents cohabiting unions as a percentage of all unions in selected countries. The table shows that in the early 1980s, about 6 per cent of Canadian

Table 4.4: Cohabitations as a Percentage of First Unions by Selected Periods in Selected Countries

Country	Early 1970s	Late 1970s	Early 1980s	Late 1980s
Canada	16.6	37.3	40.5	51.2
France*	29.8	50.6	64.6	—
Sweden*	—	—	94.2	—
Netherlands	—	—	—	42.9

* Before age 30.

Sources: J. Dumas and A. Belanger, *Report on the Demographic Situation in Canada 1997,* Cat. no. 91–209 (Ottawa: Statistics Canada, 1997); B. Hoem and J. Hoem, 'The Disruption of Marital and Non-Marital Unions in Contemporary Sweden', in J. Trussell, R. Hankinson, and J. Tilton, eds, *Demographic Applications of Event History Analysis* (New York: Oxford University Press, 1992), 61–93; H. Leridon, 'Cohabitation, Marriage, Separation: An Analysis of Life Histories of French Cohorts from 1968 to 1985', *Population Studies* 44 (1990): 127–44; D. Manting, 'The Changing Meaning of Cohabitation and Marriage', *European Sociological Review* 12 (1996): 53–65.

unions were non-marital cohabitations, compared to 3 per cent in the US, 5 per cent in Norway, 16 per cent in Sweden, and 5 per cent in Australia. In the mid-1980s, the rates increased to about 8 per cent in Canada and 4 per cent in the US. In the early 1990s, the rates rose to 11 per cent in Canada and 5 per cent in the US, and were at 16 per cent in Finland, 4 per cent in Portugal, and 23 per cent in Sweden. By the mid-1990s, the rates kept rising—to 14 per cent in Canada, 6 per cent in the US, 27 per cent in Denmark, 22 per cent in Finland, and 25 per cent in Iceland. Clearly, Canada is not alone. The prevalence rate of Canadian cohabitation is higher than in the US, lower than in the Nordic countries, and perhaps comparable to (West) Germany.

Table 4.4 focuses our attention on first unions. We can see that in the early 1970s, 17 per cent of first unions formed in Canada were non-marital cohabitations, compared to 30 per cent in France. The Canadian rate increased to 37 per cent in the late 1970s, compared to 51 per cent in France. In the early 1980s, the rate further increased to 41 per cent in Canada. The corresponding figures for France and Sweden are 65 per cent and 94 per cent, respectively. It appears that Canada lags behind Sweden, and perhaps France, in the prevalence of cohabitation.

Table 4.5 looks at comparative data on cohabitation by age. Partly because of limited time of observation for the youngest age group (15–19), we will focus on age 20 and older. We observe that, without exception, cohabitation is most common in the 20–4 age group. Further, across the countries, the rate of cohabitation generally declines with age. Except for Sweden, less than 10 per cent of all unions are cohabitations for people aged 40 and older. Canada appeared to

Table 4.5: Cohabitations as a Percentage of All Unions, by Age, Selected Countries

Country	Year	15–19	20–4	25–9	30–4	35–9	40+
Canada	1986	70	39	19	11	8	3
	1991	81	53	27	16	12	5
US	1992	20	12	10	10	10	6
Denmark	1986	45	24	12	4	2	0
Finland	1985	—	50	25	12	7	7
	1990	89	72	44	23	15	7
Sweden	1985	—	78	48	28	17	12
	1989	—	78	50	28	21	—
Norway	1987	—	59	23	8	5	5
Netherlands	1986	—	37	16	7	4	3
France	1985	—	40	17	9	6	4
	1988	—	49	23	12	6	6
Portugal	1991	23	10	6	5	5	3
Great Britain	1980	—	11	6	2	3	2
	1986	—	24	10	7	4	4
	1989	—	32	14	9	6	3

Sources: K.E. Kiernan and V. Estaugh, *Cohabitation: Extramarital Childbearing and Social Policy* (London: Family Policy Studies Centre, 1993); United Nations, *1995 Demographic Yearbook* (New York: UN, 1997).

have a higher rate than the US, Denmark (only in the mid-1980s, see Table 4.3), the Netherlands, Portugal, and Great Britain, but a lower rate than Finland and Sweden. Canada seemed to have a comparable rate to those of Norway and France. Clearly, Sweden leads the industrial countries considered here in the prevalence of cohabitation. A close look at Swedish data indicates that the age pattern of cohabitation changed little between 1985 and 1989, suggesting that cohabitation in Sweden is more likely to be an alternative form of family living than a transitional phase to legal marriage (see Chapter 10 for more discussion on the Swedish experience in this area).

Summary

Cohabitation is not a new social invention in Canada or elsewhere. It has been practised, though in different forms, in virtually all human societies and across historical time. However, the recent surge in cohabitation is most likely unprecedented in Canadian history. In this chapter, we have examined cohabitation trends using Canadian census data since 1981, when the census began collecting information on cohabitation. Our analysis has shown that the incidence of cohabitation has increased dramatically since 1981, whether in absolute numbers or relative percentages. The increase in numbers has been particularly evident in the province of Quebec. Indeed, nearly half of all Canadian cohabitors (43 per cent) recorded in the 1996 census were living in Quebec, where most Francophone Canadians live. However, in relative terms, Canada's two northern territories, with significantly higher percentages of Aboriginal populations, have the highest cohabitation prevalence rates. The English provinces vary little in the prevalence rate of cohabitation.

Age and gender patterns of cohabitation are evident across the regions. Generally, cohabitation is a common phenomenon among young and single (never-married) Canadians, although there has been an increase in cohabitation in all age groups (age 20 and over). Among older Canadians, cohabitation is popular among previously married people, particularly those who are separated or divorced. It is also clear that cohabitation is more common among men than women and that the gender difference appears to be widening over time. Men are increasingly more likely than women to live in a cohabitational relationship.

Canada is certainly not alone in the evolution of cohabitation as a popular alternative form of family living. Similar developments are observable in many Western industrial countries. Overall, the prevalence of Canadian cohabitation is behind countries such as Sweden, comparable to countries such as France, and ahead of countries such as Great Britain and the United States. It seems that Canada is leading the English-speaking world in the prevalence of cohabitation. However, considered apart from French-speaking Quebec, Canada compares evenly with the US and Britain.

5 | Changing Attitudes towards Union Relationships

In the last chapter, we saw an overall increase in non-marital cohabitation in Canada since the early 1980s. Although this increase has been rapid and is unprecedented, it is not necessarily universal across social and demographic strata. There are distinct age, gender, and regional patterns of cohabitation. Cohabitation appears to be more prevalent among younger Canadians than older Canadians, among men more than women, and among Quebec residents more than non-Quebec residents. Canada is not alone. Rapid increases in non-marital cohabitation have been observed in other industrial societies as well.

As we noted in Chapter 2, a sociological explanation of the rise in cohabitation focuses on the changing societal norms concerning non-marital sexual behaviour and the institution of marriage. The basic sociological argument is that modernization (industrialization) gradually transforms individuals' material aspirations from essentially physiological needs to psychological ones, including such things as love, freedom, self-fulfilment, privacy, and companionship (Burch and Matthews, 1987; Lesthaeghe and Surkyn, 1988). The shift in material tastes is believed to lead to an erosion of traditional social norms and bring with it new values and attitudes towards family behaviour.

Studies have shown that attitudes towards gender roles and family life have changed in recent decades. There has been an increasing acceptance of non-marital sex, unmarried parenthood, permanent non-marriage, divorce, voluntary childlessness, and egalitarian gender roles (Cherlin and Walters, 1981; Goldscheider and Waite, 1991; Morgan and Waite, 1987; Thornton, 1985, 1989; Thornton and Freedman, 1979, 1982; Thornton et al., 1983; Veevers, 1979). Research also indicates that these changing attitudes play no small part in recent changes in family behaviour (Axinn and Thornton, 1993; Mason et al., 1976; Plotnick, 1992; Thornton et al., 1983; Thornton and Freedman, 1982).

In this chapter, we look at the patterns and determinants of attitudes towards non-marital sexual behaviour and the importance of marriage. Some key questions that we will address are: What are the social norms regarding non-marital sexual and marital behaviours? Have these norms changed over time? Who are the people who tend to hold more liberal attitudes towards family behaviour? We will begin with a brief discussion of the data and methodology used in this chapter. We will then examine attitudes towards premarital sex and non-marital cohabitation, look at cohort and regional patterns of these attitudes, and investigate their determinants. Because the question of the importance of marriage was asked in both the 1984 Canadian Fertility Survey and the 1995 General Social Survey, we are able to examine attitudes towards the importance of marriage at two points in time, and see whether these attitudes have changed. We will explore also the determinants of these attitudes.

Data and Methods

Data used in this chapter come from the CFS and GSS–95. As noted in Chapter 3, the CFS included a series of questions on respondents' attitudes towards non-marital cohabitation, marriage, child-bearing, and other family issues. The GSS–95 repeated the question about the importance of marriage, but not the questions on premarital sex and cohabitation. The GSS–90 did not include any attitudinal items. To examine the patterns of attitudes, the entire samples of the CFS and the GSS–95 were used. Recall that the CFS includes only women in their child-bearing ages (18–49), whereas the GSS–95 includes women and men aged 15 and older. Both surveys excluded residents living in the two northern territories and in institutions.

To collect information on attitudes towards premarital sex, CFS respondents were asked, 'In your opinion, is it acceptable to have a sexual life before getting married for young women?' 'And for young men?' Response categories included 'yes' and 'no' for both questions. The two questions are examined separately in the descriptive analysis. However, in the multivariate analysis, they were coded as a dichotomous variable (yes/no) indicating whether the respondent gave an affirmative answer to either or both questions.

As for non-marital cohabitation, the respondents were asked, 'Do you find that it is acceptable or not for a man and woman to decide to live together without marriage (a) if they want to make sure that their future marriage will last? And (b) if they are attracted to one another but do not want to make any long-term commitments?' The questions used the same response categories as for premarital sex (i.e., yes/no) and were coded in a similar fashion.

The question on the importance of marriage in the CFS was, 'In order for you to be generally happy in life, is it very important, important, not very important or not at all important to be married?' The response categories were 'very important', 'important', 'not very important', and 'not at all important'. The GSS–95 used the same question and response categories, except that it did not include the word 'generally' in the question. As the responses were recorded ordinally, it was treated as a continuous variable in the multivariate analysis.

As Valerie Oppenheimer (1994: 309) noted, two types of attitudinal questions are commonly used to assess attitudes towards family issues. One is an 'evaluative'

Figure 5.1: Percentage Approval of Premarital Sex for Women

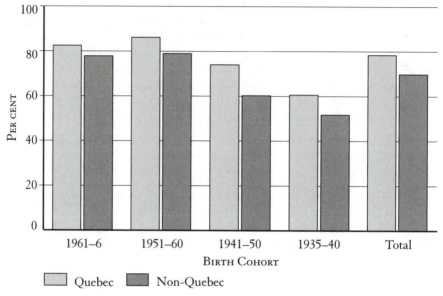

Source: The 1984 Canadian Fertility Survey.

type of question, which is designed explicitly to establish a person's moral position. If shared by a majority, responses could be interpreted as social norms. The second is a 'preference' type of question, which asks people to predict their own future behaviour. These questions generally reflect the individual's preferences and are not necessarily normative. Using these definitions, the attitudinal questions analysed in this study should fall in the first category, and may be viewed as social norms if generally shared. Therefore, any change in the responses to these questions may provide evidence of normative changes in the society.

In the multivariate analysis, we consider a number of individual-level variables that may influence the formation of attitudes towards family behaviour. Selection of these explanatory variables is not arbitrary. Rather, they were chosen on the basis of the theoretical frameworks reviewed in Chapter 2. Accordingly, we consider three groups of determinants: (1) socio-economic status (SES), (2) cultural background, and (3) demographic and family characteristics. This principle is followed throughout the study. Occasionally, explanatory variables are added to the analytical model on the basis of prior research findings and/or other theoretical developments not expressly discussed in Chapter 2. To be sure, the analyses are necessarily limited by the selection of variables available in the surveys. I have no pretension of providing definitive answers to the research questions posed earlier.

The empirical analysis was carried out in two stages. In stage one, I conducted a series of descriptive analyses of the attitudes, emphasizing their age and

Figure 5.2: Percentage Approval of Premarital Sex for Men

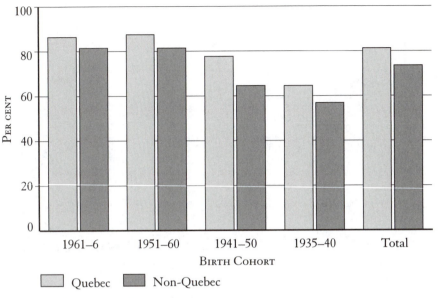

Source: The 1984 Canadian Fertility Survey.

regional patterns. In stage two, I estimated a series of multivariate models. I first estimated two binary logit models for approval of premarital sex and cohabitation, respectively.[1] I then estimated three ordinary least squares (OLS) models for the importance of marriage.[2] The multivariate analyses not only help us explore and identify the determinants of these family attitudes, they also serve the purpose of re-evaluating (confirming) the descriptive findings by removing the potential confounding effects of other characteristics.

Attitudes Towards Non-marital Sexual Behaviour

We first examine attitudes towards premarital sexual behaviour and non-marital cohabitation. The analyses were solely based on the CFS data. We start with a descriptive account of these attitudes, then conduct a multivariate analysis to examine the determinants of these attitudes.

Age/Cohort and Regional Patterns

Figure 5.1 presents the percentage approving of premarital sex for women. It is clear that a majority of the respondents (women aged 18–49) think that it is acceptable for young women to have a sexual life before marriage. It is also evident that the approval rate is generally higher among the younger than the older cohorts, although the 1951–60 cohort (aged 24–33) appears to have the highest approval rate. Regional patterns are unmistakable. As would be

Figure 5.3: Percentage Approval of Non-Marital Cohabitation for Successful Marriage

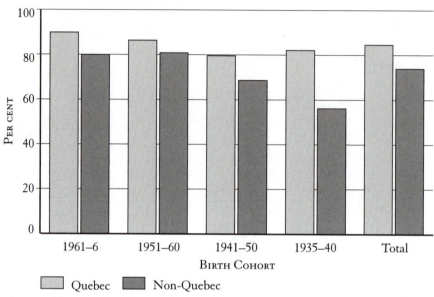

BIRTH COHORT

Quebec   Non-Quebec

Source: The 1984 Canadian Fertility Survey.

expected, the approval rate in Quebec is considerably higher than in the rest of Canada, with an overall difference of 8 percentage points (78 per cent for Quebec and 70 per cent for non-Quebec women). It should be pointed out that, given the data shown here, we cannot separate age- and cohort-effects.

Figure 5.2 shows the comparable distribution for approval of premarital sex for men. The age/cohort and regional patterns are similar to those shown in Figure 5.1. We can see that a large majority of women in their child-bearing ages approve of premarital sex for men; and the approval rate is generally higher among younger cohorts than older cohorts, and among Quebec rather than non-Quebec women. It is also interesting to note that there seems to be a greater acceptance of premarital sex for men than for women (i.e., compare Figure 5.1 with Figure 5.2). For example, overall, 81 per cent of Quebec women feel that premarital sex is acceptable *for men*, compared to 78 per cent expressing the same sentiment *for women*. The corresponding figures for non-Quebec women are 74 per cent and 70 per cent, respectively. These findings support the notion that there may be greater social sanctions against premarital sexual behaviour for women than for men.

While premarital sex is accepted by the majority of Canadian women (in their child-bearing ages), do women also accept the idea that unmarried women and men may live together premaritally to ensure the success of their marriage? Clearly, a large majority of the respondents gave an affirmative answer (see

**Figure 5.4: Percentage Approval of Non-Marital Cohabitation
for Mutual Attraction**

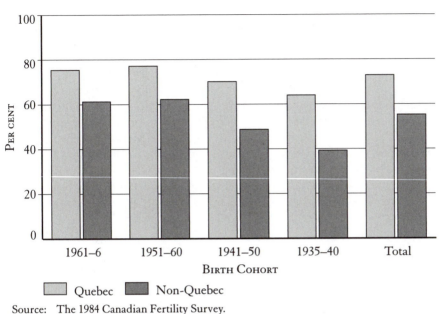

Source: The 1984 Canadian Fertility Survey.

Figure 5.3). Again, the approval rate is higher in Quebec than elsewhere in Canada. However, while the approval rate declines with age for non-Quebec women, the age pattern is not entirely clear for Quebec women (see the two oldest cohorts). Perhaps the sharpest contrast between Quebec and non-Quebec women is found among those who were born in the period 1935–40, the oldest cohort in the study. For Quebec women of this cohort, the approval rate is 82 per cent, compared to 56 per cent of non-Quebec women. How do we make sense of these findings? One possible explanation is that this cohort of Quebec women lived through the era of the Quiet Revolution (beginning in the early 1960s) when they were in their early twenties, a life-cycle stage in which new ideas and values are most permissible and acceptable.

While a majority of women believe it is acceptable for couples to live together premaritally to ensure the success of a future marriage, do women also accept the notion that unmarried couples may live together simply because they are attracted to each other but have no intention of making a long-term commitment? Seventy-three per cent of Quebec women said 'yes', compared to only 55 per cent of non-Quebec women (Figure 5.4). It is evident that the support for 'non-committal' cohabitation is considerably less than for 'premarital cohabitation'. The approval rate is again higher among younger and Quebec women.

In sum, the CFS data suggest a widespread acceptance of premarital sex and non-marital cohabitation among Canadian women, especially among younger and Quebec women. There is also a general acceptance of non-marital cohabitation when couples intend to marry. The acceptance of 'premarital cohabitation' is consistent with the view that cohabitation may be an extended courtship leading to marriage. People cohabit because they want to try out the relationship and see whether they are compatible as a couple living in a family unit.

Determinants of Approval of Non-marital Sexual Behaviour

To examine the determinants of the attitudes towards premarital sex and cohabitation, the response categories of the attitudes were coded as two dichotomous variables indicating whether the respondent gave an affirmative answer to either or both questions on premarital sex, and on cohabitation, respectively. Because the response variables are binary, I estimated two binomial logit models to fit the CFS data. Logit models estimate the log-odds that a value of the independent variable is associated with the dependent variable, all else being equal. Odds ratios can be calculated from logit models by taking the anti-log (e^β) of parameter estimates. Using premarital sex as an example, the anti-log of a parameter estimate reflects the odds of acceptance of premarital sex. A simple transformation, $100 \times (e^\beta - 1)$, can be interpreted as the percentage change in the odds of the acceptance of premarital sex for a one-unit change in a given explanatory variable, holding all other variables constant. For example, the parameter estimate for educational status in the model of premarital sex is .034 (see Table 5.1). The anti-log of .034 is 1.035, which can be interpreted as: for each additional year of formal education, the odds of the acceptance of premarital sex are increased by 3.5 per cent ($100 \times [1.035 - 1]$), holding all other variables constant. Similarly, for a dichotomous variable, a comparable interpretation becomes the percentage change in the odds of the acceptance of premarital cohabitation for having some characteristic. For example, the parameter estimate for working outside the home in the model of premarital sex is .193. The anti-log of .193 yields a value of 1.213, which means that the odds of the acceptance of premarital sex are 21 per cent ($100 \times [1.213 - 1]$) higher for women working outside the home than for women who do not.[3]

The results of the two logit models are shown in Table 5.1. Column 1 shows the parameter estimates for the model of acceptance of premarital sex. Column 2 shows the anti-logs (the odds ratios) of the estimates. The corresponding estimates for acceptance of non-marital cohabitation are presented in columns 3 and 4.

We first look at the SES indicators. Table 5.1 shows that employment status has a significant positive effect on the acceptance of premarital sex, and a positive, but not significant, effect on the acceptance of non-marital cohabitation. As noted, women working outside the home are more likely to approve of premarital sex than women who do not. Educational attainment has a significant positive impact on acceptance of both premarital sex and non-marital cohabitation. Also as noted, a one-year increase in formal education raises the odds of the acceptance of premarital sex by 3.5 per cent, and of non-marital cohabitation by 2.4 per cent. Further, household income also has a significant positive effect on premarital sex, but not on non-marital cohabitation. Educational enrolment has a negative but not significant impact on both attitudinal items.

Four cultural indicators were considered in the analyses: religion, church attendance, nativity, and region. It is clear that religion has a significant effect on both attitudinal items. Catholics appear to have a greater acceptance of both premarital sex and non-marital cohabitation than Protestants and women with other religious orientations. These results are inconsistent with the notion that Catholics are more conservative than Protestants when it comes to family values. However, they are consistent with recent findings on the declining role of Catholicism in Canadian family life, particularly in Quebec (Balakrishnan and Chen, 1990; Lipset, 1990; Wu and Baer, 1996). The results also show that Catholics are not different from women without religious orientations.

In addition to religion, church attendance, a useful indicator of religiosity, is also an important predictor. As anticipated, frequent church attendance fosters negative (conservative) attitudes towards premarital sex and non-marital cohabitation. Further, nativity (place of birth) has an impact on the approval of cohabitation. Canadian-born women are about 24 per cent more likely to approve of non-marital cohabitation than are immigrant women. Finally, consistent with the earlier findings on regional attitudinal patterns, we observe that Quebec women tend to hold more liberal attitudes towards premarital sex and cohabitation than non-Quebec women. The regional effects are strong and consistent.

Turning to demographic determinants, we observe that marital status has a significant effect on both attitudinal items. As would be expected, married women are less likely to accept premarital sex and non-marital cohabitation than cohabiting and separated/divorced women, but are not different from widowed women. Compared with single women, married women are also more conservative on the question of premarital sex, but are not different from single women when it comes to premarital cohabitation.

Age/cohort effects are significant and positive. Generally, the approval rate of premarital sex and cohabitation declines with age, although the 1951–60 cohort (second youngest cohort) appears to be the least conservative on both attitudinal questions. Moreover, women living in rural areas are less likely to accept premarital sex than urban women, although they do not differ significantly when it comes to premarital cohabitation.

In short, our regression analyses suggest that the approval rates of premarital sex and non-marital cohabitation increase with SES and age, but decrease with church attendance. Rates are also higher among women who are Catholic, non-immigrant, cohabiting, or separated/divorced, and who are residing in Quebec or in urban areas.

Attitudes Towards Marriage

We now turn to values of the importance of marriage. As noted, the question on the importance of marriage was asked in both the CFS and the GSS–95. Thus, we

Table 5.1: Binomial Logit Models of Approval of Premarital Sex and Cohabitation

Variable	Premarital Sex		Cohabitation	
	ß	exp(ß)	ß	exp(ß)
	1	2	3	4
SOCIO-ECONOMIC STATUS				
Employed outside home				
Yes	0.193*	1.213	0.040	1.041
No†				
Educational status	0.034***	1.035	0.024***	1.024
(years of formal education)				
School enrolment				
Yes	−0.253	0.777	−0.046	0.956
No†				
Household income	0.001*	1.001	0.0004	1.000
(in $100s, 0 = none, ...,				
996 = $99,600 or more)				
Income missing				
Yes	−0.466***	0.627	−0.193*	0.824
No†				
CULTURAL BACKGROUND				
Religion				
Protestant	−0.271**	0.763	−0.325***	0.723
Other	−1.159***	0.314	−0.718***	0.488
None	−0.020	0.980	−0.366	0.694
Catholic†				
Church attendance	−0.589***	0.555	−0.621***	0.537
(in 5 levels, 1 = never, ...,				
5 = at least once a week)				
Nativity				
Canadian-born	0.041	1.042	0.213*	1.238
Foreign-born†				
Region				
Atlantic	−0.562***	0.570	−0.702***	0.496
Ontario	−0.468***	0.626	−1.007***	0.365
Prairie	−0.703***	0.495	−1.109***	0.330
BC	−0.704***	0.495	−0.966***	0.381
Quebec†				

DEMOGRAPHIC CHARACTERISTICS

Marital status				
Cohabiting	1.177***	3.243	1.442***	4.229
Separated/Divorced	0.562***	1.754	0.677***	1.967
Widowed	0.273	1.314	0.419	1.521
Single	0.684***	1.981	0.126	1.134
Married†				
Birth cohort				
1961–6	0.643***	1.902	0.847***	2.333
1951–60	0.939***	2.558	0.860***	2.363
1941–50	0.260*	1.297	0.358**	1.430
1935–40†				
Rural residence				
Yes	–0.192*	0.825	–0.096	0.909
No†				
Intercept	2.474***		3.355***	
– 2 Log Likelihood	4887.2		4396.2	
Model chi-square	1124.4***		911.6	
df	22		22	

Note: All dummy variables are coded as 1 = yes, 0 = no.
†   Reference category.
*   p < .05
**   p < .01
*** p < .001 (two-tailed test)
Source: The 1984 Canadian Fertility Survey.

are able to use data from both surveys in the descriptive analysis. In the multi-variate analysis, only data from the GSS–95 were used because of their recency and better representation of the population. Again, we begin with a descriptive analysis of aggregate trends and focus on their age-, period-, cohort-, and regional patterns. We then look at the results of the multivariate analysis.

Changing Patterns of Attitudes Towards Marriage

Table 5.2 presents percentage distributions for women's opinions on the importance of marriage for Canada as a whole, for Quebec, and for the rest of Canada. The survey question and response categories are provided in the table as well. To assist our discussion of age-period-cohort-regional patterns, we focus on the response categories A and B (i.e., those who reported that it is *very important*, and *important*, to be married).

Table 5.2 shows some age effects on the importance of marriage.[4] For example, for Canada as a whole we observe that in 1984, 39 per cent of women aged 18–28 rated marriage as *very important*, and this percentage rises to 48 per cent for women aged 40–50. Similar patterns are also observed when we break down the data by region. An overall increasing effect with age is discernable in 1995 as well, although the effect is not entirely linear across the age groups. The age effects seem to be reversed for the response category of *important* in 1984 (see column 2), and the patterns are unclear for the comparable distributions in 1995 (see column 7). Overall, there is some evidence that the rating of the importance of marriage increases with age. Older women are more likely than younger women to report that it is *very important* to be married for a happy life.

Period effects are more evident than age effects. For example, in 1984, 39 per cent of women aged 18–28 rated marriage as *very important* (see column 1). The comparable figure for 1995 is 34 per cent (see column 6).[5] The same pattern holds for Quebec and non-Quebec women (see columns 1 and 6). Considering the response category of *important*, we see a reduction in rating marriage as *important* for Quebec women, but an increase for non-Quebec women (see columns 2 and 7). The percentage distributions change little for Canada as a whole (see columns 2 and 7). In short, there are relatively fewer people (women) who feel that it is *very important* to get married today than a decade ago. This period effect is more evident in Quebec than elsewhere in Canada.

Cohort effects may be observed by following the distribution of a given characteristic for a given age group across surveys. Using women who were 18–28 years of age in 1984 as an example (see column 1), women in this cohort would turn 29–39 years of age in 1995. If sampling variations in the surveys are negligible, we may compare percentage distributions across the surveys. For this cohort of women (who were born in 1956–66 and were 18–28 years old in 1984), we see that 39 per cent rated marriage as *very important* in 1984, but the percentage declined to 35 per cent in 1995. A similar pattern is observed for the cohorts of 1945–55 and 1934–44, who were aged 29–39 and 40–50 in 1984. This downward pattern holds when we break down the distributions by region. However, cohort patterns become less clear when we look at the category of *important* (columns 2 and 7). We observe a reduction in rating marriage as *important* for the youngest cohort (aged 18–28 in 1984), but an increase in the rating for the oldest cohort (aged 40–50 in 1984). For the middle age cohort (29–39 in 1984), we see a reduction in Quebec, but an increase elsewhere in Canada. Overall, we observe some cohort change in rating the importance of marriage. If cohort change can be interpreted as a sign for social change in society (Ryder, 1965), then there is some evidence of a change in normative attitudes towards marriage in Canadian society. Marriage has become somewhat less important in Canadian life.

Regional effects are unmistakable. Comparing the numerical figures between Quebec and the rest of Canada, we see that the percentage rating marriage as *very important* is considerably lower for Quebec women than for non-Quebec women (column 1). For example, in 1984, 26 per cent of Quebec women aged 18–28 rated marriage as *very important*, compared to 44 per cent of non-Quebec women in the same age group. This pattern is consistent for the other age

Table 5.2: Importance of Being Married for a Happy Life: Women, 1984–1995

Question: In order for you to be happy in life, is it very important (A), important (B), not very important (C), or not at all important (D) to be married?

Age	1984 A 1	B 2	C 3	D 4	Total 5	1995 A 6	B 7	C 8	D 9	Total* 10
CANADA										
15–17	—	—	—	—	—	16.13	44.84	33.35	5.69	100%
18–28	39.09	32.04	22.24	6.63	100%	33.70	32.34	30.11	3.86	100%
29–39	39.41	27.97	23.12	9.49	100%	34.54	27.81	31.02	6.63	100%
40–50**	48.37	26.80	17.89	6.94	100%	31.93	28.78	33.36	5.93	100%
51–61	—	—	—	—	—	37.43	34.37	24.88	3.33	100%
62 or older	—	—	—	—	—	44.45	38.55	14.61	2.39	100%
Total	41.35	29.32	21.56	7.76	100%	35.05	32.56	27.66	4.72	100%
N†	2,190	1,553	1,142	411	5,296	1,835	1,843	1,664	350	5,710
QUEBEC										
15–17	—	—	—	—	—	14.41	27.83	52.01	5.74	100%
18–28	26.44	34.17	26.98	12.41	100%	23.18	25.42	41.68	9.72	100%
29–39	26.15	29.65	26.89	17.31	100%	16.92	22.01	48.07	13.00	100%
40–50**	37.94	29.71	17.65	14.71	100%	19.86	25.72	41.24	13.19	100%
51–61	—	—	—	—	—	27.20	33.88	30.77	8.14	100%
62 or older	—	—	—	—	—	37.79	42.18	14.22	5.81	100%
Total	29.05	31.41	24.74	14.80	100%	23.89	29.15	36.91	10.05	100%
N†	418	452	356	213	1,439	387	500	647	193	1,727
NON-QUEBEC										
15–17	—	—	—	—	—	16.71	50.61	27.01	5.67	100%
18–28	43.61	31.28	20.55	4.56	100%	37.11	34.58	26.35	1.95	100%
29–39	44.59	27.35	21.63	6.43	100%	40.46	29.75	25.29	4.50	100%
40–50**	52.26	25.62	18.06	4.06	100%	36.29	29.89	30.51	3.31	100%
51–61	—	—	—	—	—	41.29	34.55	22.65	1.52	100%
62 or older	—	—	—	—	—	46.94	37.20	14.75	1.11	100%
Total	45.96	28.54	20.37	5.13	100%	38.97	33.76	24.41	2.85	100%
N†	1,773	1,101	786	198	3,858	1,466	1,343	1,017	157	3,983

*   Total may not add up to 100 per cent due to rounding.
**   Age 40–9 for the 1984 CFS.
†   Weighted percentages, unweighted N.
Sources: The 1984 Canadian Fertility Survey and the 1995 General Social Survey.

groups and for the 1995 data as well. However, a slightly higher proportion of Quebec women than non-Quebec women rated marriage as *important* in 1984, although this trend was reversed in 1995. A comparison of the marginal distributions (see the totals for each group) between the two regions tells a similar story. In short, there is fairly consistent evidence that Quebec women place less emphasis on marriage than non-Quebec women. These findings are congruous with our earlier results on the attitudes towards premarital sex and non-marital cohabitation.

Table 5.3 provides comparable findings on the importance of marriage for men using the 1995 data. Considering response category A (*very important*), we see some evidence that the rating of the importance of marriage increases with age, although the increase is not monotonic. This age effect pattern holds in both Quebec and the rest of Canada. Age effects become less evident for response category B (*important*). Moreover, as with women, regional trends are apparent. With age held constant, we observe a lower rating of marriage among Quebec men than non-Quebec men (see response A). Marginal distributions confirm this trend. Finally, there is evidence that women appear to place less emphasis on the importance of marriage than men do (see the 1995 marginal distributions for Canada as a whole in Tables 5.2 and 5.3). While the differences may seem small, as will be shown below, these differences are statistically significant after removing the effects of all other variables.

In brief, our results provide evidence supporting the view that Canadians have placed less emphasis on marriage over time. This tendency is stronger among younger people and people residing in Quebec. Having said this, we should not lose sight of the larger picture: a majority of Canadians feel that it is *very important*, or *important*, to be married, no matter how we arrange our data. Marriage is not going out of style soon.

Determinants of Attitudes on Importance of Marriage

While we observed that the pattern of values on the importance of marriage varies by age and region, the age and regional effects could be spurious due to the influences of other variables not considered in the analysis. For example, because older people tend to be married, and because married people are likely to place more importance on marriage, the positive effect of age may be attenuated and even disappear when marital status is taken into account. To eliminate this and other potential confounding effects, and to identify other determinants of marriage attitudes, I estimated three ordinary-least-squares (OLS) models with the importance of marriage as the response variable. The first OLS model fits the data for the whole sample. In anticipation that the effects of the determinants may be gender-based, two gender-specific models were estimated. The interpretation of OLS estimates is straightforward: the parameter, b, indicates the change in the response variable (increase or reduction) for a one-unit change in a given explanatory variable, holding all other variables constant. Table 5.4 presents the results of the analyses.

Table 5.3: Importance of Being Married for a Happy Life: Men, 1995

Question: In order for you to be happy in life, is it very important (A), important (B), not very important (C), or not at all important (D) to be married?

| Age | Birth cohort | Response | | | | Total* |
		A	B	C	D	
CANADA						
15–24	1971–80	26.12	44.36	25.71	3.80	100%
25–34	1961–70	36.18	31.58	26.98	5.26	100%
35–44	1951–60	33.99	32.42	27.61	5.99	100%
45–54	1941–50	32.89	40.64	22.43	4.05	100%
55–64	1931–40	43.85	41.37	13.03	1.75	100%
65–74	1921–30	53.87	38.66	5.73	1.74	100%
75 and over	<1921	49.72	42.97	7.12	0.19	100%
Total		36.14	37.55	22.20	4.11	100%
N**		1,604	1,660	1,147	258	4,669
Chi-sqaure = 274.4, *d.f.* = 18, (p < .001)						
QUEBEC						
15–24	1971–80	14.13	39.79	36.34	9.56	100%
25–34	1961–70	19.92	23.62	42.11	14.36	100%
35–44	1951–60	21.60	27.72	36.22	14.46	100%
45–54	1941–50	19.22	40.27	29.69	10.82	100%
55–64	1931–40	36.75	46.44	12.32	4.48	100%
65–74	1921–30	48.42	44.44	4.10	3.03	100%
75 and over	<1921	31.43	61.08	7.49	0.00	100%
Total		23.80	35.67	30.09	10.44	100%
N**		280	434	435	167	1,316
Chi-sqaure = 176.6, *d.f.* = 18, (p < .001).						
NON-QUEBEC						
15–24	1971–80	29.94	45.84	22.28	1.94	100%
25–34	1961–70	41.61	34.24	21.93	2.23	100%
35–44	1951–60	38.38	34.08	24.56	2.98	100%
45–54	1941–50	38.01	40.78	19.71	1.51	100%
55–64	1931–40	46.46	39.50	13.29	0.74	100%
65–74	1921–30	55.72	36.70	6.29	1.30	100%
75 and over	<1921	55.97	36.78	7.00	0.25	100%
Total		40.42	38.2	19.46	1.92	100%
N**		1,324	1,226	712	91	3,353
Chi-sqaure = 144.1, *d.f.* = 18, (p < .001).						

*   Total may not add up to 100 per cent due to rounding.
** Weighted percentages, unweighted N.
Source: The 1995 General Social Survey.

Table 5.4: Ordinary Least Squares Models of Importance of Marriage

Variable	All	Women	Men
SOCIO-ECONOMIC STATUS			
Social class (in 16 levels, 1 = farm labourers, …, 16 = self-employed professionals)	−0.007*	−0.009	−0.005
Social class missing			
Yes	0.072*	0.087	0.035
No[†]			
Educational status (in 10 levels, 1 = none, …, 10 = bachelor or higher)	−0.024***	−0.020**	−0.027***
School enrolment			
Yes	0.057	0.040	0.079
No[†]			
Personal income (in 21 levels, 0 = none, …, 20 = $100,000 or more)	−0.009*	−0.010	−0.008
Income missing			
Yes	0.057*	0.068	0.051
No[†]			
CULTURAL BACKGROUND			
Religion			
Protestant	0.068*	0.041	0.099*
Other	0.031	0.136	−0.062
None	−0.132**	−0.088	−0.171**
Catholic[†]			
Church attendance (in 5 levels, 1 = never, …, 5 = at least once a week)	0.094***	0.100***	0.089***
Nativity			
Canadian-born	−0.132***	−0.058	−0.214***
Foreign-born[†]			
Region			
Atlantic	0.417***	0.402***	0.435***
Ontario	0.494***	0.551***	0.429***
Prairie	0.545***	0.570***	0.516***
BC	0.550***	0.508***	0.602***
Quebec[†]			

DEMOGRAPHIC AND FAMILY CHARACTERISTICS

Gender			
Men	0.225***	—	—
Women[†]			
Marital status			
Cohabiting	−1.331***	−1.202***	−1.456***
Separated/Divorced	−0.340***	−0.308***	−0.436***
Widowed	−1.168***	−1.228***	−1.054***
Single	−1.245***	−1.258***	−1.214***
Married[†]			
Birth cohort			
1971 or later	0.437***	0.491***	0.335**
1961–70	−0.022	−0.014	−0.057
1951–60	−0.323***	−0.309***	−0.363***
1941–50	−0.292***	−0.266**	−0.346***
1931–40	−0.160*	−0.143	−0.195
1921–30	−0.020	−0.033	−0.001
<1921[†]			
Had a happy childhood			
Yes	0.077***	0.066***	0.091***
No[†]			
Intact family			
Yes	0.002	−0.001	−0.001
No[†]			
Mother's education (in 10 levels, 1 = none, …, 10 = bachelor or higher)	−0.006	−0.011	−0.0001
Father's education (in 10 levels, 1 = none, …, 10 = bachelor or higher)	−0.006	−0.005	−0.008
Father's education missing			
Yes	−0.066	−0.095*	−0.035
No[†]			
Intercept	3.643***	3.596***	3.931***
R square	0.301***	0.289***	0.321***

Note: Dummy indicator for missing values of mother's education is also included as covariate, which is not significant at the .05 level. All dummy indicators are coded as: 1 = yes, 0 = no.

[†] Reference category.

* $p < .05$

** $p < .01$

***$p < .001$ (two-tailed test)

Source: The 1995 General Social Survey.

We first look at the SES indicators. Social class is a numerical measure based on a respondent's occupation, the so-called Pineo social class scale. Table 5.4 shows that social class has a negative effect on the importance of marriage (see column 1), although the effect becomes non-significant in both gender-specific models. A similar negative effect is found for personal income. Educational status has a negative effect as well; and the negative effect remains significant in both gender-specific models. However, school enrolment does not have a significant effect. These results suggest that individuals with high SES tend to place less emphasis on the importance of marriage than those with low SES. The effects of SES do not seem to vary by gender, although only educational status has a significant effect in both gender-specific models.

Turning to cultural indicators, we observe that religion has an impact on the importance of marriage. Consistent with our results on premarital sex and cohabitation, Catholics tend to place less emphasis on marriage than Protestants (column 1). This tendency remains for men (column 2), but becomes non-significant for women (column 3). Catholics also appear to place less emphasis on marriage than people with no religious orientations, although Catholic women do not seem to differ from non-Catholic women on their attitudes towards marriage (column 2).

The effect of church attendance is consistent across the models. As would be expected, frequent churchgoers tend to emphasize the importance of marriage more than others. Further, non-immigrants appear to place less emphasis on marriage than immigrants, although the negative effect becomes non-significant for women. Also, consistent with our earlier findings, marriage appears to be less important for Quebecers than non-Quebecers.

Table 5.4 also shows that the estimate for gender is positive and significant, suggesting that men tend to place more emphasis on the importance of marriage than women (column 1). As would be expected, the rating of marriage is higher among married people than unmarried people. Moreover, age/cohort effects are 'U'-shaped. The youngest cohort appears to place more emphasis on marriage than any other cohort, while the middle-age cohorts place the least emphasis on marriage. Although the finding for the youngest cohort could signal a change in the attitudes towards marriage, it may also be that many of the young people have not married and have not experienced marital problems. Younger people also tend to be more idealistic and romantic about intimate relationships than older people.

For the variables measuring family background, only happy childhood has a significant influence. We observe that respondents who reported having a happy childhood tend to value marriage more than others. Other family characteristics, such as parental divorce and education, do not have a significant impact on attitudes towards the importance of marriage.

In short, our multivariate analysis suggests that a positive attitude towards marriage is associated with low SES, regular church attendance, and with being Protestant, immigrant, non-Québécois, married, the youngest, and having a happy childhood. Moreover, men appear to have more favourable attitudes towards marriage than women do—this is consistent with Goldscheider and Waite's (1986) notion that men may have a greater preference for marriage than women.

Summary

In this chapter we have examined the patterns of attitudes towards premarital sex, non-marital cohabitation, and the importance of marriage. We found that a majority of women in their child-bearing ages (18–49) approve of premarital sex and non-marital cohabitation. We also observed that a majority of adult men and women feel that it is important to be married. These results seem to suggest that while non-marital cohabitation is acceptable, it is not necessarily seen as a substitute for marriage, but rather as a prelude to marriage. Indeed, as we will show in Chapter 8, most cohabiting respondents in the GSS–95 reported that they intended to marry their partners.

We have also shown that the pattern of attitudes towards marriage has changed over time. There is clear evidence that people now place less emphasis on marriage than they did a decade ago. If these attitudes can be interpreted as reflecting social norms, then we can see changes in the societal norms about the institution of marriage. The centrality of marriage seems to have weakened. Similar trends are observed also in Europe (e.g., Lesthaeghe and Surkyn, 1988) and the United States (e.g., Goldscheider and Waite, 1991; Thornton, 1989).

We have identified several individual-level characteristics associated with these attitudes. Generally, an increased acceptance of non-marital sexual behaviour is observed among people of high SES and among those who are young, unmarried, Canadian-born, Catholic, less religious, and living in Quebec and/or in urban areas. A reduced emphasis on the importance of marriage is found among those with high SES, an unhappy childhood, and who are middle-aged, unmarried, Canadian-born, non-Protestant, less religious, and/or residing in Quebec. Taken together, these results indicate that those who share the notion that non-marital sexual behaviour is acceptable tend to value marriage less. If these values and attitudes may lead to behavioural changes, as suggested by the sociological theory, then we should expect that these individual attributes may also have a bearing on the formation of non-marital cohabitation, a hypothesis that will be examined in the next chapter.

6 | The Transition to Cohabitation

It was not too long ago that marriage was perhaps the most important decision that young persons made as they entered into adulthood. Marriage marked a clear transition from childhood to adulthood, was associated with being an adult and assuming other adult roles, and normally led to a separation from the financial and residential dependence of childhood (Goldscheider and Waite, 1986: 91). However, many young people now delay the entrance into marriage, and some forgo it altogether. Perhaps this is because marriage has become a less central event in the transition to adulthood, or perhaps the idea that marriage is a life-long commitment has become unrealistic, as the incidence of divorce is so high. The decline in marriage has made non-marital cohabitation an attractive lifestyle choice. While the decision to cohabit may not be as difficult to make as the decision to marry, 'moving in together' is an important step in the development of coupling relationships: it entails the sharing of a common residence, usually a pooling of financial resources, and generally involves the obligation of exclusive sexual intimacy. For many it is far more painful and difficult to dissolve a cohabiting relationship than it is to break up a date or even an engagement.

Why do people choose to cohabit? To answer this question, we may assume that people are rational and that they make rational choices regarding their union behaviour. Given the constraints, people will choose to cohabit only if they feel that they are better off cohabiting than remaining in their current state. By the same token, people will dissolve a cohabitation when they feel that they will be better off (at least not worse off) being single, given the costs of dissolution. We may add to our initial assumption that searching for a mate is not conceptually different from searching for a job: both require time, energy, and money. Only a small number of all potential matches are perfect. People assess their own assets, such as physical attractiveness and earnings, and trade in the (marriage or cohabitation) market for a mate whose assets either complement or substitute for their own (Lichter et al., 1992: 782; also see Becker, 1981; Hutchens, 1979; Oppenheimer, 1988). In this chapter, we consider several individual characteristics known to affect marital search and the decision to marry and assume that they have similar influences on the decision to cohabit.[1]

As we noted in Chapter 4, the recent increase in non-marital cohabitation is unprecedented in Canada and many other industrial countries. Over the past two decades, considerable scholarly attention has been devoted to the examination of cohabitation patterns and trends (e.g., Bumpass and Sweet, 1989; Carmichael, 1990; Landale and Forste, 1991; Leridon, 1990; Liefbroer, 1991; Ramsøy, 1994; Spanier, 1985; Tanfer, 1987; Thornton, 1988) and to the factors influencing the transition to cohabitation (e.g., Axinn and Thornton, 1993; Bumpass and Sweet, 1989; Clarkberg, 1995; Hoem, 1986; Landale and Forste, 1991; Raley, 1995; Thornton et al., 1992; Thornton et al., 1995). However, with few exceptions (e.g., Balakrishnan et al., 1993; Le Bourdais and Marcil-Gratton, 1996; Rao, 1990; Turcotte and Goldscheider, 1998), the transition to cohabitation has not been explored in Canada.

The objective of this chapter is to examine the transition to cohabitation. The key questions to be addressed are: (1) How many people make the transition to cohabitation? (2) When do people make such transitions? (3) Does the timing of the transition differ between premarital and post-marital cohabitation? (4) Who cohabits? What are the characteristics of cohabitors? (5) Do the determinants of premarital and post-marital cohabitation differ? (6) Does the transition to cohabitation differ between men and women? To answer these questions, we employ survey data from two rounds of the GSS. Our analysis begins with a brief review of the data sources and analytical models. In the second section, we look at the age patterns and determinants of premarital cohabitation. In the third section, we examine post-marital cohabitation. The last section includes a brief discussion of the findings.

Data and Methods

The data used to study premarital cohabitation came from the GSS–95. As noted in Chapter 3, the GSS–95 involved a nationally representative survey of 10,749 women and men aged 15 and over. The residents of the two northern territories and those in state institutions were excluded from the survey. As cohabitation prior to marriage is relatively rare among middle-aged and elderly people, I restricted the sample to respondents who were under 35 years of age at the time of the survey (i.e., in 1995). Using this constraint, the final study sample included 2,055 women and 1,760 men.

The section on post-marital cohabitation is based on an earlier study that used the GSS–90 (Wu and Balakrishnan, 1994). As we noted, the GSS–90 was also a national survey of respondents aged 15 and over, excluding the residents of the two territories and institutions (N = 13,495). To study post-marital cohabitation, the sample was restricted to respondents who ended a first marriage through either a separation or a divorce. The study did not include widowed respondents, primarily because only a very small number of widowed persons ever cohabited following the death of their spouses.[2] With these constraints, the study sample included 930 women and 650 men.[3]

In both surveys, respondents were asked to provide detailed information on their union formation experiences. Using a technique known as 'a life history calendar' (Freedman et al., 1988), respondents' complete marriage and cohabitation histories were reconstructed.[4] To analyse the timing of premarital cohabitation, we reconstructed the union histories of the respondents until they reached age 35. Respondents who made the transition into cohabitation prior to that age were coded as 1; those who had not were coded as 0. To study the timing of cohabitation, an exposure time (also known as duration or survival time) variable was constructed. For those who made the transition, exposure time (the time during which the respondent was exposed to the 'risk' of cohabitation) was measured from age 15 to the age at the entry into the union. For those who had not yet cohabited by the time of the survey (the censored cases), exposure time was measured up to the time of the survey.[5] Age was measured in months.

Similarly, for post-marital cohabitations, the respondents were assigned a value of 1 if they made the transition to cohabitation after (first) marital disruption and 0 otherwise. To measure exposure time, we decided to use the date of separation rather than the date of divorce to determine the timing of marital dissolution. As Bumpass et al. (1990) noted, there are two reasons for this practice. First, divorce is often contingent upon variation in the legal process. Second, there are substantial variations among subgroups in the timing and likelihood of divorce, given separation. Therefore, for those who cohabited after marital disruption, exposure time was measured from the time of marital separation, or divorce if separation data are unavailable. Where post-marital cohabitation did not occur, exposure time was measured from the date of marital disruption to the survey date.[6] Time was measured in months.

The primary statistical tools used in the analysis are survival model techniques.[7] Our analysis proceeds in two stages. In stage one, we estimate the timing and rate of cohabitation using ordinary life-table techniques. The life tables estimate the probability of cohabitation at each age (duration), computed in whole months, and provide the description of these probabilities in terms of the cumulative experience of cohabitation by successive ages (durations). Life table techniques were designed specifically to incorporate censored observations into the estimation. Individuals who enter into cohabitation contribute exposure to the 'risk' at each age (duration) until the time of the union formation. Individuals who have not yet cohabited (who are censored) also contribute exposure at each age (duration), up to the time of the survey.

In stage two, we focus on the associations between cohabitation and each of the individual-level determinants considered in the study. For premarital cohabitation, I estimated two gender-specific proportional hazard (PH) models of age dependence, estimating the effects of explanatory variables on the 'risk' (hazard rate) of cohabitation (Cox, 1972; Kalbfleisch and Prentice, 1980). The PH model is a general non-parametric model and has the advantage of allowing the form of the baseline hazard function to remain unspecified (Cox, 1972). For post-marital cohabitation, I estimated a series of parametric hazard models of duration dependence, also known as (accelerated) failure time models (Kalbfleisch and Prentice, 1980). I chose the Weibull distribution as the baseline hazard function because the Weibull distribution is a generalization of the exponential distribution, which, unlike the exponential distribution, does not assume a constant hazard rate. As with the hazard distribution of remarriage (e.g., Wu, 1992), the hazard of post-marital cohabitation could be a monotonic decreasing function since marital dissolution.

The Transition to Premarital Cohabitation

In Chapter 4 we saw that the incidence of cohabitation has increased dramatically since 1981, when the Canadian census began collecting information on non-marital cohabitation. The 1996 census found that 7.7 per cent of Canadians aged 15 and older were cohabitating at the time of the census. While the census data provide a snapshot of the phenomenon of cohabitation, they underestimate the Canadian experience of cohabitation due to its transient nature. Since cohabitations generally are short-lived (see Chapter 8), we would suspect that the proportion of Canadians who cohabited sometime in their life should be much higher than the figure reported 'currently cohabiting' in the census. While the 1996 census did not ask (non-cohabiting) people whether they ever cohabited, this information is available in the GSS–95. To make it comparable to census data, we will use the whole sample, appropriately weighted to reflect the distribution of the Canadian population in 1995.

Figure 6.1 provides the percentage distribution of respondents who had ever cohabited. Overall, about 36 per cent of Quebec women and 25 per cent of women elsewhere in Canada (including those who were cohabiting at the time of the survey) reported that they had cohabited at some time in their lives. The corresponding figures for men are 41 per cent and 26 per cent. Both age/cohort and regional effects are evident. The percentage having ever cohabited generally declines with age cohort, except for the youngest age cohort. The lower percentage for the youngest cohort is primarily due to the limited observation period (i.e., they were censored at the survey time). The higher percentage, those ever having cohabited in Quebec, is consistent across age and gender groups. It is also interesting to observe that while Quebec men (41 per cent) have a substantially higher rate than Quebec women (36 per cent), the comparable rates for non-Quebec women and men are virtually identical (25–6 per cent). Certainly, these age and regional patterns of having ever been in a cohabitation cannot tell us whether these patterns would remain if we were to look at premarital and post-marital cohabitation separately.

The Timing of Premarital Cohabitation

How many people cohabit, and how soon do they form a cohabiting relationship? Figure 6.2 shows the life table estimates of the cumulative experience of cohabitation separately for women and men. As noted, life table techniques are

Figure 6.1: Percentage Ever Having Been in a Cohabiting Relationship

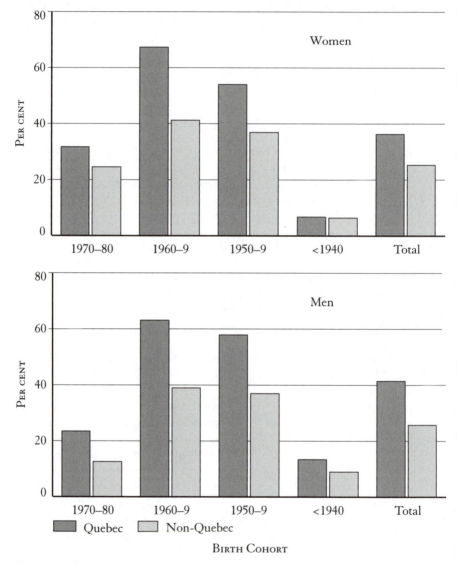

Source: The 1995 General Social Survey.

capable of incorporating censored observations into the estimation and provide a description of the cumulative cohabitation experience. The figure shows that the rate of cohabitation is fairly low before age 20 and accelerates in the twenties. For example, by age 18, about 8 per cent of women and 3 per cent of men had entered into a cohabitational relationship. By age 20, the percentages rise to 21 per cent and 9 per cent for women and men, respectively. By age 25, the corresponding

Figure 6.2: Life Table Estimates of Cumulative Proportion of Premarital Cohabitation

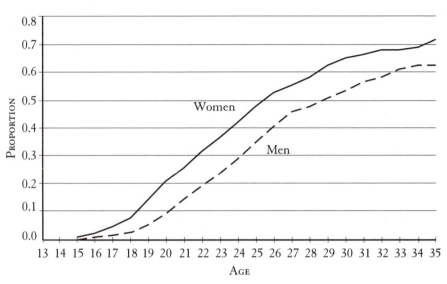

Source: The 1995 General Social Survey.

figures for women and men jump to 48 per cent and 35 per cent; by age 30, the comparable numbers are 65 per cent and 54 per cent. It is clear that when we take the censored observations into consideration, we observe a different picture: the rate of cohabitation is considerably higher than we saw in Figure 6.1. Moreover, gender differences in the entry into cohabitation also are apparent. We see that women are more likely to enter, and enter more rapidly, into cohabitation than are men. These findings are consistent with the age patterns of first marriage, as women tend to marry men older than themselves.

The Determinants of Premarital Cohabitation

While women appear to be more likely than men to cohabit prior to marriage, not all women are equally likely to cohabit. There is considerable heterogeneity in cohabitation among women and men. To identify the factors that may influence the decision to cohabit, we consider a set of individual-level variables known to affect the entry into marital union and hypothesize that they may influence the entry into premarital cohabitation as well. Based on our theoretical review in Chapter 2, explanatory variables are again divided into three categories: socio-economic status (SES), cultural background, and demographic and family characteristics.[8]

Table 6.1 presents the parameter estimates from two proportional hazard models of premarital cohabitation for women and men, respectively. The interpretation of parameter estimates is similar to that for the binary logit models we

Table 6.1: Proportional Hazard Models of Entry into Premarital Cohabitation

Variable	Women	Men
SOCIO-ECONOMIC STATUS		
Employed[†]		
Yes	0.372***	0.512***
No[‡]		
Educational status	−0.060***	0.006
(in 10 levels, 1 = none, …,		
10 = bachelor or higher)		
School enrolment[†]		
Yes	−0.362***	−0.326**
No[‡]		
CULTURAL BACKGROUND		
Religion		
Catholic	−0.243**	−0.125
Protestant	−0.308**	−0.210
Others	−0.726*	−0.747*
No religious affiliation[‡]		
Nativity		
Canadian-born	0.887***	0.694***
Foreign-born[‡]		
Region		
Quebec	0.594***	0.662***
Rest of Canada[‡]		
DEMOGRAPHIC AND FAMILY CHARACTERISTICS		
Birth cohort		
1960–4	−0.263**	−0.199
1965–9	−0.519***	−0.362**
1970–80[‡]		
Pregnancy[†]		
Yes	0.825***	0.670***
No[‡]		
First birth[†]		
Yes	−0.030	1.374***
No[‡]		
Second birth[†]		
Yes	−0.164	0.464
No[‡]		

Third or later birth[†]		
Yes	0.612	−0.352
No[‡]		
Had a happy childhood		
Yes	−0.162***	−0.121**
No[‡]		
Number of siblings	−0.024	0.031
Intact family		
Yes	−0.310***	−0.020
No[‡]		
Mother's education	0.004	−0.022
(in 10 levels, 1 = none, ...,		
10 = bachelor or higher)		
Father's education	−0.040**	−0.000
(in 10 levels, 1 = none, ...,		
10 = bachelor or higher)		
−2 Log Likelihood	8199.9	5935.3
Model chi-square	389.6***	240.1***
df	21	21

Note: Dummy indicators for missing values of father's and mother's education are also included as covariates. Both indicators are not significant at the .05 levels. All dummy indicators are coded as 1 = yes, 0 = no.

[†] Time-varying covariate.

[‡] Reference category.

* p < .05

** p < .01

***p < .001 (one-tailed test)

Source: The 1995 General Social Survey.

have already seen. A positive estimate indicates an increased hazard rate of cohabitation, whereas a negative estimate suggests a reduced rate. A similar transformation, $100 \times (e^{\beta} - 1)$, can also be interpreted as the percentage change in the hazard rate of premarital cohabitation for a one-unit change in a given explanatory variable, holding all other variables constant.

We will look at SES indicators first. Employment has a significant positive effect on the hazard rate of cohabitation for both women and men. Working outside the home appears to increase the hazard rate of cohabitation by 45 per cent ($100 \times [e^{0.372} - 1]$) for women and 67 per cent ($100 \times [e^{0.512} - 1]$) for men. A positive employment effect for women is inconsistent with Becker's independence hypothesis that economically independent women may have less to gain

Figure 6.3: First Marital Disruption by Type of Dissolution

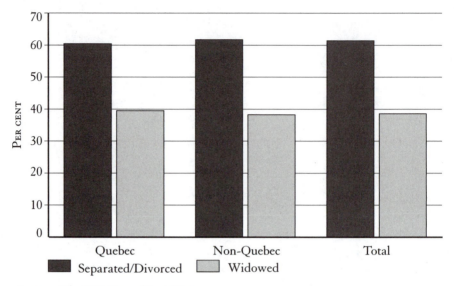

Source: The 1990 General Social Survey.

(financially) from marriage (cohabitation) than women who are not (Becker, 1981). However, consistent with our speculation in Chapter 2, increased earnings may facilitate or encourage cohabitation as an attractive alternative to marriage for these women. Educational attainment appears to have a significant negative effect for women and a positive, but not significant, effect for men. Also, as we predicted in Chapter 2, school enrolment has a negative effect for both women and men, which supports the view that school attendance tends to be incompatible with family living (Thornton et al., 1995).

Turning to cultural background, we see that religion has a significant effect on the hazard rate of cohabitation, although the effects are generally not significant for men. Women with no religious affiliation tend to have a higher hazard rate than religious women, whether Catholic (as we anticipated earlier), Protestant, or other religious orientations. Further, nativity has a positive effect for both genders, suggesting that immigrants (born outside Canada) tend to have a lower rate than non-immigrants. This is also consistent with the notion that immigration tends to disrupt social networks and negatively impact cohabitation formation (see Chapter 2). Also consistent with our earlier findings, Quebecers have a higher hazard rate than non-Quebecers.

Several demographic characteristics are important as well. We find that the hazard rate of cohabitation is higher among the youngest cohort than the two older cohorts, which is consistent with the overall increase in cohabitation in recent years. As child-bearing history is an important determinant in the process of first marriage (e.g., Goldscheider and Waite, 1986; Thornton, 1991), we consider several indicators measuring pregnancy and fertility histories. It is clear that pregnancy has a significant positive effect on the hazard of cohabitation, which supports the 'shotgun marriage' hypothesis.[9] Further, the entry into parenthood (first birth) appears to increase the hazard rate of cohabitation for men but not for women. Higher birth orders do not appear to have much of an impact on the hazard rate.

Three family background indicators influence the process of premarital cohabitation as well. Having a happy childhood (a self-reported measure) reduces the hazard rate of cohabitation. Growing up in an intact family also reduces the chances of women cohabiting. Moreover, father's education has a significant impact on women: women with better-educated fathers are more likely to cohabit than women with less-educated fathers. These findings suggest that family stability and childhood environment may have a long-lasting impact on children's union behaviour.

In short, our descriptive analysis of the GSS–95 data on premarital cohabitation is consistent with our earlier analysis of Canadian census data. The analysis confirms the finding of an overall increase in premarital cohabitation in recent years. The rate of cohabitation is higher among women and younger cohorts. The (hazard) rate of premarital cohabitation is also higher among those who are employed, less-educated (women), non-students, have no religious orientation, Canadian-born, Quebecers, are pregnant (or their partners are pregnant), are entering into parenthood (men), had a less happy childhood, and come from a broken family or a low social class family background (women).

The Transition to Post-marital Cohabitation

While one reason that young people cohabit premaritally may be to try out the couple lifestyle, the same cannot be said for those who have already been married. In this section we examine cohabitational behaviour after marital disruption. As noted, we focus our analysis on those who dissolved their first marriage through separation or divorce. However, it would be worthwhile to examine the percentage breakdown of people who actually dissolved their first marriage through separation (divorce) and through widowhood. Figure 6.3 presents prevalence levels for the two exits from marriage.

The exit pattern of marital dissolution is clear: more marriages are ended by marital separation (divorce) than by widowhood. At the national level, nearly two-thirds of dissolved marriages do so through marital breakdown and one-third through the death of a spouse. There is virtually no regional difference in the type of marital dissolution.

Once a marriage has ended, people may choose to do one of three things: cohabit, remarry, or remain unmarried. Table 6.2 shows the prevalence of post-marital union formation for separated or divorced respondents by gender and selected age groups. It is clear that the rate of 'currently cohabiting' decreases with age for both women and men. For example, over 24 per cent of women

Table 6.2: Prevalence of Postmarital Unions (%)

Union Type/Age	Women				Men			
	<35	35–44	45–54	55+	<35	35–44	45–54	55+
Currently cohabiting	24.1	15.3	10.8	2.8	38.2	18.9	15.1	7.3
Ever cohabited	46.7	42.2	30.9	13.8	55.9	46.7	42.8	22.5
Ever remarried	35.4	39.9	34.3	45.9	29.4	48.6	53.9	48.6
Remarried preceded by cohabitation	68	69.2	60	25.7	65	58.3	52.4	31.1

Note: N = 1,580 (930 women; 650 men).
Source: The 1990 General Social Survey.

aged 35 and younger are currently cohabiting, compared to less than 3 per cent of women aged 55 and older. The comparable numbers for men are 38 per cent and 7 per cent, respectively. A similar trend is observed for any post-marital cohabitational experience. Over 46 per cent of women aged 35 and younger had cohabited after marital disruption, compared to less than 14 per cent of women aged 55 and older. The comparable figures for men are 56 per cent and 23 per cent. Further, unlike premarital cohabitation, the overall rate of post-marital cohabitation is higher for men than for women.

To illustrate the whole picture of post-marital union formation, the rate of remarriage was also estimated. The estimates are shown in Table 6.2. Overall, about one-third of women and one-half of men remarried. However, the rate of remarriage appears to be erratic across age cohorts. While the youngest cohort has the lowest rate for both genders, the rate changes little over the older cohorts. There may be two reasons for this age pattern. First, the lower rate of remarriage for younger people is rooted in the aggregate downward trend in remarriage (Wu, 1994). Second, the lower rate for the youngest cohort may reflect the limited time of observation (due to censoring).

Do these cohabitations lead to remarriages?[10] Apparently, many do. Table 6.2 shows that except for the oldest age group (55+), a majority of remarriages were preceded by cohabitation. While these data do not tell us how many post-marital cohabitations did not eventually lead to remarriages, nor how many people actually remarry, this finding has two implications. First, together with the high rate of remarriage, it indicates the resilience of marriage as a social institution. High rates of marital disruption could reflect dissatisfaction with particular marriages, not necessarily disillusionment with the institution. Second, divorced people may become particularly cautious when it comes to making marital decisions, and many see cohabitation as a trial marriage. Are marriages preceded by cohabitation more successful (longer lasting) than those that were not? As we will see in Chapter 9, the answer is unequivocally 'no'.

Figure 6.4: Life Table Estimates of Cumulative Proportion of Post-marital Cohabitation

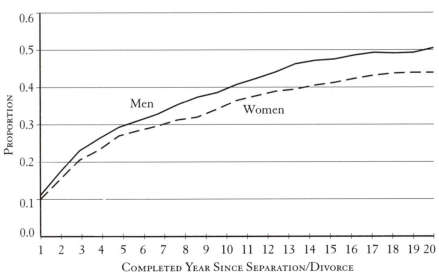

Source: The 1990 General Social Survey.

The Timing of Post-marital Cohabitation

The prevalence rates of cohabitation in Table 6.2 are unable to tell us when people cohabit after marital disruption. Again, we resort to life table techniques. Figure 6.4 shows life table estimates of the cumulative experience of post-marital cohabitation separately for women and men. Overall, we observe that the rate of cohabitation rises quickly in the first few years after marital disruption has occurred, then the rate of increase declines. For example, within one year after marital disruption, 10 per cent of women and 11 per cent of men have entered into a cohabitational relationship. After 3 years, the rate rises to 21 per cent for women and 24 per cent for men. After 6 years, the rates are only up to 29 per cent and 32 per cent for women and men, respectively. After 10 years, the corresponding rates are 36 per cent for women and 40 per cent for men.

The entry into premarital and post-marital cohabitation differs in two important ways. First, the shape of the cumulative curve varies. For premarital cohabitation, the entry is slow in the teens and accelerates in the twenties. For post-marital cohabitation, however, the entry is rapid in the first few years (following marital disruption) and decelerates in later years. These union formation patterns mirror those of first marriage and remarriage, respectively (e.g., Bumpass et al., 1990; Coale, 1971; Hernes, 1972; Wu, 1994). As with marriage, the slow entry into premarital union may reflect 'a minimum age (at sexual union) defined by law, religion, or custom' in the society (Coale, 1971: 204). The rapidly declining 'risk' of post-marital cohabitation in later years suggests that opportunities for cohabitation generally decline with age, perhaps because aging tends to lessen one's eligibility for coupling, particularly in view of rising rates of morbidity and mortality (Smith et al., 1991). A similar accelerating (negative) aging effect is also found in studies of remarriage (e.g., ibid.; Uhlenberg, 1989; Wu, 1995).

The second feature emerging from comparing the two union formation patterns is the effect of gender. For premarital cohabitation, gender effects are obvious: women enter into cohabitation more rapidly than men do. However, for post-marital cohabitation, the direction of the effect is reversed and considerably attenuated. Again, these cohabitation patterns parallel the patterns of first and second marriages. In the case of first marriage, women tend to marry at younger ages than men do. As for remarriage, similar norms about age differences between partners place older women in a disadvantaged position—they seek to marry men of their own age or older, whereas men want to marry women of their own age or younger. Largely due to sex differences in life expectancy at older ages, as women age there is a 'short supply' of men who are older, while at the same time, aging women are in 'excess supply' in terms of the pool available to appropriately aged men. However, it is worth pointing out that gender differences are considerably less evident for post-marital cohabitation than for remarriage, suggesting that a greater proportion of divorced men may opt to marry than to cohabit.

The Determinants of Post-marital Cohabitation

To examine the determinants of post-marital cohabitation, we estimated a series of failure time models. We consider the effects of three groups of explanatory variables known to influence the process of remarriage: SES, cultural, and demographic characteristics.

Table 6.3 shows the parameter estimates for the failure time models. Models 1 and 3 do not include duration of first marriage, but do include age at first marriage, whereas models 2 and 4 are the reverse. Age at first marriage, age at marital disruption, and duration of first marriage are not simultaneously incorporated in one model because each of the three measures is fully determined by the other two. Further, caution should be exercised when interpreting the parameter estimates. Because a Weibull regression models the natural logarithm of the 'survival' times, a positive estimate indicates a longer duration of survival—that is, a longer interval of remaining 'single', or alternatively, a delayed union. If we equate shorter intervals with higher (hazard) rates, a negative estimate should indicate a higher hazard rate of cohabitation. Conversely, a positive estimate suggests a lower cohabitation hazard rate. The anti-log transformation (i.e., $100 \times [e^{\beta} - 1]$) may also be used to interpret the estimates.

Table 6.3 shows that education does not have a significant effect for either gender. While earlier we saw that premarital cohabitation tends to select less-educated women, educational status clearly has little to do with post-marital cohabitation. The non-significant effect of education may actually support the notion that education tends to have an ambiguous effect for women when it comes to

Table 6.3: Accelerated Failure Time Models of Post-marital Cohabitation

Independent Variable	Women		Men	
	Model 1	Model 2	Model 3	Model 4
SOCIO-ECONOMIC STATUS				
Educational attainment				
Elementary school or less	0.680	0.680	0.262	0.262
Some high school	0.048	0.048	0.038	0.038
College or more[†]				
CULTURAL BACKGROUND				
Religion				
Catholic	−0.058	−0.058	0.221	0.221
Protestant	−0.148	−0.148	−0.048	−0.048
Other/None[†]				
Region				
Quebec	0.345	0.345	−0.383*	−0.383*
Rest of Canada[†]				
DEMOGRAPHIC CHARACTERISTICS				
Presence of children				
Yes	0.519**	0.519**	−0.016	−0.016
No[†]				
Age at first marriage	0.123**	—	0.026	—
Age at marital dissolution (age at separation is used if it is available)	0.049**	0.172**	0.051**	0.077**
Duration of first marriage (in years)	—	−0.123**	—	−0.026
Year of marital dissolution				
<1971	1.915**	1.915**	1.910**	1.910**
1971–9	0.858**	0.858**	1.033**	1.033**
1980 or later[†]				
Intercept	0.783	0.783	2.598**	2.598**
Scale parameter (d)	1.232**	1.232**	1.204**	1.204**
−Log Likelihood (Weibull)	757.06	757.06	527.71	527.71

Note: All dummy variables are coded as 1 = yes, 0 = no.
† Reference category.
* $p \leq .10$
** $p \leq .01$ (one-tailed test)
Source: The 1990 General Social Survey.

marital behaviour (Becker et al., 1977; also see Chapter 2). On the one hand, better-educated women (women with high SES) tend to gain less from marriage/cohabitation, as the independence hypothesis predicts. On the other hand, an elevated SES may increase their eligibility as they are financially more attractive. The result is that education may have little net effect on union formation.

Two cultural indicators are considered: religion and region. Clearly, religion plays no significant role in the process of post-marital cohabitation, while region has a significant effect only for men. Holding all other variables constant, 'survival' time for Quebec men is 32 per cent ($100 \times [e^{-.383} - 1]$) shorter than for non-Quebec men. Alternatively, we may say that the hazard rate of post-marital cohabitation is 32 per cent higher for Quebec men than for non-Quebec men.

Table 6.3 shows that demographic variables have a stronger impact on the timing of post-marital cohabitation than socio-economic or cultural variables. We observe that having children at the time of marital disruption tends to delay the entry into cohabitation by about 68 per cent. This supports Becker's (Becker et al., 1977) idea that children are marriage-specific capital and become worth considerably less in the event of divorce. Age at first marriage also has a significant effect for women. The older a woman was when she married for the first time, the less likely it is that she will cohabit after marital disruption. A similar deterrent effect is found for age at marital disruption for both genders. The effect of duration of first marriage is positive for women, consistent with the view that women who have longer first marriages may expect more (gains) from potential cohabiting partners. Year of marital dissolution, a measure of period effect, has a strong impact for both women and men. Those who dissolved their marriages in earlier periods are less likely to cohabit than those who did so in recent years. This is consistent with the overall rising trends in cohabitation. Finally, the scale parameter (d) is greater than unity. This suggests that the hazard of post-marital cohabitation declines over time, which is consistent with our earlier life table results (see Figure 6.4).

In brief, analysis of the GSS–90 data suggests that an increasing number of women and men now choose to cohabit after marital disruption. Many do so fairly soon after disruption, and many also subsequently marry their cohabitation partners. The hazard rate of post-marital cohabitation appears to increase with the duration of first marriage (indicating a shorter period until cohabitation), but decreases with age at first marriage (women), age at marital disruption, and year (period) of marital disruption. The rate is also higher among Quebec men than non-Quebec men, indicating that they spend less time in the single state following marital disruption.

Discussion

In this chapter we examined the transition to cohabitation. Analysis of the GSS data has shown an overall increase in cohabitation. This increase is consistent, whether we focus on the never-married population or the ever-married population, confirming the aggregate trends in cohabitation presented in Chapter 4. In general, premarital, rather than post-marital, cohabitation appears to be more prevalent and pervasive. This observation is based on the finding that over 70 per cent of men and 60 per cent of women are likely to enter a premarital cohabitation by age 35. In contrast, only 45 per cent of women and 51 per cent of men will do so within 20 years following marital disruption.[11] Also important in this regard is that gender effects are strong in premarital cohabitation, but considerably weaker in post-marital cohabitation. These gender patterns mirror those of first and second marriages: never-married women enter into cohabitation at a faster pace than their male counterparts, while the converse is true for the separated/divorced population. Another noteworthy finding is that the tempo of entry into premarital cohabitation is much slower than that of post-marital cohabitation, which is also consistent with the patterns of first and second marriage, respectively.

Multivariate (survival) analyses identified several important characteristics associated with the transition to premarital cohabitation. The hazard rate of premarital cohabitation is particularly high among people who are employed outside their homes, are not students, have no religious orientations, are Canadian-born, are pregnant (or their partners are pregnant), and had a less happy childhood. As anticipated, some of the determinants are gender-specific. For example, the transition to parenthood increases the hazard rate of premarital cohabitation for men but not for women, suggesting that 'single' parenthood may be more acceptable among women than among men. Cohabitation also appears to attract women who are less educated and came from a broken and/or a low social class family.

The single most important determinant of post-marital cohabitation is age. Our survival analysis shows clearly that the hazard of post-marital cohabitation is inversely related to two age-related variables: (duration) time since marital disruption and age at marital disruption. This finding is consistent with studies on remarriage that found age to be a crucial factor impeding the entry into remarriage (e.g., Bumpass et al., 1990). Younger persons may use age as an indicator for physical attractiveness of the potential partner. Older persons may use age as an indicator for the health status and longevity of the potential spouse (Smith et al., 1991: 371). Another important determinant is year of marital dissolution. If year of dissolution is indeed an indicator of social change, then our findings suggest changes in the norms regarding family life in our society. Moreover, several determinants are also gender-specific. Higher rates of post-marital cohabitation are found among Quebec men, and the presence of children at marital disruption only negatively affects women—probably because women are normally the custodians of their children. Further, women who entered into first marriage at older ages and/or who have shorter durations of first marriages tend to delay their entry into a post-marital cohabitation, perhaps due to their lower taste for family living or lower desire to be in a couple relationship (Waite et al., 1986).

7 | Child-bearing in Cohabitational Relationships

Procreation has been one of marriage's most important functions in virtually every human society and across perhaps all historical times. If the emergence of non-marital cohabitation is to lead eventually to the replacement of the institution of marriage, then it must, among other things, provide some kind of socially acceptable living arrangement for performing the function of population replacement. This chapter examines child-bearing intentions and experience in Canadian cohabiting families.

Recent data from Canadian vital statistics show that while overall fertility has declined slowly over the last two decades, non-marital fertility has increased sharply. For example, from 1974 to 1994, the total fertility rate declined from 2.2 to 2.0 births per woman aged 20 and over (Ford and Nault, 1996: 42). However, during the same period, non-marital fertility increased from 0.2 to 0.9 births. Indeed, the percentage of non-marital births constituted as many as one-third of all children born in 1994, compared to only 6 per cent in 1974. These diverging trends in marital and non-marital fertility can be traced back to as early as the turn of the century (e.g., Balakrishnan and Wu, 1992; Beaujot and McQuillan, 1982).

While the decline in Canadian fertility rarely makes it to the evening news, the increase in non-marital fertility has not eluded media attention. With the increase in non-marital fertility, it is understandable that we are bombarded with media exposés depicting teenage pregnancy and teenage parenthood as a social 'epidemic'. However, it may come as a surprise to media commentators and to the public that teenage fertility has actually declined in recent years. For example, between 1974 and 1994, the teen fertility rate (the number of births per 1,000 women aged 15–19) declined from 34.8 to 25.1 (Ford and Nault, 1996: 41). How do we explain these data? The rise in non-marital fertility and the decline in teen fertility are consistent with my unconfirmed view that much of the increase in non-marital fertility in recent decades may have been largely a consequence of the increase in non-marital cohabitation and that more and more children have been born into cohabiting families over time. If I am correct, then cohabitation is slowly but surely becoming a substitute for legal marriage as a social institution where children are born, raised, and socialized to become members of our society.

Why do cohabiting couples want children? It is probably safe to assume that the reasons behind fertility decisions of cohabiting couples are not much different from those of marital couples. As with the decision to cohabit, we assume that child-bearing decisions are rational and that couples balance the benefits and costs when they decide whether they want to have one (or an additional) child. The benefits of children may include such things as children's help around the home or elsewhere, security in old age, and continuation of family names, which were particularly relevant in historical times (pre-industrial eras). The costs of children include direct monetary expenditures and, perhaps even more importantly, the time commitments necessary for child-bearing and child-rearing, which are known as opportunity (shadow) costs. The decline in marital fertility has been interpreted as a consequence of the decline in the benefits (value) and the increase in the costs of children, particularly the rising opportunity costs for the mother (for reviews of theoretical advances in explaining fertility change, see, e.g., Burch, 1996; Davis, Bernstam, and Ricardo-Campbell, 1986; Hirschman, 1994). In this chapter we examine several individual-level determinants of fertility and anticipate that these same determinants also influence child-bearing intentions and decisions among cohabiting couples.

We focus on two important aspects of cohabiting fertility: child-bearing intentions and child-bearing experience within cohabiting relationships. The main questions addressed in this chapter include: How many cohabitors intend to have children? How many cohabitors are uncertain about their fertility plans? What are the determinants of fertility intentions among cohabitors? Do people choose to have children born into their relationships, and if so, who are they? The analysis again starts with a review of the data sources and analytical models used. Then we look at child-bearing intentions among cohabiting women and men. Next, we examine child-bearing experience among cohabiting women. We focus on the timing of first births in cohabitational relationships and explore its determinants.

Data and Methods

Our analysis of child-bearing intentions uses data from the GSS–95. A description of the survey was provided in Chapter 3. The measurement of child-bearing intentions was based on the question: 'Do you intend to have a/another child sometime?'[1] The question was asked to the respondents only if: (1) they were currently in a marital or cohabiting union; and (2) the female partner was under the age of 50. Following prior research on child-bearing intentions (e.g., Miller, 1992; Sloane and Lee, 1983), I excluded the respondents/their partners who were currently pregnant and those who were sterilized either due to a natural cause or through a surgical procedure.[2] To examine the determinants of child-bearing intentions among cohabitors, I further restricted the sample to respondents who were cohabiting and had no children of their own at the time of the survey. With these restrictions the study sample includes 150 women and 132 men (N = 282).

The study of child-bearing experience draws on an earlier study using data from the GSS–90 (Wu, 1996). A description of this survey was also given in Chapter 3. The analysis was limited to women respondents who cohabited prior to their first marriage (if they had a first marriage). There are two reasons for this restriction. First, excluding post-marital cohabitation reduces the complexity of the study. Second, a relatively small number of women had cohabited subsequent to a marital disruption (see Chapter 6). Furthermore, predictors of child-bearing behaviour may well be different for first cohabitation than for subsequent cohabitations. Therefore, where more than one premarital cohabitation can be identified, the first cohabitation is used. The final study sample includes 1,517 women.

The dependent variable in the *intention* study was measured as a categorical variable, indicating whether the respondent gave a 'yes', 'no', or 'don't know' response to the survey question on intention. While the patterns and determinants of fertility intentions have been well documented in the literature (e.g., Axinn et al., 1994; Laumon et al., 1988; Miller, 1992), little is known about uncertainty in child-bearing intentions. As Morgan (1981) noted, patterns of uncertainty in fertility decisions are important not only because ignoring them introduces biases in the estimates of intended fertility, but because aggregate uncertainty has important policy implications. For example, if substantial numbers of couples indicate that they are uncertain about whether they want a (another) child, rather than deciding that no (further) children are intended, it is possible that these couples may choose to have a (another) child if there are positive reinforcements. 'Uncertain' couples are the most likely to be influenced by period-specific factors, such as socio-economic conditions and population policy. While uncertainty in fertility intentions has been discussed mainly in the context of marriages, the importance of uncertainty can be readily extended to cohabiting couples, particularly in light of the possible surge in cohabitational fertility.[3]

The dependent variable in the *experience* study is a dichotomous measure indicating whether a woman gave birth within the cohabiting union. To study the timing of child-bearing experience, a duration (survival) time variable was constructed. Survival time for the 'risk' of the first birth (within the cohabitation) was counted from the date of the initiation of cohabitation to the date of the first birth.[4] Where a birth did not occur within cohabitation, survival time was measured from the date of the beginning of cohabitation to the date of the interview. For women who did not give birth and whose unions dissolved through separation, legal marriage, or the death of their partner, survival time was measured from the initiation of cohabitation until the date of its termination. Time was measured in months.

The empirical analysis proceeds in two steps. In the first step, descriptive analyses of child-bearing intentions and child-bearing experiences were conducted. In the second step, analytical (multivariate) analyses were carried out. The primary statistical tools used in the *intention* study were multinomial logit model techniques (Maddala, 1983). Specifically, I estimated a series of generalized logit models by specifying the ratio of the probability of taking the ith alternative (e.g., giving a 'yes' response) to the probability of taking some standard alternative (e.g., giving a 'no' response). In line with prior studies (Morgan, 1981, 1982; Sloane and Lee, 1983), I estimated models for two contrasts: the probability of giving a 'no' response versus the probability of giving the other two responses (i.e., 'yes' and 'don't know').

Survival model techniques were employed to examine child-bearing experiences within cohabitations. The descriptive analysis uses the life table procedures as discussed in Chapter 6. To examine possible period effects, separate life tables were calculated for selected years when respondents started cohabiting. To examine the determinants of first births in cohabitations, Cox's (1972) proportional hazard (PH) model techniques were used.

Child-bearing Intentions

Survey questions targeting behavioural intentions are sometimes viewed as attitudinal questions that reflect personal preferences for certain behaviour (Oppenheimer, 1994). However, the importance of fertility intention studies extends beyond monitoring attitudinal changes in child-bearing preferences. One key application of these studies is to use the aggregate intention patterns for population projection, although the validity of this practice is widely debated among demographers (e.g., Bongaarts, 1992; Hendershot and Placek, 1981; Westoff, 1990; Westoff and Ryder, 1977). The debate focuses on the predictive ability of the preference and intention questions asked in fertility surveys. The usefulness of these questions has been challenged on the grounds that individuals' ideal family sizes may change over time and in response to the changing social contexts in which child-bearing decisions are made (Tan and Tey, 1994). Critics have also pointed to the significant number of unwanted births in survey data as evidence of the ineffectiveness of intentions as predictors of actual fertility and of the difficulty in accessing contraception (Bongaarts, 1992: 102).

In response to this challenge, population researchers have made considerable efforts to develop and assess the survey measurement of fertility preferences, desires, and intentions. In a recent review of this literature, Bongaarts (1992: 102) showed that most preference and intention questions in surveys are generally valid and useful: 'Survey measures of women's desire to continue child-bearing are considered generally reliable, and although desired family size is subject to some bias . . . , it, too, largely serves its intended purpose.' Several studies since Bongaarts further confirm that fertility is primarily an intended behaviour and that fertility intentions provide fairly accurate forecasts of subsequent fertility (e.g., Miller and Pasta, 1995; Schoen et al., 1997; Tan and Tey, 1994; Thomson, 1997). Developments in contraceptive technology and new

Figure 7.1: Number of Children Intended among Cohabitors

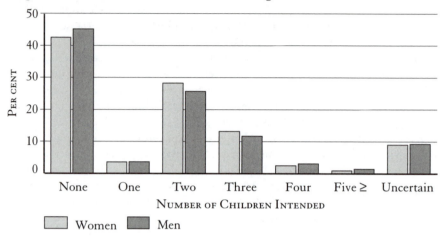

Source: The 1995 General Social Survey.

treatments for infertility have now made fertility less constrained by physical and biological factors. Couples can use contraceptive methods to control their fertility, and many infertile couples can be effectively treated to become parents. Therefore, it is reasonable to believe that conscious fertility intentions govern the reproductive process. Bearing these issues in mind, let us now examine fertility intentions among cohabiting individuals.

Age, Gender, and Regional Patterns

We begin with a 'snapshot' of child-bearing intentions among the cohabiting population in 1995. Figure 7.1 provides data on the total number of children intended among *current* cohabitors, including the children that they had already and the child that they were expecting if the female partner was pregnant at the time of the survey (step- and adopted children were not included). No sample-selection restrictions (such as those discussed above) were applied to this sample of cohabitors except that the female partner is under age 50.

Figure 7.1 shows that over 40 per cent of the cohabitors intend no children at all, over 25 per cent intend two children, about 12 per cent intend three children, and 9 per cent are uncertain about their fertility plans. Less than 4 per cent of the cohabitors intend one child, and about the same fraction of cohabitors want four or more. It is also worth noting that there are only slight gender variations in fertility intentions. Overall, less than half of the cohabitors intend to have one or more children.

Research has shown that fertility intentions and uncertainty vary with age, parity (the number of children that couples already have), and partner's gender (e.g., Mason and Taj, 1987; Morgan, 1981, 1982; Schoen et al., 1997). To examine the effects of these personal traits, Table 7.1 shows fertility intentions and uncertainty

Table 7.1: Child-bearing Intentions among Childless Cohabitors by Age, Sex, Region

Intend to have children	Women				Men			
	<25	25–9	30–4	35+	<25	25–9	30–4	35+
Quebec								
Yes	89.4	81.5	62.2	17.3	95.8	87.4	82.1	30.5
Uncertain	0.0	4.0	25.2	21.3	0.0	0.0	17.9	15.9
No	10.6	14.5	12.6	61.4	4.2	12.6	0.0	53.6
Total	100	100	100	100	100	100	100	100
Non-Quebec								
Yes	93.2	80.2	41.1	45.2	84.0	54.3	66.1	41.0
Uncertain	4.4	16.9	32.3	0.0	0.0	6.7	16.9	0.0
No	2.4	2.9	26.6	54.8	16.0	39.0	16.9	59.0
Total*	100	100	100	100	100	100	100	100

*   May not total to 100 per cent due to rounding.
Source: The 1995 General Social Survey.

among childless cohabitors (N = 282). In anticipation of regional differences in intentions, separate tables are presented for Quebec and elsewhere in Canada.

It is clear that child-bearing intentions and uncertainty vary with age. For example, in Quebec, 89 per cent of women cohabitors under age 25 intend to have children, compared to 82 per cent aged 25–9, 62 per cent aged 30–4, and 17 per cent aged 35+. However, for the same sample of Quebec women, uncertainty increases with age until the mid-thirties and declines thereafter. The percentage of those intending no children also increases with age, with 61 per cent of (childless) cohabiting Quebec women wanting no children at age 35 and older. Similar patterns of intentions and uncertainty are also observed for women outside Quebec, except for uncertainty levels at ages 35 and older. Age patterns for men generally resemble those of women.

Gender and regional patterns are less evident. In Quebec, it appears that a higher percentage of men than women intend one or more children. A higher percentage of Quebec women than men intend no children. Uncertainty is also higher among Quebec women than men. While the gender pattern for uncertainty in Quebec holds true elsewhere in Canada, the effect of gender is less clear for the other two response categories. On balance, outside Quebec it seems that a higher percentage of women than men desire children, except for ages 30–4 where the pattern is reversed.

In short, the data show that nearly half of the cohabitors desire children. This percentage rises to over 60 per cent for childless cohabitors (not shown in the table). Overall, the percentage of cohabitors wanting children declines with age, and the reverse is true for uncertainty (up to age 35). While gender patterns are not consistent for wanting children, uncertainty levels do differ consistently between women and men. Women are less certain than men about wanting children, particularly when they approach age 35. Overall regional patterns also are mixed. When ignoring the effects of gender and age (the results are not shown), relatively more childless cohabitors in Quebec (67 per cent) want children than those outside Quebec (58 per cent), and uncertainty levels are about the same (9–10 per cent) in and outside Quebec.

The Determinants of Child-bearing Intentions

The regional patterns of fertility intentions can be more easily identified in the multivariate analysis. Following prior research, we examine a set of personal characteristics believed to influence fertility intentions. Again, the explanatory variables are grouped into three categories: SES, cultural, and demographic and family.

Table 7.2 shows the parameter estimates from two multinomial logit models of fertility intentions and uncertainty for women and men, respectively. As noted, models have been estimated for two probability contrasts: (1) 'yes' versus 'no' (intention models) and (2) 'uncertain' versus 'no' (uncertainty models). In anticipation of gender differences in intentions (e.g., Schoen et al., 1997; Wu and Wang, 1998), separate models were estimated for women and men. The interpretation of parameter estimates is similar to the binomial (logit) models discussed in Chapter 5. As with binomial models, multinomial models estimate the log-odds that a value of the explanatory variable is associated with the dependent variable, all else being equal. The two probability contrasts were modelled simultaneously, in the sense that three response options are assumed to be competing choices. For numerical explanatory variables, a now familiar transformation, $100 \times (e^{\beta} - 1)$, can be interpreted as the percentage change in the odds of choosing a 'yes' (or 'don't know') response versus choosing a 'no' response for a one-unit change in the explanatory variable. The comparable transformation for categorical variables is: $100 \times (e^{2 \times \beta})$.[5]

We first look at SES variables. Table 7.2 shows that among the SES indicators, only personal income has a significant impact on intentions and uncertainty. We observe that for women, personal income has a negative effect in both the intention and uncertainty models (columns 1 and 2), suggesting that an increase in a woman's income raises the likelihood of *not* wanting any children. For men, the reverse is true. As an example, the coefficient for women's income in the intention model suggests that a one-unit increase in women's income (approximately $5,000) is likely to reduce their odds of intending a child by 32 per cent ($100 \times [e^{-.381} - 1]$). The negative effect of women's income supports the notion that the (opportunity) costs of bearing children are particularly high for mothers with high earnings. These findings also support Becker's (1981) independence hypothesis that an increase in women's SES reduces their economic dependence on their spouses, which in turn reduces the incentive to invest in union specific capital, such as children.

Among the cultural indicators, religion and region show some influence on intentions and uncertainty for women but not for men. Protestant women appear to be less likely to want a child than women with other or no religious orientations. Catholic women are less certain about their fertility plans than others. The most consistent cultural variable is region. We observe that Quebec women are less likely to want children than women outside Quebec.

Several demographic and family variables show significant effects. Table 7.2 shows that for women, age appears to have a negative curvilinear effect on intent for a child, suggesting an inverted U-shaped relationship between intentions (uncertainty) and age. That is, the levels of intentions and uncertainty are likely low in (very) young ages, rise rapidly in probably the twenties, and decline in the thirties. While the signs on the estimates for men are consistent with the ones for women, the effects are significant only in the uncertainty model. Moreover, age heterogamy (age-discrepant union) appears to encourage the intent for children, particularly for unions in which the male partner is older. However, the reverse seems to be the case for men along heterogamous union status (different marital statuses at the time of cohabitation). Finally, an increase in the duration of cohabitation seems to reduce men's intent for children, although only one estimate (uncertainty model) is significant.

A few family characteristics are significant as well. We observe that having a happy childhood tends to raise the likelihood of wanting children, particularly for women. For men, the intent for children also increases with the number of siblings. It is also interesting to note that an increase in father's education increases the desire for children, whereas the effects of mother's education are generally negative and non-significant.

In sum, our multivariate analysis suggests that for cohabiting women, the desire for children is higher among those who have lower personal income, are non-Protestants, reside outside Quebec, are likely in their twenties, are the younger union partner, had a happy childhood, and have more educated fathers. For cohabiting men, the desire for children increases particularly with personal income, number of siblings, and father's education. For both women and men, uncertainty about having children generally increases with the desire for children.

Child-bearing Experience

We have noted that many cohabiting individuals, particularly childless cohabitors, desire to have children. However, the data we have examined thus far do not permit us to determine whether these cohabitors want children to be born into cohabitations rather than some other state. Do women actually bear children while cohabiting? This section examines child-bearing experience among cohabiting women.

As noted, our analysis focuses on first births in cohabitations. However, it would be useful to have an overview of all children ever born to women who

Table 7.2: Multinomial Logit Models of Child-bearing Intentions among Childless Cohabitors

Variable	Women		Men	
	Yes vs No	Yes vs Uncertain	Yes vs No	Yes vs Uncertain
SOCIO-ECONOMIC STATUS				
Employed				
Yes	−0.053	−0.816	—‡	—‡
No†				
Educational status	0.074	0.205	−0.058	−0.265
(in 10 levels, 1 = none, …, 10 = bachelor or higher)				
School enrolment				
Yes	0.817	0.397	0.595	0.568
No†				
Personal income	−0.381**	−0.503***	0.202**	0.597**
(in 21 levels, 0 = none, …, 20 = \$100,000 or more)				
CULTURAL BACKGROUND				
Religion				
Catholic	0.790	1.180*	0.184	0.777
Protestant	−0.952*	−0.519	−0.037	0.379
Other/None†				
Church attendance	0.155	−0.642	0.165	−0.369
(in 5 levels, 1 = never, …, 5 = at least once a week)				
Region				
Quebec	−1.388**	−1.988***	0.248	0.267
Rest of Canada†				
DEMOGRAPHIC AND FAMILY CHARACTERISTICS				
Age	0.704*	2.076***	0.193	2.797*
Age square	−0.016**	−0.035***	−0.005	−0.039*
Heterogamy in age				
Men older	0.992**	1.208**	−0.570	−1.172
Women older	1.080*	0.761	0.152	0.885
Age-homogeneous union†				
Heterogamy in union status				
Yes	−0.363	−0.228	−1.305***	−2.806**
No†				

Duration of union (in years)	0.050	0.054	−0.105	−0.191*
Had a happy childhood Yes No[†]	1.094***	1.615***	0.366	1.945*
Number of siblings	0.190	0.321	0.247*	0.867***
Intact family Yes No[†]	0.364	0.596	—[‡]	—[‡]
Mother's education (in 10 levels, 1 = none, ..., 10 = bachelor or higher)	−0.117	−0.216	−0.211	−0.672*
Father's education (in 10 levels, 1 = none, ..., 10 = bachelor or higher)	0.534**	0.492*	0.390**	0.921**
Intercept	-9.252	−35.269***	−3.346	−64.436**
Likelihood Ratio (chi square)		137.66		106.21
df		46		40

Note: Dummy indicators for missing values of personal income (women only), father's education, and mother's education are also included as covariates. All three indicators are not significant at the .05 level. The parameters for nativity (not shown in the table) cannot be estimated for all models; and the parameters for missing values of personal income cannot be estimated for the two models of men. All dummy variables are coded as 1 = yes, 0 = no.

[†]   Reference category.
[‡]   Parameter cannot be estimated.
*   p < .10
** p < .05
***p < .01 (one-tailed test)
Source: The 1995 General Social Survey.

were cohabiting at the time of the survey (none of the constraints discussed earlier are applied here, other than all women are under age 50). Figure 7.2 provides data from the GSS–95 on children ever born to cohabiting women by age and region. We observe that most cohabitors under age 30 (58–9 per cent) are childless. However, for older women (age 30+), this percentage drops to 30 per cent in Quebec and 35 per cent elsewhere in Canada. Age is clearly the most important determining factor, although regional effects are mixed. On balance,

Figure 7.2: Number of Children Ever Born to Women Cohabitors

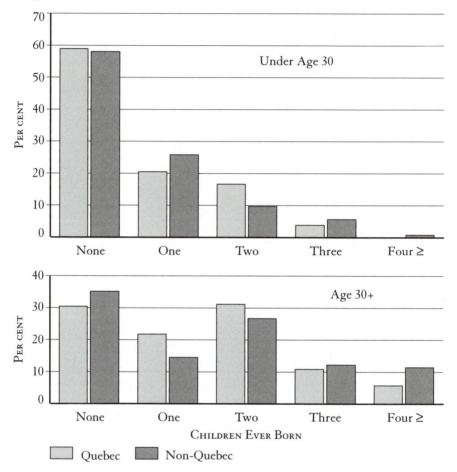

Source: The 1995 General Social Survey.

older Quebec women are more likely than their counterparts outside the province to be mothers, and are more likely to have one or two children. The opposite appears to be the case for women having three or more children.

The Timing of First Births

The data shown in Figure 7.2 tell us the proportion of cohabitors who are also mothers, but they cannot tell us the timing of births or whether the mothers had their children with their cohabiting partners. To address these issues (and reduce the complexity of the analysis), we focus our attention on the timing of first births within first cohabitations before (first) marriage. As noted, life table procedures were employed for the descriptive analysis.

Table 7.3: Life Table Estimates of the Cumulative Child-bearing Experience of Cohabiting Women

Months Since Start of Cohabitation	Year Cohabitation Inititated			
	<1970	1970–9	1980–4	1985+
6	0.052	0.004	0.006	0.014
12	0.074	0.033	0.023	0.030
24	0.162	0.052	0.041	0.044
36	0.243	0.081	0.085	0.062
48	0.266	0.089	0.094	0.074
60	0.266	0.094	0.095	0.114
72	0.266	0.094	0.106	—
84	0.266	0.096	0.110	—
96	0.266	0.109	0.115	—
108	0.266	0.111	0.115	—
120	0.266	0.115	0.120	—
N	53	341	370	569

Note: Survival curves for the four periods—before 1970, 1970–9, 1980–4, and 1985 or later—are significant at the .001.

Source: The 1990 General Social Survey.

Table 7.3 provides the life table estimates for the cumulative experience of child-bearing separately by year of the start of cohabitation. It indicates that about 7 per cent of the women who entered a cohabiting relationship before 1970 gave birth within one year of the initiation of cohabitation. The percentages for women who commenced their relationships between 1970 and 1979, between 1980 and 1984, and after 1984 are 3 per cent, 2 per cent, and 3 per cent, respectively. After three years, those percentages rise to 24 per cent, 8 per cent, 9 per cent, and 6 per cent, respectively. Overall, women who entered a cohabiting relationship before 1970 had a higher rate of first in-union births than women who commenced cohabiting relationships in later periods. However, with the recent surge in cohabitation, it is fairly safe to say that the total number of births born into cohabitations in recent years is considerably higher than in earlier periods.

The Determinants of First Births

The determinants of first births in cohabitations are examined in multivariate analysis, using survival model techniques. Explanatory variables include those known to influence marital fertility (e.g., education and religion), as well as variables that are presumably relevant in the context of non-marital cohabitation (e.g., year of start of cohabitation) (see, e.g., Davis et al., 1986; Hirschman, 1994).

Table 7.4: Proportional Hazard Model of Child-bearing within Cohabitation Relationships

Variable	ß	exp(ß)
EDUCATIONAL STATUS		
College diploma or higher	−0.920***	0.399
High school or some college	−0.601***	0.548
Some high school or less[†]		
CULTURAL BACKGROUND		
Religion		
Catholic	−0.009	0.991
Protestant	−0.182	0.833
Other/None[†]		
Ethnic origin		
British	−0.289	0.749
French	−0.124	0.883
Other[†]		
Year of immigration to Canada		
<1972	0.088	1.092
1972 or after	0.684**	1.981
Native (Canadian) born[†]		
Region		
Quebec	0.525**	1.691
Rest of Canada[†]		
DEMOGRAPHIC AND FAMILY CHARACTERISTICS		
Age at start of cohabitation	−0.145***	0.865
Partner's age		
Five or more years older	−0.289	0.749
Two or more years younger	0.267	1.306
Age-homogeneous partnership[†]		
Partner's marital status		
Single	−0.977***	0.376
Previously married[†]		
Parity at start of cohabitation		
Zero	0.201	1.222
One	0.174	1.190
Two or more[†]		

Number of siblings	0.037***	1.038
Year of start of cohabitation		
<1970	0.722**	2.058
1970–9	−0.205	0.814
1980–4	0.086	1.090
1985+[†]		
− 2 Log Likelihood	1672.7	
Model chi-square	109.08***	
df	19	

Note: All dummy variables are coded as 1 = yes, 0 = no.
[†] Reference category.
*   p < .10
**   p < .05
***p < .01 (one-tailed test)
Source: The 1990 General Social Survey.

In presenting the results of the analysis, the explanatory variables are again divided into three categories (SES, cultural, and demographic and family).

Table 7.4 presents the parameter estimates from a proportional hazard model of first births within cohabitations. As noted in Chapter 6, a positive parameter estimate indicates an increased rate of child-bearing, whereas a negative estimate suggests a reduced rate. A simple transformation, $100 \times (e^{\beta} - 1)$, can also be interpreted as the percentage change in the hazard rate of child-bearing for a one-unit change in a given explanatory variable, holding all other variables constant.

Table 7.4 shows that the only SES variable considered in the model is educational status. As anticipated, education has a negative effect on the hazard rate of first births. Specifically, the hazard rate is about 60 per cent ([.399–1] $\times$ 100) lower for college-educated women than for women with less than a high school education. This finding is consistent with both the opportunity costs and the independence hypotheses noted in the intention study.

We consider four cultural variables: religion, ethnic origin, immigrant status, and region. The effects of religion and ethnicity do not reach a significance level of 10 per cent, although immigrant status and region are statistically significant. It appears that women who immigrated to Canada in 1972 or later have a higher hazard rate than women born in Canada, and that women who immigrated before 1972 are not significantly different from Canadian-born women. It is possible that the higher rate of first births among immigrant women is attributable to the influence of cultural traditions in their home countries. For example, in many Latin American countries, cohabiting unions are essentially common-law marriages (e.g., Landale and Forste, 1991).

While earlier we found that cohabiting women in Quebec are less enthusiastic about wanting children than women elsewhere in Canada, they are actually more likely to have children born into cohabitations.[6] The higher rate of first births in Quebec is consistent with the findings that the overall rate and stability of cohabitation are higher in Quebec than elsewhere in Canada (see Chapters 4 and 8).

Turning to demographic and family characteristics, we see that age at cohabitation initiation has a significant negative effect. For cohabiting women, a one-year increase in the age at initiation of cohabitation is likely to decrease the hazard rate by 14 per cent ([.865–1] x 100). This negative effect could reflect the decline in fecundity as age increases, as well as a possible delay at initiation of sexual activity (e.g., Jones et al., 1986).[7] Moreover, partner's (pre-cohabitational) marital status has an impact as well. Single women who cohabit with previously married men are more likely to give birth while cohabiting than those who cohabit with single men. Also, we see that the hazard rate increases with the number of siblings. This is consistent with the hypothesis of an intergenerational effect: women from large families are more likely to bear a child within cohabitation due to the influence of the child-bearing experience of their parents.

Finally, consistent with the earlier life table analysis, women who entered into a cohabiting union before 1970 were more likely to bear a child within the union than women who formed a cohabiting union in more recent years. It could be that because entry into cohabitation before 1970 was less common it was also more selective. Cohabitation in those years may have been particularly selective of individuals who viewed it as an alternative lifestyle to legal marriage. Therefore, because these cohabitational relationships were more marriage-like, they would be more likely to provide a suitable and stable environment for child-bearing and child-rearing.

In short, the multivariate analysis shows that the hazard rate of first cohabitational births decreases with educational status and age at initiation of cohabitation, but increases with the number of siblings. A high rate of first births is also common among (more recent) immigrant women, (single) women cohabiting with previously married men, and women who began their first cohabitation prior to 1970.

Discussion

The survival of any human society is determined by its ability to replace itself. For centuries, marriage has been the primary social institution stipulating the appropriate environment in which children are born and grow up. If cohabitation develops into an alternative to legal marriage, then we should expect that child-bearing and child-rearing will become an integral part of cohabiting family life. In this chapter we examined child-bearing intentions and first cohabitational births. We saw that nearly half of cohabiting persons are certain that they want children, and 9 per cent are ambivalent about their fertility plans. Nearly 5 per cent of recent cohabiting women gave birth within two years of the initiation of cohabitation. This percentage rose to 16 per cent for women who began cohabiting before 1970. These numbers are by no means trivial in either a relative or absolute sense. It has now become clear that child-bearing is not a 'rare' event in the cohabiting family. Indeed, much of the increase in non-marital fertility in recent years can be attributed to the rise in cohabitation and the fact that more children have been born into cohabitations than ever before. These findings warrant a call for redefining non-marital fertility. It is unrealistic to continue to view children born in cohabitations as the same as children born out of 'union-lock'.

While our data show few gender differences in child-bearing intentions (see Figure 7.1), the influences of several determinants of these intentions do differ between women and men. For example, higher personal income reduces the desire for children among women but increases this desire among men. As noted, the negative effect of income for women supports Becker's independence hypothesis, whereas the positive effect of income for men is in line with the notion that a rise in income encourages parents to want more and higher-quality children (e.g., Becker, 1960).[8] Moreover, age is a far more important predictor of child-bearing intentions for women than it is for men. Intentions and uncertainty initially increase with age and then decline rapidly. These results tell a consistent story: intentions and uncertainty rise when the female partner is relatively young and having a child is a possibility. Intentions decline, and certainty (about remaining childless) increases, when the 'biological clock' advances and the possibility of having children diminishes. The generally negative effect of aging is also consistent with the widely supported finding that fecundity declines rapidly with age (e.g., Menken, 1985). Indeed, our finding that women in relationships with older men tend to have a greater desire for children is consistent with the negative effect of aging.

Why do cohabiting women want children? While we have argued that child-bearing decisions are largely contingent on balancing the benefits and costs of children, another explanation also is plausible. Women, particularly single young women (who constitute the majority of our study sample), may desire to become parents as a means of reducing the uncertainty they face in their lives. In Chapter 2 we discussed the uncertainty reduction theory and argued that when marriage and career prospects are poor, women may resort to cohabitation as a means of reducing uncertainty. In fact, as Friedman and her colleagues (1994) convincingly argued, parenthood is also an effective global strategy to reduce uncertainty. This is because, like marriage and careers, children may also embed persons in abiding social relations that likely lead to a reduction in uncertainty. Of all strategies, parenthood is the most likely to be a lifelong commitment, as a commitment to a career or a marriage (cohabitation) can be retracted.

Several findings from our analysis of child-bearing are supportive of the uncertainty reduction hypothesis.[9] For example, education has a negative effect on the hazard rate of first births (becoming a parent). This is consistent with the notion that an increase in educational status leads to stable careers, which are alternative means of uncertainty reduction. Also, the desire for children increases when single women cohabit with previously married men. It may be that heterogamy in personal traits, such as age, education, and union status, tends to be a source of conflict between partners (Udry, 1974), thus raising the level of uncertainty within the relationship. The arrival of a new child may reduce (or shift) some of this conflict. Moreover, women who have recently immigrated are also more likely to resort to parenthood as a means of uncertainty reduction, partly because voluntary international migration is a process of uprooting, whereby the social networks in the home country are disrupted (Kuo and Tsai, 1986). Immigrants, therefore, tend to have fewer family ties and smaller social networks, and generally face more obstacles in adjusting to life. Consequently, they have higher levels of uncertainty. Family ties and social networks in the receiving country tend to increase with duration of residence, and the effect of immigration status is likely to diminish over time. This is consistent with our finding that the negative effect of immigrant status is more salient for recent immigrants than for early immigrants.

8 | The Transition out of Cohabitation

When people move in together, some 'live happily ever after'. However, this is not always the case. Things can go wrong, and couples may split. Certainly, not all cohabitational relationships end in union separation; many cohabiting couples marry each other. This chapter examines the dissolution of cohabitation. We focus on two competing transitions out of cohabitation: union separation and legal marriage.

We have noted in several places that there are two competing views on the meaning of non-marital cohabitation. One perceives cohabitation essentially as an extension of courtship leading to marriage and as 'a form of "engagement" ' (Rindfuss and VandenHeuvel, 1990: 705). In this context, cohabitation can also be seen as some sort of 'trial marriage' whereby cohabiting couples try out 'married' life, rehearse marital roles, and assume marriage-like responsibilities (Teachman and Polonko, 1990: 208). If things go well, these couples marry. However, if the trial does not turn out as anticipated, couples may choose to dissolve the relationship. This form of relationship is appealing because couples are subject to fewer legal consequences if they choose to separate. Empirical evidence supports this view. For example, using data from the 1987–8 National Survey of Families and Households (NSFH), Bumpass et al. (1991) show that most American cohabitors say that they expect to marry their partners. Cohabitors also seem to have lower levels of marital satisfaction (DeMaris and Leslie, 1984), marital commitment, and perceived stability (Booth and Johnson, 1988), and express greater acceptance of divorce than non-cohabitors (Axinn and Thornton, 1992).

The second position views cohabitation as a substitute for legal marriage. It suggests that cohabitors are a select group of persons who are fundamentally different from non-cohabitors (e.g., ibid.; Teachman and Polonko, 1990). In other words, it is not the experience of having cohabited that makes cohabitors unique, but 'a preexisting disposition towards lesser commitment' shared by (all) cohabitors that sets them apart from non-cohabitors (Teachman and Polonko,

1990: 208). Empirical evidence is also supportive of this view. Several researchers have shown that cohabitors are less committed to a long-term relationship and are more willing to terminate an unhappy one than non-cohabitors (e.g., Axinn and Thornton, 1992; Booth and Johnson, 1988; Bumpass et al., 1991; Tanfer, 1987). Others have noted that the arrival of a child or the desire to have a child marks the key difference, as cohabiting couples may marry to legitimize children (e.g., Bachrach, 1987; Carlson, 1985).

In this chapter we intend to shed light on this debate by examining marriage intentions among cohabitors. In particular, we address such questions as: How many cohabitors intend to marry? How many cohabitors are ambivalent (uncertain) about marriage? Do cohabiting men have a greater desire for marriage than cohabiting women? Are previously married cohabitors more ambivalent and negative about marriage than never-married cohabitors?

While marriage intention is an important issue, we are not limited simply to asking what cohabitors intend to do. Rather, we will also look at what they actually do and examine how and why cohabitations are dissolved. As previously noted, our analysis focuses on two competing outcomes of cohabitational relationships, namely, union separation and legalization through marriage. Other key questions that we will address are: How long do cohabiting relationships last? How do cohabitations end? That is, how many cohabitations end in separation, and how many end in marriage? Who are the cohabitors likely to separate, and who are the ones likely to marry?

As noted in Chapter 2, the underlying assumption regarding union decisions is that cohabitors balance the gains and losses when deciding whether to remain cohabiting, to separate, or to marry their partner. The avoidance of losses and the seeking of gains, whether these are financial, social, or psychological (emotional), are the primary motives behind union decisions. Couples dissolve a union when they feel that they will be better off being 'single' despite the costs of terminating the relationship. We also noted that uncertainty often presides over union decisions. Union dissolution may not be fully anticipated and can result from unexpected events. Thus, the optimal union decision at any moment is likely to be the one that maximizes the gain one expects to receive over one's lifetime, given the realization up to that moment (Becker et al., 1977: 1143).

To facilitate our understanding of the process of union dissolution, we further assume that there are no fundamental differences between the uncoupling processes of marriage and cohabitation and that theories (and the determinants) of marital disruption are relevant to the process of terminating a cohabiting union (Becker et al., 1977; Lillard and Waite, 1993; Morgan and Rindfuss, 1985; South and Spitze, 1986). By the same token, theories of marriage can be used to understand the transition from cohabitation to legal marriage (e.g., Becker, 1981; Burch and Matthews, 1987; Goldscheider and Waite, 1986; Levinger, 1976; Oppenheimer, 1988). In this chapter we consider several individual-level characteristics known to influence marital union formation and dissolution, and assume that they influence non-marital union as well.

The discussion begins with a review of data sources and analytical models. We then examine the transition to union separation, focusing on transition timing and determinants. Next we turn to the transition to legal marriage. We look at marriage intentions and uncertainty among cohabiting individuals, and examine the timing and determinants of the transition to marriage.

Data and Methods

The materials in this chapter are based primarily on an earlier study (Wu and Balakrishnan, 1995). The data were taken from the GSS–90, although the GSS–95 was used in the descriptive analysis. The GSS–90 collected detailed information on union histories, from which survival data on union dissolution were constructed. To study the process of transition out of cohabitation, the sample has been restricted to respondents who experienced cohabitation prior to first marriage (if first marriage ever occurred). The reasons for this constraint are similar to those used in excluding post-marital cohabitations in the child-bearing study (Chapter 7). Accordingly, where there was more than one cohabitation before the first marriage, we used the first cohabitation. With this restriction, our study sample included 1,521 women and 1,494 men.

The primary dependent variable is union dissolution, coded as a multinomial variable, indicating whether a cohabitation ended in marriage, separation, or widowhood or was intact at the time of the survey. As a very small proportion of cohabitations are ended by the death of one partner (as Figure 8.2 will show), we focus on two probability outcomes: the hazard of separation and the hazard of marriage. However, widowhood was modelled as a competing 'risk' in the sense that widowed cohabitors are subject to the same 'risks' of separation and marriage prior to the time of widowhood.[1] A survival time variable measuring the exposure to the risk of disruption (or marriage) from the date of the initiation of cohabitation to the date of union disruption (or marriage) was again constructed. Where a union remained intact, survival time was measured up to the date of the interview. For cohabitations that ended in the death of one partner, survival time was measured up to the time of 'widowhood'. Time was measured in a series of eight-month intervals.[2]

Survival model techniques were employed to analyse survival data on union transitions.[3] We used a double-decrement life table procedure to estimate overall 'survival' rates, separation rates, and marriage rates (Chiang, 1984). Cox's proportional hazard (PH) model techniques were used to examine the determinants of the union transitions.

The Transition to Union Separation

Like marriage, a cohabitation relationship has a beginning and an end. Unlike marriage, however, there is a third way to end a cohabitation—that is, legalizing the relationship (note that both can be terminated by separation/divorce or the

Figure 8.1: Life Table Estimates of Proportion of Cohabitors Surviving

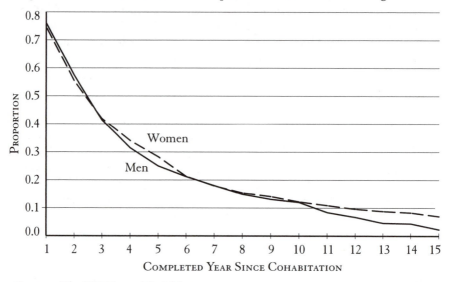

Source: The 1990 General Social Survey.

death of one or both partners). Although Canadian marriages are perhaps more likely to end in the death of one spouse than in divorce, the same cannot be said for Canadian cohabitations.[4] Cohabitations are known to be short-lived (e.g., Burch and Madan, 1986), but how long do they actually last?

How Long Do Cohabitations Last?

Figure 8.1 presents the life table estimates of cohabitation 'survival' rates, computed from a conventional double-decrement life table.[5] The estimates are computed and presented in terms of cumulative proportions of those who have remained in the relationship by duration since the initiation of the relationship. It is clear that the 'survival' curves for both genders decline rapidly with time, suggesting high rates of dissolution. For example, for women, only 75 per cent of cohabiting relationships survive the first year. The comparable figure for men is 76 per cent. After three years, only slightly over 40 per cent of cohabitations (for both genders) have survived. After five years, the proportion surviving is down to 28 per cent for women and 25 per cent for men.

The ephemeral nature of cohabiting relationships is evident. How fragile are these relationships compared to marriages? To answer this question, we analysed marital history data from the same survey (the results are not shown). Our life table estimates show that approximately 90 per cent of first marriages (N = 9,478) are expected to survive for 10 years.[6] The comparable figure for cohabitations is only 12 per cent. There is no doubt that cohabiting unions are more vulnerable and less stable than marital unions. Indeed, less than half of all cohabiting unions are expected to last for three years.[7]

Figure 8.2: Dissolution of Cohabitation by Type of Dissolution (%)

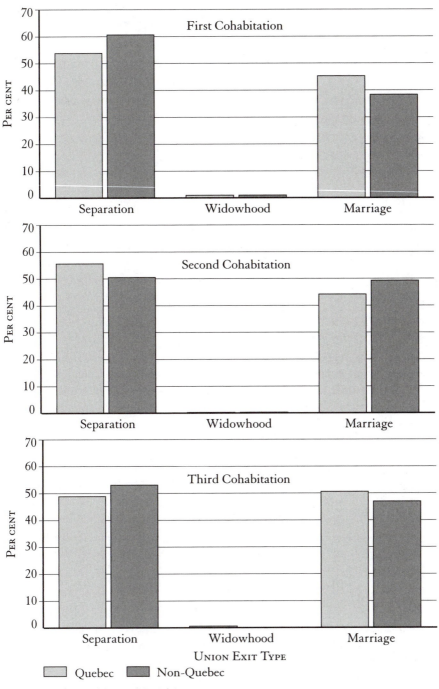

Source: The 1995 General Social Survey.

Figure 8.3: Life Table Estimates of Cumulative Proportion of Unions Separating

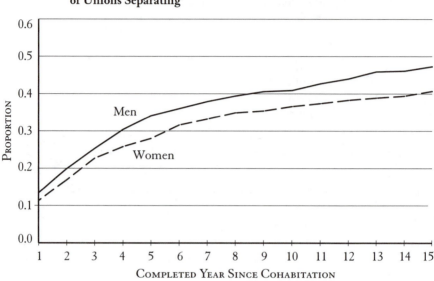

Source: The 1990 General Social Survey.

The Timing of the Transition to Separation

As noted, there are two primary ways to terminate a cohabitation relationship: union separation and legal marriage. We will look at union separation first. However, before we do that, let us take a glance at how cohabitations end at the aggregate level. Figure 8.2 shows data from the GSS-95 on ways in which cohabitation relationships are ended.[8] All three exits are considered: separation, marriage, and 'widowhood'. Note that all these cohabitations had already been terminated by the time of the survey and that ongoing relationships are not included.

Evidently, very few cohabitations are terminated as a result of the death of a partner (about 1 per cent of first cohabitations, and less for later cohabitations). It is also clear that more first cohabitations appear to end in separation than in marriage (note that this pattern is reversed in the following life table analysis) and that this tendency is more evident in non-Quebec Canada. Specifically, 54 per cent of first cohabitations in Quebec end in separation, compared to 45 per cent in marriage. The corresponding figures for non-Quebec Canada are 61 per cent and 38 per cent, respectively. The difference in the relative share of the two exits is reduced for second cohabitations and further reduced for third. Indeed, a reversed pattern emerges for third cohabitations in Quebec—that is, the third cohabitations in Quebec are more likely to end in marriage than separation.

The data in Figure 8.2 can only tell us part of the story because intact cohabitations are not included in the computation. Since unhappy relationships tend to be dissolved sooner rather than later, the cohabitations included in the computation may be a biased subsample of those who might have had higher risks of union disruption. To tackle this problem, we resort again to the life table procedure, which is capable of combining intact unions (censored cases) and dissolved unions (uncensored cases) in a way that produces unbiased and consistent estimates.

Figure 8.3 shows life table estimates in terms of cumulative proportions of unions separating. Overall, for both genders, the risk (rate) of separation rises rapidly in the early years of the relationship and levels off at longer durations. This finding is expected because incompatible relationships are likely dissolved more quickly, which supports the 'trial marriage' hypothesis noted earlier. Specifically, we see that about one-fourth of the cohabiting couples have separated within three years of the initiation of the relationship. The percentage rises to one-third at about seven years and to about 40 per cent at ten years. Moreover, men appear to be more likely than women to separate from a cohabiting relationship.

The Determinants of the Transition to Separation

While men appear to be more willing to end a cohabitational relationship through separation than women, the factors affecting the decision to end a relationship may also differ between men and women. For example, an increase in SES could raise the risk of separation for women, as the *independence* hypothesis suggests, but not necessarily so for men. Here we consider a number of individual characteristics and examine how they may affect the decision to separate. Table 8.1 presents the parameter estimates for the hazard models of union separation for women and men. Again, the interpretation of the parameter estimate uses a simple transformation, $100 \times (e^\beta - 1)$, which indicates the percentage change in the hazard rate of union separation for a one-unit change in an explanatory variable, holding all other variables constant.

We examine the effects of SES first. The data show that education has a positive but non-significant effect on union separation for both genders. School enrolment has a significant and positive effect on union separation for women but not for men. Numerically, the hazard rate of separation is 49 per cent ($100 \times [e^{.398} - 1]$) higher for student women than non-student women. This result supports the view that the student role is incompatible with the 'traditional' cohabiting (marital) role (Thornton et al., 1995), at least for women.

Turning to the cultural indicators, we observe that religion does not have a significant effect on either gender. In contrast to our earlier speculations (see Chapter 2), Catholics are as likely to terminate a cohabitation relationship as are Protestants and individuals with other/no religious orientations. Region, however, shows a significant negative effect, suggesting that the rate of separation is lower in Quebec than elsewhere in Canada. In Chapter 3, we saw that the overall rate of cohabitation is also higher in Quebec than elsewhere in Canada. Taken together, these findings suggest that cohabitations are more socially acceptable, and thus more stable, in Quebec than elsewhere in Canada, as we initially anticipated.

Table 8.1: Proportional Hazard Models of Transition out of Premarital Cohabitations via Union Separation

Variable	Women	Men
SOCIO-ECONOMIC STATUS		
Educational status (in 6 levels, 1 = elementary school or less, …, 6 = univ. grad. or higher)	0.023	0.036
School enrolment		
Yes	0.398**	0.207
No[†]		
CULTURAL BACKGROUND		
Religion		
Catholic	−0.022	0.026
Protestant	0.003	−0.148
Other/None[†]		
Region		
Quebec	−0.203**	−0.177*
Rest of Canada[†]		
DEMOGRAPHIC CHARACTERISTICS		
Age at cohabitation	−0.016**	−0.002
Partner's marital status		
Separated/Divorced	0.024	0.135
Widowed	−0.509	−0.976***
Not stated	−5.257***	−4.936***
Single/Never married[†]		
Partner's age		
Ten or more years older	−0.298**	—
Two or more years younger	0.063	—
Two or more years older	—	−0.028
Ten or more years younger	—	0.058
Age-homogeneous partnership[†]		
First birth[‡]		
Yes	−0.331***	−0.889***
No[†]		
Second or later birth[‡]		
Yes	−0.612***	−0.578**
No[†]		

Children before cohabitation		
Yes	0.180*	−0.193*
No[†]		
Year of cohabitation		
<1970	−1.499***	−1.138***
1970–9	−0.866***	−0.466***
1980–5	−0.447***	−0.312***
1986 or later[†]		
−2 Log Likelihood	3664.4	2980.1
Model chi-square	485.94***	430.39***
df	17	17

Note: All dummy variables are coded as 1 = yes, 0 = no.
[†] Reference category.
[‡] Time-varying covariate.
* $p \leq .10$
** $p \leq .05$
***$p \leq .01$ (one-tailed test)
Source: The 1990 General Social Survey.

Table 8.1 shows that several demographic variables are important determinants of union separation. For example, age at cohabitation has a negative effect for women. Women who entered first cohabitation at a younger age appear to have a greater risk of separation. Such a negative effect is consistent with the search model noted in Chapter 2. That is, the earlier a woman enters into a cohabitation, the shorter the duration of search, the higher the likelihood of divergence from an ideal match, and the fewer the benefits of remaining in the relationship (Becker et al., 1977).

We consider two measures of heterogamy: the partner's marital status prior to the entry into the union and the age difference between partners.[9] Single men who cohabit with widowed women have significantly lower rates of separation than single men who cohabit with single women. Also, the rate of separation is significantly lower when the man is 10 or more years older than his partner than when they are of more similar age. These findings are in contrast to our earlier speculations based on both the economic conceptualization of the family (e.g., Becker, 1981) and the potentially increased conflicts between partners suggested by sociological theory (e.g., Udry, 1974).

Children are known to stabilize marital unions (e.g., Morgan and Rindfuss, 1985; Morgan et al., 1988; Waite and Lillard, 1991). The presence and number of children within cohabitations also exhibit a strong deterrent effect on union separation, supporting the notion that having a *common* child increases the gains from the union relationship because 'union-specific capital' is increased. However, our data also show that having children born outside the union (pre-union births) tends to raise the risk of separation for women, although the opposite appears to be the case for men. The negative effect of pre-union births for women is understandable because these children are not 'union-specific capital'. But why is the effect positive for men? It is conceivable that men who bring children into the relationship may experience a greater desire for traditional role specification, and therefore perceive greater losses associated with returning to single parenthood.

Finally, year of cohabitation initiation was used as a period measure. The hazard rate of separation is 78 per cent lower for women who entered into cohabitation before 1970 than for those who did so after 1986. The corresponding figure for men is 68 per cent. The strong negative period effect provides evidence that cohabitations have become less stable over time.

In short, our analysis suggests that cohabitations are mostly short-lived. Only about one-fourth of cohabitations are expected to survive longer than five years, although as we will see in the next section, fewer cohabitors end their unions in separation than in marriage. Overall, men are more likely to terminate a cohabitation through separation than are women, although the rate of separation is particularly high among women students, non-Quebecers, and women who began cohabiting at young ages. The risk of separation is relatively low among men cohabiting with widows, women cohabiting with men 10 or more years older, couples with their own children, and cohabitations initiated in earlier periods.

The Transition to Marriage

We noted that cohabitation can be viewed as a 'trial marriage', whereby incompatible relationships are weeded out through separation and compatible ones may proceed to marriage. But how many cohabitors actually choose to marry each other, and what are the factors that influence their decision to marry? In this section we examine the union transition to marriage. Before we look at how many cohabitors actually marry, let us see how many cohabitors *want* to marry in the first place.[10]

Marriage Intentions

Table 8.2 shows marriage intentions among current cohabitors. As the reasons for marriage may differ depending on past marital experience, separate cross-tabulations are presented for premarital and post-marital unions. The data in the table clearly support the notion that divorced (cohabiting) people desire marriage less than do never-married (cohabiting) people. Post-marital cohabitors are considerably less likely to intend to marry than premarital cohabitors. As an illustration, our data show that 63 per cent of Quebec women who are cohabiting post-maritally do not intend to marry, compared to 52 per cent of Quebec women who are cohabiting premaritally. The corresponding figures for Quebec

Table 8.2: **Marriage Intentions among Cohabitors**
by Marital Status, Sex, Region (%)

Intent to marry	Women		Men	
	Premarital Cohabitation	Post-marital Cohabitation	Premarital Cohabitation	Post-marital Cohabitation
Quebec				
Yes	35.5	26.5	40.8	14.3
Uncertain	12.2	10.9	11.3	19.6
No	52.3	62.6	47.9	66.1
Total	100	100	100	100
Non-Quebec				
Yes	74.1	38.7	64.6	29.8
Uncertain	14.8	21.9	19.3	15.2
No	11.2	39.4	16.1	55.0
Total*	100	100	100	100

* May not total to 100 per cent due to rounding.
Source: The 1995 General Social Survey.

men are 66 per cent and 48 per cent, respectively. Similar patterns hold for non-Quebec Canada.

Gender patterns of marriage intentions are mixed. Outside Quebec, it appears that women are more likely than men to intend to marry, whether they are cohabiting premaritally or post-maritally. However, in Quebec, women who are cohabiting premaritally have lower desire to marry than their male counterparts. The reverse is true for post-marital cohabitors.

Regional patterns are more evident, though. The desire for marriage is conspicuously lower in Quebec than elsewhere in Canada. For example, 36 per cent of Quebec women who are cohabiting premaritally intend to marry, compared to 74 per cent of their counterparts outside Quebec. A similar pattern holds for men and for post-marital comparisons. If we equate those who have no intention to marry with those who see cohabitation as a substitute for marriage, then cohabitation is more likely a substitute for marriage in Quebec than elsewhere in Canada. Similarly, if we equate those who intend to marry with those who view cohabitation as a trial marriage, then cohabitation is less likely a trial marriage in Quebec than elsewhere in Canada.

It is important to note that there is considerable uncertainty in marriage intentions. Overall, the level of uncertainty tends to be higher outside of Quebec, with the exception of men in post-marital cohabitations for whom the pattern is reversed. Gender and union-history patterns of uncertainty are unclear. However, regardless of their gender or union histories, more than 10 per cent of cohabitors (in each subgroup) are uncertain about their marriage plans.

Figure 8.4: Life Table Estimates of Cumulative Proportion of Unions Marrying

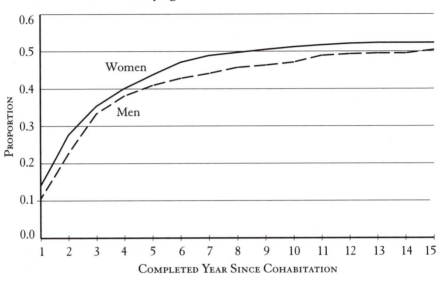

COMPLETED YEAR SINCE COHABITATION

Source: The 1990 General Social Survey.

The Timing of the Transition to Marriage

While a substantial number of cohabitors say that they intend to marry, how many actually do, and how soon into the cohabitation? Figure 8.4 presents life table estimates in terms of cumulative marriage rates. The shapes of the marriage curves are similar to those of separation: the 'risk' (rate) of marriage increases rapidly in the initial periods of cohabitation and slows about three years after the start of cohabitation. Moreover, the rate of marriage is slightly higher for women than for men, consistent with the gender pattern in the timing of first marriage. For example, we observed that 14 per cent of women cohabitors married their partners within one year of cohabitation. The comparable rate for men is 11 per cent. After three years, the rate is up to 35 per cent for women and 33 per cent for men. After five years, the corresponding rates are 44 per cent for women and 41 per cent for men.

A comparison of the two exits from cohabitation (Figures 8.3 and 8.4) suggests that cohabitors are more likely to marry than to separate. For example, 35 per cent of women and 33 per cent of men married their partner within three years of initiating cohabitation, compared to 23 per cent of women and 25 per cent of men who separated. After five years, the proportion marrying rises to 44 per cent for women and 41 per cent for men. The comparable figures for separation are 28 per cent for women and 34 per cent for men. Although the overall survival rate varies little between women and men, there is a clear gap with respect to the type of exit. Women exhibit a greater propensity to marry than men do at each duration under consideration, whereas men have a greater probability of separation than women.

The Determinants of the Transition to Marriage

To examine the determinants of marriage, again we resort to Cox's proportional hazard model techniques and use the same set of individual-level characteristics shown in Table 8.1 (the separation models). Table 8.3 presents the parameter estimates for the models of marriage for women and men. The interpretation of the parameter estimates is the same as for the models of union separation.

As with the separation models, educational status has a positive but non-significant effect on transition to marriage for both genders. School enrolment has a negative effect, although the effect is significant only for women—the hazard rate of marriage is 29 per cent ($100 \times [e^{-.348} - 1]$) lower for student women than for non-student women. Combined with our earlier findings, it seems that school enrolment undermines union stability (via spurring union separation and deterring the transition to marriage), which is consistent with the role conflict thesis noted earlier.

Table 8.3 shows that religion has a significant influence on the hazard rate of marriage for both genders. It appears that Protestants and Catholics are more likely to marry their partners than those who have other or no religious orientations. It is possible that cohabitation serves as an extended courtship to marriage more for people with Christian background than for others. The sacramental view of marriage could be more important for Christians than for others, for whom it is a ritual or formal legality, particularly those with no religious orientation.

Regional effects are strong and consistent. All else being equal, the hazard rate of marriage is 33 per cent lower for Quebec women than for non-Quebec women. For men, the corresponding figure is 49 per cent. This complements the hazard rate of cohabitation disruption, which, as was noted earlier, is lower in Quebec than in the rest of the country. Together, these findings are congruous with the notion that cohabiting relationships in Quebec are more stable and permanent than those observed elsewhere in the country.

In regard to demographic indicators, age at cohabitation has a negative effect. People who entered cohabitation at a younger age are more likely to marry their partner than those who entered at an older age. Further, never-married women have a greater propensity to marry never-married men than previously married men; the same is the case for never-married men. Moreover, the rate of marriage is significantly higher when men are 10 or more years older than their partners than it is when they are of similar age. Combined with the findings shown in Table 8.1, it appears that relationships involving older men and younger women tend to be more stable and have a greater likelihood of turning into marriage, probably because these men have a relatively higher SES (which is not necessarily reflected in educational status) and are therefore more economically attractive. Given the transitory nature of cohabitation, it is also understandable that when

Table 8.3: Proportional Hazard Models of Transition out of Premarital Cohabitations via Marriage

Variable	Women	Men
SOCIO-ECONOMIC STATUS		
Educational status (in 6 levels, 1 = elementary school or less, ..., 6 = univ. grad. or higher)	0.009	0.008
School enrolment		
Yes	−0.348*	−0.071
No[†]		
CULTURAL BACKGROUND		
Religion		
Catholic	0.190*	0.189*
Protestant	0.475***	0.231**
Other/None[†]		
Region		
Quebec	−0.405***	−0.672***
Rest of Canada[†]		
DEMOGRAPHIC CHARACTERISTICS		
Age at cohabitation	−0.031***	−0.010*
Partner's marital status		
Separated/Divorced	−0.421***	−0.291**
Widowed	−0.286	−1.766***
Not stated	−21.364	−4.733***
Single/Never married[†]		
Partner's age		
Ten or more years older	0.032	—
Two or more years younger	−0.159	—
Two or more years older	—	−0.103
Ten or more years younger	—	0.433**
Age-homogeneous partnership[†]		
First birth[‡]		
Yes	−0.476***	−0.403***
No[†]		
Second or later birth[‡]		
Yes	−0.752***	−0.775***
No[†]		

Children before cohabitation		
Yes	−0.529***	−0.716***
No[†]		
Year of cohabitation		
<1970	−0.403***	−0.454**
1970–9	0.110	0.293***
1980–5	0.090	0.036
1986 or later[†]		
−2 Log Likelihood	4229.4	3042.3
Model chi-square	588.75***	411.97***
df	17	17

Note: All dummy variables are coded as 1 = yes, 0 = no.
[†]   Reference category.
[‡]   Time-varying covariate.
* $p \leq .10$
** $p \leq .05$
***$p \leq .01$ (one-tailed test)
Source: The 1990 General Social Survey.

men are considerably older, they may have a greater desire to secure the relationship through marriage.

The effects of children are negative and significant. The presence and number of (common) children tend to reduce the likelihood of marriage. In Table 8.1 we saw that children stabilize cohabiting relationships. It appears that children not only discourage union separation but also deter the transition to marriage. The effects of pre-union births are more consistent, however. Table 8.3 shows that having children outside cohabitation reduces the hazard rate of marriage by 41 per cent for women and 51 per cent for men, which is consistent with the notion that these children do not constitute 'union-specific capital' but are likely to be sources of tension between couples. Family sociologist Jessie Bernard (1956) once said that parenting in a step-family is one of the most difficult tasks assigned to the human race. Raising 'step-children' in a cohabiting relationship may be even more challenging.

As with the separation models, year of cohabitation initiation was used as a period indicator. People who began cohabiting prior to 1970 are less likely to marry their partner than are those who did so in more recent years. It is also interesting to note that women who began cohabiting in the 1970s are more likely to marry than women who started cohabiting either prior to the seventies or in the eighties.

In short, our regression analysis identifies several factors that influence the hazard rate of the transition to marriage. The rate of marriage is particularly high among non-student women, individuals affiliated with Christian religions, and people outside of Quebec. The rate of marriage also increases with a decrease in age at entry into cohabitation, in cohabitations involving never-married men and women, and when men cohabit with women 10 or more years younger than themselves. However, the rate decreases when children are involved (either brought or born into the relationship) and when people entered into cohabitation prior to 1970.

Discussion

While few, if any, couples take (marital) vows when they begin to cohabit non-maritally, most would want the relationship to last. However, things can go wrong. In fact, things are probably more likely to go wrong in non-marital unions than in marital unions. The data presented in this chapter confirm that cohabitations are ephemeral and that most cohabiting relationships are dissolved after only a few years. While many cohabitors eventually marry their partners, about two-fifths of women and one-half of men terminate their relationships by separation. What happens to those who marry? Are their marriages more successful and stable as a result of their trial marriage? As we will see in the next chapter, premarital cohabitation actually leads to less stable marriages. Empirically, we also know that cohabiting unions are less stable than marital unions. This evidence lends support to the argument that cohabiting unions are fragile and transient and that they weaken the institution of marriage by undermining 'its central foundation of permanence' (Rindfuss and VandenHeuvel, 1990: 722).

The empirical analyses also contribute to our understanding of the debate over whether cohabitation serves as a trial marriage or a substitute for marriage. While a significant number of Canadian cohabitors wish to get married, many others, particularly Quebecers and/or previously married cohabitors, have no intention of marrying or are ambivalent about marriage. Clearly, there is some grey area between the two opposite views of cohabitation.

Our analytical findings contribute to this debate as well. Our hazard analysis models identify several individual characteristics associated with cohabitors who separate as well as those who eventually marry. Presumably, the married ones are those who are most likely to see cohabitation as a trial marriage. The implication is that cohabitors are likely a select group of people with *different* viewpoints on the role that cohabitation plays in the process of family formation. For some, it may serve as a trial marriage, while for others it is an alternative. Therefore, the two seemingly competing views regarding the place of cohabitation in the union formation process may not be mutually exclusive, but rather complementary to each other. Of course, people may change their view of cohabitation once they begin to cohabit. As will be shown in next chapter, the experience of cohabitation has a strong influence on the timing of marriage.

Several findings from the multivariate analyses merit some additional comments. First, we saw that educational status has no significant effect on either union separation or marriage. It could be that education exerts two opposing effects on the process of union dissolution, as we noted in Chapter 2. On the one hand, an increase in education, particularly for women, may reduce the gains from the union due to a decrease in the traditional division of labour within the household (Becker et al., 1977). On the other hand, cohabitations between highly educated individuals may result in greater gains from the union because of the partners' greater market-valued skills. The result is that education itself has limited *net* impact on union dissolution. The same reasoning should apply to the union formation process as well.

Second, the finding that children delay and deter the transition to marriage is somewhat surprising. Like married couples, when cohabitors move in together, they may invest in assets such as household appliances, cars, houses, and even children.[11] To secure their investments, particularly children, it is logical that couples may choose to marry each other as a means of protection. To our surprise, having children born into the relationship actually reduces the propensity to marry. How do we explain this negative effect? While the answer can never be definitive, I suspect that cohabiting couples who choose to have children are those individuals who have a stronger ideological commitment to cohabitation as an alternative lifestyle. Having (mutual) children may reinforce this commitment. Another explanation is also possible. We know that marriage traditionally served as a means of formalizing a relationship. The ritual of marriage may become less important with the birth of a mutual child. In other words, the arrival of a child may also serve to legitimate the union in the eyes of family and friends. Consequently, the probability of subsequent marriage may decrease once a child is born. This explanation is supported by some European studies (e.g., Bachrach, 1987; Carlson, 1985).

Third, we have seen that year of cohabitation initiation, used as a period indicator, has an important influence on union dissolution. Specifically, we saw that cohabitations formed prior to 1970 are particularly stable (i.e., less likely to end in either separation or marriage). Again, I suspect that the selection hypothesis may explain this phenomenon. We know that cohabitation was rare prior to the 1970s and thus was most likely to select individuals who saw cohabitation as a substitute for marriage. As the incidence of cohabitation becomes more widespread, it is likely to attract people with different views of cohabitation, either seeing it as a substitute for marriage or as a trial marriage. This may also explain the elevated rate of marriage observed for the cohabitations formed in the 1970s (see Table 8.3), as the proportion of cohabitors who took the latter view might have increased.

9 | Consequences of Cohabitation

We have noted that the rapid increase in non-marital cohabitation caught many of us by surprise. The emergence of this phenomenon not only demands an examination of the factors that give rise to this lifestyle choice, but also calls for a close look at the implications for the individuals involved in this family form and for the future of marriage. In Chapters 6 and 8 we examined the transitions into and out of cohabitation. We have already looked at the trends in cohabitation and identified the factors that influence union transitions. In this chapter we will examine the implications of cohabitation.

We focus on three dimensions of cohabitation: (1) its role in the timing of first marriage; (2) its impact on the stability of subsequent marriage; and (3) its influence on the division of household labour.[1] There are good reasons to believe that cohabitational experiences may influence the timing of marriage. As we have already noted, cohabitation tends to be selective of individuals who are more likely to reject 'traditional' family values and less committed to the long-term relationship of marriage. If the *selectivity* hypothesis is correct, then we can expect that the propensity to cohabit will be negatively associated with the propensity to marry and that the characteristics that positively influence the decision to cohabit will negatively affect the decision to marry. Then, other things being equal, premarital cohabitation should lead to a later age at marriage and raise the probability of non-marriage.

Premarital cohabitation may also delay marriage because of the very *experience* of living in a cohabitation. While it is true that it takes time to experience cohabitation, particularly when cohabitations do not later become marriages (Oppenheimer, 1994: 308), it is more than just the *time* spent in cohabitations that is relevant. For example, the experience of living together may affect the way people perceive marriage and family life (Axinn and Thornton, 1992). As we saw in Chapter 8, cohabitations generally are short-lived. The ephemeral nature of cohabiting unions may undermine the notion that intimate relationships are lasting and permanent. Therefore, it is not unreasonable to believe that the experience of cohabitation may foster less conventional attitudes regarding marriage and the family and thereby reinforce the view that cohabitation provides an alternative lifestyle to marriage. Moreover, lower motivation to marry may also be associated with the fear that the transition from cohabitation to marriage leads to a loss of autonomy (Bumpass et al., 1991).

The *selectivity* and *experience* hypotheses are also pertinent to an explanation of the relationship between premarital cohabitation and subsequent marital stability. We have observed that many cohabiting couples choose to marry each other after a short period of cohabitation. Common sense tells us that since poor matches would tend to be weeded out before becoming marriages, marriages preceded by cohabitation should be more stable than the ones that were not. However, evidence contradicts this common sense. Premarital cohabitation seems to increase the risk of marital instability (e.g., Balakrishnan et al., 1987; Bennett et al., 1988; Booth and Johnson, 1988; Lillard et al., 1995; Teachman and Polonko, 1990). Why is this relationship negative?

Applying the *selectivity* thesis, one would expect that cohabitation is likely to select individuals with characteristics conducive to marital instability. Research by Thomson and Colella (1992) has shown that cohabitors tend to perceive themselves to be poor risks for marriage. Booth and Johnson (1988) show that people with various personal problems, such as personality problems, alcohol and drug abuse, and trouble with the law, are likely to select themselves into cohabitation. These problems may subsequently lead to marital conflict and undermine marital stability. Cohabitors also express less conventional familial values and greater acceptance of divorce than non-cohabitors (Axinn and Thornton, 1992) and tend to have lower levels of marital satisfaction (DeMaris and Leslie, 1984), marital commitment, and perceived stability (Booth and Johnson, 1988). In Chapter 5, we also saw that cohabitors tend to have a greater acceptance of premarital sex and non-marital cohabitation and place less emphasis on the importance of marriage than non-cohabitors.

Applying the *experience* thesis, we should expect that selectivity alone cannot fully explain the higher risk of marital instability for married couples who cohabited premaritally. As we have noted, the experience of living together itself influences the way people perceive marriage and family life, cultivates non-traditional attitudes towards marriage, and undermines the notion that marriage is a lifetime commitment. Moreover, the decision to marry may also be influenced by pressure from family and friends and by the arrival of a child. If this line of reasoning is correct, then we can expect that the experience of cohabiting, net of the selection into cohabitation, should lead to an increased risk of marital disruption when cohabiting couples do choose to marry.

Household labour is an integral part of adult life in all families. The division of household labour is often a source of marital (union) conflict, particularly when the division of domestic labour is seen as being unfair (Pina and Bengston, 1993; Suitor, 1991). For example, studies have shown that married women, regardless of their employment status and work schedules, tend to spend more time doing household tasks than married men do (e.g., Presser, 1994; South and

Spitze, 1994; Spitze, 1988). Further, married people tend to spend more time on housework than unmarried people do (e.g., Bergen, 1991; South and Spitze, 1994).

The *selectivity* hypothesis may shed light on the division of household labour within cohabiting families as well. If cohabitors are a select group of individuals who tend to hold non-traditional familial attitudes, they are likely to lead an unconventional lifestyle (cohabitation itself has been, until recently, an unconventional lifestyle), including an unconventional division of household labour. What would an unconventional division of labour be like? In all likelihood, it would involve a more gender-balanced division of housework. There is some indirect evidence supporting this view. Research by Sweet and Bumpass (1990) shows that cohabitors tend to hold more egalitarian sex role attitudes than non-cohabitors. They are also more likely to approve of mothers who have preschool-age children working full-time and to support the care of young children in day-care centres. Thus, all else being equal, we would anticipate that cohabiting men tend to do more housework than married men, with the reverse holding true for women.

The *trial marriage* hypothesis may also predict a reduced gender gap in the division of domestic labour among cohabiting couples. To the extent that cohabitation is viewed as a trial marriage, cohabitors live in a 'marriage-like' relationship and rehearse marital roles and expectations. While cohabiting, couples may try hard to please each other, including an increased share of housework performed by the male partner (Roelants, 1998). Accordingly, the division of household labour should be more egalitarian in cohabiting families than in married families. However, if this hypothesis is correct, then we should also expect that the division is likely to shift towards a less gender-balanced one once the couple is married.[2] There is also some indirect evidence supporting this view. For example, DeMaris and Leslie (1984) showed that the level of marital satisfaction tends to be lower among couples who cohabited premaritally than couples who did not. A more recent study by Rogers and Amato (1997) also suggests that premarital cohabitation has an adverse influence on the quality of a subsequent marriage by reducing the levels of marital interaction and increasing marital conflict and problems.

In this chapter we examine some of these issues. Specifically, we test the hypothesis that cohabitational experiences, whether they lead directly to marriage or not, contribute to a delay in marriage timing. We examine the notion that premarital cohabitation has an adverse impact on marital stability. We also evaluate the contention that cohabiting couples have a more egalitarian division of household labour than married couples. In addition, we consider the validity of the *selectivity* and *experience* hypotheses in the context of marriage timing.

The chapter is ordered as follows. In the following section we briefly look at data sources and statistical models. We then examine the role of cohabitational experiences in the timing of first marriage. Next, we consider the relationship between premarital cohabitation and marital stability. Finally, we look at the division of household labour, comparing the division of household tasks between married and cohabiting families.

Data and Methods

The data used in the marriage timing section come from the GSS–90. The materials are taken primarily from a recent study (Wu, 1999b). The study sample was restricted to the respondents who were under age 35 at the time of the survey, regardless of their current marital status. The primary reason for this constraint is that cohabitation is generally a recent phenomenon and is particularly common among young people (see Chapter 4). As a result, the analysis includes 2,865 women and 2,329 men.

The GSS–95 data were used in the analyses of marital instability and the division of household labour. The GSS–90 data were also used for a descriptive table in the marital instability section. The instability study includes ever-married respondents, regardless of their current marital status. The study sample includes 4,310 women and 3,158 men. No sample selection criteria were applied to the housework study (i.e., the entire sample is used).

The dependent variable in the marriage study is marriage timing, measuring duration time (exposure time to the 'risk' of marriage) from age 15 to the date of first marriage, if marriage occurred. Where a marriage did not occur, duration time was measured from age 15 to the survey date. Duration time was measured in months. The primary independent variable is cohabitational status, coded as a dichotomy indicating whether the respondent ever cohabited, either with a current or previous partner, prior to entering first marriage, if marriage occurred.

The dependent variable in the marital instability study is a multinomial variable indicating whether a respondent's first marriage ended in separation (divorce) or widowhood, or was intact at the time of the survey. As we are primarily interested in marital instability, we focus on the risk (hazard) of marital separation (divorce).[3] Survival time was measured from the date of first marriage to the date of marital separation or divorce if the respondent was divorced without a separation or if the date of separation is unavailable.[4] Where a marriage remained intact, survival time was measured up to the time of the survey. Where a marriage ended in widowhood, survival time was measured up to the time of widowhood. Time was measured in months. The primary independent variable in the marital instability study is a dichotomous variable indicating whether the respondent cohabited with his/her partner prior to first marriage.

The main dependent variable in the housework study is the number of hours spent doing unpaid housework. The information on unpaid housework was collected using the question, 'Last week, how many hours did you spend doing the following activities? ... Doing unpaid work, yard work or home maintenance for members of this household or others.'[5] The information on the number of hours is only available as an ordinal variable in six levels, ranging from 'none' to

'60 hours or more'. Moreover, because the GSS–95 did not collect information on specific household tasks, the GSS–90 data were used to construct a descriptive table of household tasks (see Table 9.3). The primary independent variable is marital status, which was measured in six levels: (1) currently married but did not cohabit premaritally, (2) currently married and cohabited premaritally, (3) separated or divorced, (4) single, living at parental home, (5) single, living outside parental home, and (6) currently cohabiting. In each of the three studies, besides the independent variable of our primary interest, we also consider a number of other (control) variables that may influence the dependent variable in question.

The primary statistical tools used for the marriage timing and marital instability studies were survival analysis techniques. In both studies, we begin with an ordinary life table analysis to determine whether there is any observed difference between cohabitors and non-cohabitors in the timing of marriage and the timing of marital disruption, respectively. We then add a number of control variables known to be important in determining the timing of these two vital events. The goal is to determine whether the observed differences (if any) can be explained away by these control variables. In other words, we want to know whether any observed differences are attributable to differences in other socio-economic and demographic characteristics (e.g., age, education, and religion). In the controlled analyses, (accelerated) failure time model techniques were employed to examine the effect of cohabitational experiences on marriage timing (Kalbfleisch and Prentice, 1980).[6] Cox's proportional hazard model techniques were used to examine the effect of premarital cohabitation on subsequent marital instability.

In the household labour study, we start with a descriptive analysis of the gender division of household tasks for all marital statuses. We then estimate a series of ordinary least squares models to examine the differences in the time spent on housework between cohabitors and people in other marital statuses.

Cohabitation and the Timing of First Marriage

In Chapter 4 we observed a rising trend in cohabitation throughout many social strata of the Canadian population. Although we know that the upward trend in cohabitation has been coupled with a downward trend in marriage, we cannot simply infer that one trend is the cause of the other. The relationship could be essentially spurious and may represent no direct causal relationship. For example, it is possible that structural changes, such as the rise in women's labour force participation, underlie both demographic trends. In this section we empirically test this relationship using individual-level data.[7] We examine the extent to which cohabitational experiences are directly responsible for the rising delays in marriage. We also address the issue of selection into cohabitation in the process of union formation and provide direct tests of the *selectivity* and *experience* hypotheses noted previously.

Timing of First Marriage by Cohabitational Experience

We begin our investigation with a life table analysis of marriage timing by pre-marital cohabitational experience. Our goal is to determine whether there is any observed difference between premarital cohabitors and non-cohabitors in the timing of first marriage. Figures 9.1 and 9.2 provide life table estimates in terms of the cumulative experience of first marriage for women and men by age.

The diverging patterns of marriage between cohabitors and non-cohabitors for both women and men are evident. Individuals who have ever cohabited have lower rates of first marriage than those who have not. For example, Figure 9.1 shows that by age 18, 11 per cent of women non-cohabitors have married, compared to only 5 per cent of women cohabitors. By age 20, the corresponding figures rise to 29 per cent and 16 per cent, respectively. By age 25, the figures are 65 per cent and 47 per cent. Similar patterns are also observed for men (see Figure 9.2). These results provide preliminary evidence for the hypothesis that cohabitation leads to a later age at first marriage.

Multivariate Analysis

How do we account for the differences in marriage timing between cohabitors and non-cohabitors? It is possible that some (or all) of these differences may reflect pre-existing characteristics that influence the decision to cohabit, as suggested by the *selectivity* hypothesis. The unique experience of living together non-maritally could also be responsible for the delays in marriage timing, as claimed by the *experience* hypothesis.

To determine the role of cohabitation in union formation, we begin by modelling the self-selection into cohabitation. Biases in regression estimates introduced through self-selection have been extensively discussed in the literature, and several procedures have been proposed to correct selectivity (see, e.g., Greene, 1993; Heckman, 1979). James Heckman's (1976, 1979) two-stage procedure was followed to correct the selection into cohabitation.[8] Using Heckman's procedure, a new explanatory variable, known as the hazard rate, was constructed. The parameter estimate for the selection factor indicates: (1) whether there is a selection into cohabitation, and (2) the extent to which the selection into cohabitation affects marriage timing. In other words, the statistical significance of the hazard rate indicates whether or not the selection into cohabitation has a significant impact on marriage timing.

Table 9.1 presents four failure time models of marriage timing. Models 1 and 3 do not control for the selection into cohabitation, and models 2 and 4 correct for selectivity. Further, as noted in Chapter 6, caution should be exercised in the interpretation of the parameter estimates in the table. Because the Weibull model uses the natural logarithm of the survival times as the response values, a positive estimate indicates a longer interval of remaining single or a delayed entry into first marriage. Again, a now familiar transformation, $100 \times (e^{\beta} - 1)$, can be used to interpret the effect of a given explanatory variable on the timing of first marriage.

**Figure 9.1: Life Table Estimates of Timing of First Marriage
by Cohabitational Experience, Women**

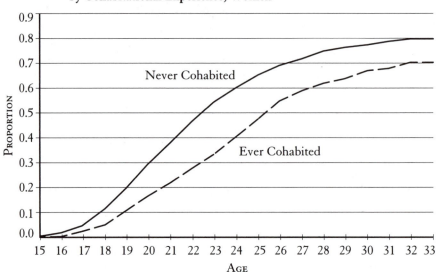

Source: The 1990 General Social Survey.

Models 1 and 3 in Table 9.1 show that the effect of cohabitation is positive and significant. The timing of first marriage is *decelerated* by 26 per cent (100 x [e$^{.234-1}$]) for women who ever cohabited premaritally compared with women who had not. The corresponding figure for men is 19 per cent (100 x [e$^{.173-1}$]). These results are consistent with our earlier life table estimates and support the hypothesis that the experience of cohabitation leads to a later age at marriage.

The delay in marriage timing associated with non-marital cohabitation could be due to a self-selection process. This hypothesis is tested by introducing a correction factor (the hazard rate) capturing the selectivity into cohabitation to the models of marriage timing. The parameter estimates from this specification are shown in models 2 and 4 in Table 9.1. Consistent with the *selectivity* hypothesis, the hazard rate has a significant impact on marriage timing.

Apart from self-selection, the experience of cohabiting itself may also delay the timing of first marriage. This hypothesis is tested by examining the effect of cohabitation on marriage timing after removing the effect of selectivity (see models 2 and 4). Models 2 and 4 show that the estimates of cohabitation are positive and significant, supporting the experience hypothesis. Indeed, comparisons of the estimates of cohabitation across the models suggest that the effect of cohabitation on marriage timing remains virtually unchanged after correcting for selectivity. It is also interesting to note that the effects of cohabitation and selectivity vary little between women and men, although the latter effect appears to be more evident for men ($p < .001$) than for women ($p < .05$). Overall, these

**Figure 9.2: Life Table Estimates of Timing of First Marriage
by Cohabitational Experience, Men**

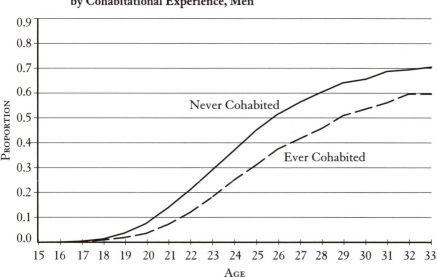

Source: The 1990 General Social Survey.

findings appear to suggest that the bias introduced by self-selection into cohabitation has a significant, though not substantial, influence on marriage timing.

The parameter estimates of the remaining factors are generally consistent with other studies. Since there is considerable evidence of selection into cohabitation, these variables in models 2 and 4 need to be considered further. Overall, with the exception of education and presence of children, the effects of these other variables are fairly comparable between women and men.

As would be anticipated, the scale parameter (σ) is less than unity in all models, suggesting that the rate of first marriage increases with age. Educational status and school enrolment have negative (delaying) effects on marriage timing, although the effects for men are generally not significant after correction for selectivity. Catholics tend to marry later than Protestants, which is consistent with Sander's (1993) finding for American women. However, Catholics appear to marry earlier than people with no religious affiliation and do not differ significantly from people with other (non-Protestant) religious orientations. Delays in marriage are also greater among people born in Canada and residing in the province of Quebec. While the presence of children delays marriage timing for women, the opposite appears to be true for men. This positive effect of children for men may reflect a greater desire to marry among single men with dependent children. This may be indicative of a greater preference among men for marriage generally (Goldscheider and Waite, 1986) and for traditional role specification within the family.

Table 9.1: Accelerated Failure Time Models of Timing of First Marriage

	Women		Men	
Variable	Model 1	Model 2	Model 3	Model 4
Ever cohabited				
Yes	0.234***	0.235***	0.173***	0.180***
No[†]				
Socio-economic Status				
Educational status				
Elementary school or lower	−0.662***	−0.612***	−0.083	−0.065
Some high school	−0.519***	−0.495***	−0.175***	−0.035
High school	−0.469***	−0.485***	−0.210***	−0.142**
Some post-secondary	−0.328***	−0.296***	−0.133**	−0.019
College/trade school diplomas	−0.232***	−0.240***	−0.128**	−0.043
Bachelor's degree or higher[†]				
School enrolment				
Yes	0.501***	0.412***	0.244**	0.020
No[†]				
Cultural Background				
Religion				
Protestant	−0.102***	−0.100***	−0.085**	−0.111***
Other	−0.012	−0.048	0.198*	0.143
None	0.140**	0.189***	0.109**	0.236***
Catholic[†]				
Nativity				
Canadian-born	0.052	0.099*	0.093*	0.185***
Foreign-born[†]				
Region				
Quebec	0.084*	0.159**	0.203***	0.521***
Rest of Canada[†]				
Demographic Characteristics				
Presence of own children				
Yes	0.154**	0.153**	−0.106*	−0.102*
No[†]				
Presence of pre-union children				
Yes	0.431***	0.524***	0.173	0.769***
No[†]				
Hazard rate (λ)	—	−0.257*	—	−0.840***

Scale parameter (σ)	0.510***	0.510***	0.377***	0.383***
Intercept	5.098***	5.195***	5.159***	5.424***
–Log Likelihood (Weibull)	2116.8	2114.8	1194.2	1185.6

Note: All dummy variables are coded as 1 = yes, 0 = no.
† Reference category.
* p < .05
** p < .01
***p < .001 (one-tailed test)
Source: The 1990 General Social Survey.

In short, our multivariate analysis provides support for both the *selectivity* and *experience* hypotheses. We observe that the experience of cohabitation delays the entry into first marriage. The delaying effect remains virtually unchanged after correction for the selection into cohabitation, suggesting a minimal influence of self-selection (into cohabitation) on marriage timing.

Cohabitation and the Risk of Divorce

Partly because many cohabiting couples eventually marry each other (see Chapter 8), considerable research attention has been directed to the linkage between premarital cohabitation and subsequent marital stability. We have noted that empirical research on this relationship has been consistent in suggesting that premarital cohabitation is associated with lower marital stability (Bennett et al., 1988; Booth and Johnson, 1988; Lillard et al., 1995; Teachman and Polonko, 1990). In this section, we re-examine this linkage using more recent Canadian data from the GSS–95.[9]

Timing of Marital Disruption by Premarital Cohabitational Status

We again begin with an ordinary life table analysis of the timing of disruption (separation) by premarital cohabitational experience. Recall that marital disruption is specified as the timing of marital separation or divorce (if divorce occurred without a legal separation). Our goal is the same as in the marriage timing study. That is, we want to know whether there is any observed relationship between premarital cohabitation and subsequent marital instability. Figures 9.3 and 9.4 show life table estimates of marital instability for women and men by marital duration.

The impact of premarital cohabitation is again evident. Couples that lived together before marriage experience substantially greater risks of marital disruption than couples that did not. Specifically, for women, 5 per cent of marriages preceded by cohabitation experienced marital disruption within two years, compared to 1.5 per cent of the marriages that were not (see Figure 9.3). After five years, the comparable figures grow to 14 per cent and 5 per cent for cohabitors and non-cohabitors, respectively. After 10 years, the figures are 30 per

Figure 9.3: Life Table Estimates of Timing of Marital Disruption by Premarital Cohabitational Experience, Women

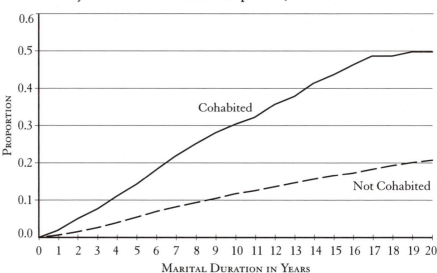

Source: The 1990 General Social Survey.

cent and 12 per cent. Overall, the risk of marital disruption for premarital cohabitors is about two to three times higher than for non-cohabitors. A similar pattern is also observed for men (see Figure 9.4).

Multivariate Analysis

The influence of premarital cohabitation on marital instability is clearly visible in the life table analyses. However, the effect of premarital cohabitation could reflect differences in other individual characteristics that are responsible for marital disruption. For example, as was noted in Chapter 6, women who work outside the home have a greater propensity to cohabit. Becker's (1981) independence hypothesis also suggests an increased risk of marital disruption as women gain (greater) financial independence. Therefore, it could be that the effect of premarital cohabitation on marital disruption simply reflects the influence of women's economic independence and may actually have little to do with cohabitation itself. Multivariate analysis will allow us to clarify the complexity of these relationships.

Table 9.2 shows proportional hazard models of marital instability for women and men. As anticipated, the effect of premarital cohabitation is positive and highly significant. For women, the hazard rate of marital disruption is 80 per cent ($100 \times [e^{.587-1}]$) higher among premarital cohabitors than non-cohabitors. The corresponding figure for men is 152 per cent ($100 \times [e^{.925-1}]$). Note that these effects are *net* effects in the sense that the influences of other covariates in the models have been removed. Comparing the parameter estimates for women and

Figure 9.4: Life Table Estimates of Timing of Marital Disruption by Premarital Cohabitational Experience, Men

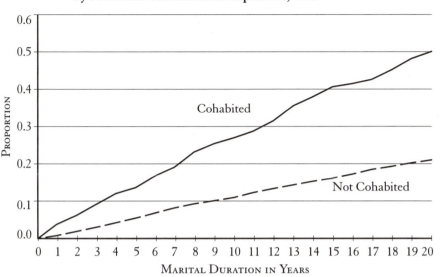

Source: The 1990 General Social Survey.

men also suggests that premarital cohabitation has a stronger influence on men than on women.[10] Earlier we saw that the risk of marital disruption is about two to three times higher for premarital cohabitors. It appears that some of the (observed) influence of cohabitation is reduced when other individual characteristics are controlled for, although a strong cohabitation effect remains.[11]

In addition to the circumstance of premarital cohabitation with the current spouse, let us consider another premarital cohabitation indicator. In a series of questions on spouse's marital status at the time of marriage, GSS–95 respondents were also asked whether their spouses had ever cohabited with anyone else prior to the current marriage, regardless of whether the couple themselves cohabited premaritally.[12] Accordingly, a dichotomous variable, with '1' for a 'yes' response, and '0' for a 'no' response, was included in the analysis. Table 9.2 shows that for both women and men, a spouse's prior cohabitation with other persons also has a strong negative impact on marital stability. This finding provides further evidence that premarital cohabitation, whether or not with a current spouse, leads to subsequent marital instability.

The influences of other covariates are generally consistent with the literature and are discussed briefly here. Table 9.2 shows that premarital cohabitation duration has a significant negative effect for men, but not for women. The longer the couple cohabited premaritally, the more stable their marriage, which is consistent with the trial marriage hypothesis. Both women's employment and educational status have a destabilizing effect on marriage, supporting the *independence* hypothesis. An increase in men's education also raises the risk of

Table 9.2: Proportional Hazard Models of Premarital Cohabitation and Subsequent Marital Instability

Variable	Women	Men
COHABITATIONAL STATUS		
Cohabited with spouse		
Yes	0.587***	0.925***
No[†]		
Spouse cohabited with others		
Yes	0.544***	0.736***
No[†]		
Duration of cohabitation (in years prior to marriage if cohabited)	0.003	−0.098*
SOCIO-ECONOMIC STATUS		
Employed[‡]		
Yes	0.666***	0.125
No[†]		
Educational status (in 10 levels, 1 = none, …, 10 = bachelor or higher)	0.040**	0.062***
School enrolment[‡]		
Yes	0.440***	0.089
No[†]		
CULTURAL BACKGROUND		
Religion		
Catholic	−0.296**	−0.244*
Protestant	−0.342***	−0.290**
Other/None[†]		
Nativity		
Canadian-born	0.196*	0.207*
Foreign-born[†]		
Region		
Quebec	0.103	0.131
Rest of Canada[†]		
DEMOGRAPHIC AND FAMILY CHARACTERISTICS		
Premarital birth		
Yes	0.361**	0.148
No[†]		
One boy[‡]		
Yes	0.124	−0.516***
No[†]		

One girl[‡]		
Yes	0.100	−0.416**
No[†]		
Two boys[‡]		
Yes	−0.179	−0.248
No[†]		
Two girls[‡]		
Yes	−0.118	−0.096
No[†]		
One boy and one girl[‡]		
Yes	−0.021	−0.173
No[†]		
Three or more children[‡]		
Yes	−0.063	0.095
No[†]		
Children under 6[‡]		
Yes	−0.131	−0.312**
No[†]		
Heterogamy in age		
Husband 6+ years older	−0.098	0.700***
Wife 2+ years older	0.682***	−0.411*
Age-homogeneous marriage[†]		
Heterogamy in marital status		
Yes	0.099	0.224
No[†]		
Had a happy childhood		
Yes	−0.228***	−0.151***
No[†]		
Intact family		
Yes	−0.222**	−0.195*
No[†]		
− 2 Log Likelihood	13446.3	8772.3
Model chi-square	491.3***	311.5***
df	23	23

Note: All dummy variables are coded as 1 = yes, 0 = no.

[†]   Reference category.

[‡]   Time-varying covariate.

* $p < .05$

** $p < .01$

***$p < .001$ (one-tailed test)

Source: The 1995 General Social Survey.

marital disruption. A similar detrimental effect is also found for school enrolment, supporting the *role conflict* thesis noted earlier.

Turning to cultural variables, we observe that the risk of marital disruption is lower for Catholics and Protestants than for those of other religions or with no religious orientation. The risk is also lower for foreign-born Canadians than for native-born Canadians. Unlike the various aspects of cohabitation we have observed so far, region does not have a significant impact on marital disruption. Although this result suggests that Quebec marriages may be as stable as the marriages outside the province, it is important to note that the marriage rate is also lower in Quebec than elsewhere in Canada (Belanger and Dumas, 1998: 14–15). The implication is that marriages in Quebec are likely to be more selective, and may be particularly selective of people who have a strong commitment to each other and/or to the institution of marriage. In other words, the institution of marriage may have been more weakened in Quebec, in part because fewer people there are now marrying than elsewhere in Canada.

Demographic characteristics also determine the risk of marital disruption. Consistent with other studies (e.g., Becker et al., 1977; Lillard and Waite, 1993; Morgan and Rindfuss, 1985; Morgan et al., 1988), we find that children stabilize marriage. For men, the presence of a child and having preschool-age children both have a stabilizing effect on marriage. However, an increase in the number of children does not seem to improve stability. Moreover, for women, the presence of premarital children destabilizes marriage, probably because these children are not marital-specific capital (Becker et al., 1977). Further, age-discrepant marriages are less stable than age-homogeneous marriages, although differences in marital status between spouses (upon marriage) show no significant impact. Finally, as would be anticipated, having a happy childhood and growing up in an intact family both have a long-term positive influence on the stability of marriage.

In short, our analysis confirms the relationship between premarital cohabitation and subsequent marital instability. We have observed an elevated risk of marital instability (roughly doubled) for couples who cohabited premaritally. The risk of disruption may increase even further when spouses *also* cohabited with other people prior to marriage. It is important to note that about half of the observed difference in the risk of disruption (two to three times greater for cohabitors) can be explained by the other covariates considered in the hazard models.

Cohabitation and the Division of Household Labour

Little was known about housework until about two decades ago, when social scientists began to document housework patterns and how domestic labour is divided within the family (South and Spitze, 1994). The focus of these studies has been primarily on married couples, perhaps because of an interest in gender equity (ibid., 327; also see Blair and Lichter, 1991; Goldscheider and Waite, 1991; Presser, 1994; Ross, 1987).[13] Studies have been fairly consistent in suggesting that married men tend to do less housework than married women (e.g., Antill and

Table 9.3: Gender Division of Selected Household Chores

| | Household Chores | | | | | | | |
| | Meal Preparation | | Meal Cleanup | | Cleaning/ Laundry | | Outside Maintenance | |
Share of Housework	Women	Men	Women	Men	Women	Men	Women	Men
Cohabiting Couples								
None	4.3	23.6	10.2	20.1	3.5	28.8	58.5	20.5
Less than ¼	4.1	14.3	3.5	11.3	1.7	16.2	9.8	0.6
Less than ½	10.4	17.6	9.1	19.0	7.4	19.4	10.7	2.1
½ or more	52.3	37.0	53.7	43.4	59.2	33.3	17.8	28.1
All	28.9	7.5	23.6	6.2	28.2	2.3	3.3	48.6
Total	100	100	100	100	100	100	100	100
Married Couples								
None	3.0	37.8	7.6	28.4	4.8	45.8	63.3	15.5
Less than ¼	1.9	22.3	3.8	17.1	1.6	17.0	12.0	2.1
Less than ½	6.9	16.7	9.7	20.1	4.4	15.6	8.7	2.3
½ or more	48.1	20.6	48.7	30.3	45.4	19.0	12.1	32.3
All	40.1	2.6	30.3	4.1	43.8	2.7	3.9	47.8
Total	100	100	100	100	100	100	100	100

Note: Weighted percentages.
Source: The 1990 General Social Survey.

Cotton, 1988; Presser, 1994; Shelton and John, 1993; South and Spitze, 1994; Spitze, 1988). In this section we examine the division of housework in the family. As noted, we anticipate that cohabiting couples distribute housework more equitably than married couples.

Division of Household Tasks

We begin our analysis with a descriptive account of selected household tasks performed by cohabiting couples and married couples. Since the GSS–95 did not collect data on specific household tasks, we rely on data from the GSS–90. Table 9.3 shows the share of four household tasks between women and men in cohabiting and married families.

Among cohabiting couples, 29 per cent of cohabiting women reported that they do all the cooking (meal preparation) at home, compared to only 4 per cent who reported that they do not cook at all. A reverse pattern is found for cohabiting men (8 and 24 per cent). Clearly, women do more meal preparation than men do in the cohabiting family. Similar gender patterns are also observed for meal cleanup and housecleaning/laundry. However, gender patterns for outside maintenance are reversed, where 59 per cent of cohabiting women reported that they do not do any outside maintenance work, compared to only 21 per cent of

Figure 9.5: Mean Number of Hours Spent Doing Housework Last Week

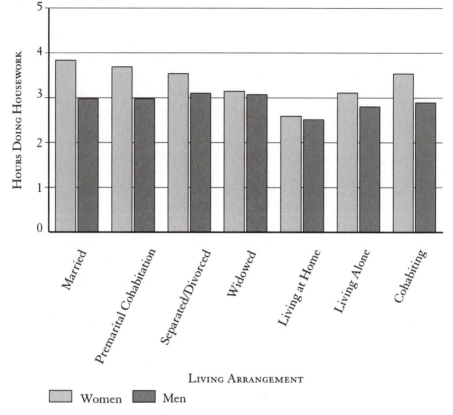

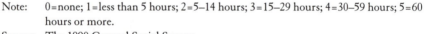

LIVING ARRANGEMENT

☐ Women   ■ Men

Note: 0=none; 1=less than 5 hours; 2=5–14 hours; 3=15–29 hours; 4=30–59 hours; 5=60
         hours or more.
Source: The 1990 General Social Survey.

cohabiting men. Indeed, nearly half of cohabiting men reported that they perform all outside maintenance work, compared to only 3 per cent of women performing the same task. The gender patterns of household tasks are similar among married couples (Table 9.3).

Do cohabiting couples have a more equitable gender division of housework than married couples? In other words, do cohabiting men contribute more than married men, or do cohabiting women contribute less than married women? There is no simple answer to this question. It appears that the division is slightly more equitable in the cohabiting family when it comes to inside housework, but the distribution for outside maintenance varies little between married and cohabiting men. However, the difference in outside maintenance may reflect that cohabiting couples are less likely to own a home (or live in a house) than married couples (Rindfuss and VandenHeuvel, 1990). On balance, the division of housework may be somewhat more equitable in cohabiting families than in married families.

Hours Spent Doing Housework

While there is little dispute that women do more housework inside the house and that men do more outside maintenance, these data cannot tell us whether women actually do more than men do. It could be that men spend more time on household maintenance than women do on household chores, though common sense tells us otherwise. One way of resolving this issue is to ask people the amount of time they spend on housework. Figure 9.5 shows data from the GSS–95 on hours spent doing housework. It is somewhat unfortunate that the final version (released for public use) of the GSS–95 does not retain the data on the actual number of hours spent doing housework reported by the respondent. Thus, caution must be exercised in the interpretation of the results reported here. The vertical axis in the figure represents a six-level ordinal scale of the number of hours spent doing housework.

As noted, we consider seven marital status groups. The married are divided into two groups, dependent on whether they cohabited premaritally. Singles (never-married) are also divided into two groups, dependent on whether they live at the parental home. The remaining three groups include separated/divorced, widowed, and cohabiting people. Again, our focus is on gender patterns in the three coupled groups.

Gender patterns in time spent doing housework are unmistakable: women spend more time doing housework than men do in each marital category. As would be anticipated, the gender difference is more evident for coupled families than for 'uncoupled' individuals. There is virtually no gender difference for widowed persons and for people living at the parental home. Moreover, the gender gap varies little between the three coupled groups. This implies that no evidence supports the hypothesis that cohabiting couples have a more equitable division of household labour between partners.

Multivariate Analysis of Time Spent Doing Housework

Our focus has been on the effect of marital status on the division of household labour. We are particularly interested in gender equity between married and cohabiting couples. So far we have not seen evidence that cohabiting couples enjoy a more equitable division of household labour than married couples. Would a multivariate analysis provide a different conclusion?[14]

Table 9.4 presents three ordinary least squares models of hours spent on housework. Column 1 includes the entire sample with gender as an explanatory variable. Columns 2 and 3 present separate models for women and men in anticipation of gender differences in the effects of the covariates. As noted in Chapter 5, the parameter estimate in the OLS model indicates the change in the dependent variable (hours spent doing housework) for a one-unit change in a given explanatory variable, holding other variables constant.

Table 9.4: Ordinary Least Squares Models of Hours Spent in Housework per Week

Variable	All	Women	Men
MARITAL STATUS			
Married	0.021	0.017	0.002
Premaritally cohabited	−0.068	−0.079	−0.045
Separated/Divorced	0.030	−0.180**	0.200**
Widowed	−0.134*	−0.388***	0.289**
Single living at home	−0.494***	−0.627***	−0.370***
Single living alone	−0.177***	−0.349***	−0.063
Cohabiting†			
SOCIO-ECONOMIC STATUS			
Hours worked last week	−0.009***	−0.009***	−0.007***
Worked last week			
Yes	0.018	−0.018	0.127*
No†			
Work evening/night shift			
Yes	−0.019	0.025	−0.047
No†			
Work Saturday/Sunday			
Yes	0.064*	0.059	0.066
No†			
Educational status	−0.003	−0.012*	0.013*
(in 10 levels, 1 = none, ...,			
10 = bachelor or higher)			
School enrolment			
Yes	−0.129**	−0.203***	0.053
No†			
Household income	−0.039***	−0.066***	−0.023**
(in 12 levels, 1 = none, ...,			
12 = $100,000 or more)			
Income missing			
Yes	−0.067**	0.044	−0.163***
No†			
Home ownership			
Yes	0.147***	0.134**	0.139**
No†			
CULTURAL BACKGROUND			
Religion			
Catholic	−0.286	−0.158	−0.465
Protestant	−0.283	−0.092	−0.549
Other	−0.290	−0.062	−0.582
None†			

Church attendance (in 5 levels, 1 = never, …, 5 = at least once a week)	0.015*	0.014	0.013
Nativity			
Canadian-born	0.028	0.027	0.059
Foreign-born[†]			
Region			
Quebec	−0.201***	−0.199***	−0.209***
Rest of Canada[†]			
DEMOGRAPHIC CHARACTERISTICS			
Gender			
Men	−0.466***	—	—
Women[†]			
Age	0.038***	0.046***	0.027***
Age square (× 1,000)	−0.433***	−0.489***	−0.311***
No. of children under 6	0.234***	0.351***	0.115***
No. of children age 6–11	0.134***	0.219***	0.036
No. of children age 12–18	0.083***	0.153***	0.016
Male adult child (19+) in household			
Yes	0.038	0.153*	−0.095
No[†]			
Female adult child (19+) in household			
Yes	0.099*	0.133*	0.066
No[†]			
Respondent Disabled			
Yes	−0.125***	−0.167***	−0.023
No[†]			
Living in a house			
Yes	0.098***	0.093*	0.089*
No[†]			
Intercept	3.362***	3.244***	2.958***
R square	0.189	0.220	0.072

Note: Dummy indicator for missing values of church attendance is also included as a covariate. It is not significant at the .05 level. All dummy variables are coded as 1 = yes, 0=no.

[†] Reference category.

* $p < .05$

** $p < .01$

***$p < .001$ (two-tailed test)

Source: The 1995 General Social Survey.

Table 9.4 shows that cohabitors tend to spend more time doing housework than the widowed and never-married singles (see column 1). They are, however, not significantly different from the married or the separated/divorced. The differences between the three coupled groups remain non-significant in both gender models (see columns 2 and 3). These results are consistent with the descriptive analysis presented above, providing no support for the hypothesis that the share of housework is more equitable in the cohabiting family than in the married family.

As noted, we separate the married by their premarital cohabitational status. Part of the reason for this configuration was to provide an indirect test of the trial marriage hypothesis. We argued that cohabiting couples may have a more equitable share of housework during their 'trial' as a means of potentially improving 'marriageability' in the eyes of the other partner. However, once they are married and the 'trial' is over, the division of household labour may become less equitable. The negative estimate for men who cohabited premaritally (see column 3) is indeed consistent with this hypothesis, although the estimate does not reach an acceptable level of statistical significance.

The influences of other determinants are generally consistent with the literature and are discussed briefly below. Table 9.4 shows that employment has a negative effect on the time spent doing housework. The more time one spends at work, the less one spends doing housework. It is also interesting to note that employed men actually do more housework than unemployed men. Inconsistent with Presser (1994), though, employment schedules (whether working evening/night shifts) do not have a significant impact. However, working on weekends appears to increase the time spent doing housework. The effect of education is gender-specific. An increase in education raises men's involvement in housework but reduces women's involvement, which is consistent with South and Spitze (1994). School enrolment also reduces the time spent on housework, supporting the available time hypothesis (e.g., Presser, 1994). An increase in resources, particularly women's resources, should lead to less involvement in domestic labour, partly because it is more economically efficient to 'purchase' domestic labour or to allocate it to the spouse who earns less (Becker, 1973). Using household income as an indicator of resources, our data support this hypothesis. Moreover, as anticipated, home ownership increases the time spent on housework, partly because the amount of housework may also increase.

Turning to cultural indicators, we observe that religion does not have a significant effect. Church attendance, an indicator of religiosity, increases the time spent on housework, although the effect is not significant in either gender model. While nativity does not show a significant impact, there are regional differences in housework patterns: Quebecers appear to spend significantly less time doing housework than non-Quebecers.[15]

The time spent on housework is also determined by demographic factors. Consistent with our descriptive analysis, women spend more time doing housework than men. Age has a negative curvilinear relationship, reflecting life-cycle changes: the time spent on housework rises initially with age, peaks during middle age, and declines in old age. Consistent with this view, we also observe that the presence and number of (young) children increase the time spent on housework; and physical disability reduces such time. Finally, living in a house increases the time spent doing housework, probably because the amount of living space is also increased.

In short, non-marital cohabitation has a minimal impact on the division of household labour within the family. There is no evidence supporting the hypothesis that cohabiting couples have a more equitable division of housework than married couples. However, there is strong evidence that women, regardless of marital status, do more and spend more time on housework than men. This gender disparity remains after we remove the effects of other explanatory variables.

Discussion

In this chapter we set out to test a series of hypotheses pertaining to the influence of cohabitation on the timing of marriage, marital instability, and the division of household labour. Our empirical analysis provides support for the hypothesis that premarital cohabitation has a delaying effect on the timing of marriage. Cohabitational experiences delay the timing of first marriage by 26 per cent for women and 19 per cent for men. This delaying effect may have been a consequence of cohabitors consisting of a select group of individuals who share certain characteristics that reduce their propensity to marry (the selectivity hypothesis), and/or a consequence of the time spent in cohabitations (the experience hypothesis). Our analysis supports both hypotheses. There is direct evidence that cohabitation is self-selective, and that the selection into cohabitation affects the timing of first marriage. The fact that the delaying effect of cohabitation remains strong and virtually unchanged after we remove the effect of self-selection offers evidence that the experience of cohabitation itself affects the timing of marriage and that self-selection into cohabitation has a significant but limited influence on marriage timing. It is also worth noting that premarital cohabitation and selectivity have similar influences on young Canadian men and women.

Both the selectivity and experience hypotheses predict that couples who lived together prior to marriage may experience an increased risk of marital instability. Our analysis is consistent with this prediction. We saw that the observed risk of marital disruption is about two to three times higher for premarital cohabitors than for non-cohabitors, although about half of the observed difference can be attributed to other explanatory variables. While couples who cohabited before marriage may have an elevated risk of marital disruption, having a spouse who cohabited with someone else raises the risk of marital disruption to a similar level. This 'spousal' effect remains whether or not the couple themselves cohabited premaritally, reinforcing the notion that living together as a form of trial marriage has a detrimental impact on subsequent marital stability.

These results have far-reaching implications for the future of marriage. For example, as the incidence of cohabitation continues to rise, we should expect that age at first marriage will increase. More people may delay marrying, and probably more may forgo it all together. As the rate of cohabitation continues to rise, we should also expect a rising number of marriages will be preceded by cohabitation. As these marriages tend to have a greater risk of disruption, other things being equal, the divorce rate may also increase over time. However, we have noted that the rising trend in cohabitation has been matched fairly well by a declining trend in marriage. We also know that more cohabitations end in separation than in marriages, and many cohabiting couples have no intention of marrying at all (Chapter 8). The implication is that the marriage rate may stay low and that marriages may become increasingly selective. As a consequence, marriages could become more stable over time. In fact, this positive (indirect) effect of cohabitation may have offset the negative effect of premarital cohabitation on the stability of marriage. This probably explains why the Canadian divorce rate reached its peak in the late 1980s and has been declining slowly ever since.

While cohabitation may have an impact on marriage timing and on marital instability, it has virtually no influence on the division of household labour. Cohabiting couples do not have a more equitable division of domestic labour than married couples, although both differ from unattached individuals. Using the 1987–8 National Survey of Families and Households, South and Spitze (1994) also reported that American cohabiting men and women do not differ significantly from their married counterparts when it comes to the time spent doing housework. Do cohabitors also closely resemble the married in other dimensions of family life as well? Apparently not. For example, research by Rindfuss and VandenHeuvel (1990) demonstrated that cohabitors are more similar to singles than to the married in fertility expectations, school enrolment, employment, and home ownership.[16] Clearly, more Canadian research is needed to examine these and other dimensions of cohabitation, such as the sharing of financial resources, the time spent together, and union (marital) adjustment.

10 | The Future of Cohabitation

Non-marital cohabitation is not a new social phenomenon. For centuries throughout the Western world heterosexual couples have lived together outside formal marriage. Indeed, historically, some form of cohabitation must have preceded the requirement of a matrimonial ceremony (Holland, 1998). Cohabitation may originally have been the normative form of family living. Even after marriage became the norm, informal cohabitation continued to coexist with formal marriage and the line between the two family forms was blurred for a long period of time. For example, in England the distinction between marriage and cohabitation remained unclear until the passage of Lord Hardwicke's Act in 1754, which stipulated more stringent requirements for formal marriage (Holland, 1998: 1–2).[1]

However, the recent increase in cohabitation is unprecedented in the contemporary history of the Western world. The rising prevalence of cohabitation raises public concerns about the implications of this re-emerging family form and about the institution of traditional marriage. The objective of this book is to address some of these concerns from a social demographic perspective. The main conclusion of this work is that non-marital cohabitation is no longer a rare phenomenon and is practised in all walks of life. The definition of the family should be expanded to include unmarried heterosexual couples, whether or not they have children, who may belong to one or both partners.

In this concluding chapter we review the major findings of this study and discuss their implications for individuals and society. We speculate on the future trends of cohabitation and briefly look at the Swedish experience. Because Sweden has a long-standing tradition of non-marital cohabitation as a family form and has the highest cohabitation rate in the Western world, the Swedish experience may provide insights into the future course of Canadian cohabitation. In the final section, we discuss policy issues. We look at the rights and obligations of Canadian cohabitors, present the rationale for family law reform, and make policy recommendations.

Major Findings

As we noted in Chapter 1, our data came from two primary sources: Canadian censuses and national surveys. Census data from 1981 onward were used to document the trends in cohabitation. Two national surveys, the GSS–90 and GSS–95, were utilized extensively in individual-level analyses in an attempt to understand the factors that influence changes in these trends. Another national survey, the CFS, was used in the analysis of attitudes towards family issues.

Trends

National data on cohabitation were not available until 1981, when the Canadian census began collecting information about non-marital heterosexual relationships. However, it was not until the 1991 census that individuals were explicitly asked whether they lived in a common-law relationship. Census data provide indisputable evidence that cohabitation has been on the rise over the past two decades. Between 1981 and 1996, the percentage of all Canadians aged 15 and over cohabiting doubled from 4 per cent to 8 per cent.

Cohabitation is most prevalent in the province of Quebec and the two northern territories. In 1981, 8 per cent of all Quebec couples were living in cohabitations. This figure rose to 24 per cent in 1996. Indeed, in 1981, about one-third of all Canadian cohabiting couples were residing in Quebec. Quebec's share rose to 43 per cent in 15 years. Although relatively small in absolute numbers, cohabitation rates in the Yukon (27 per cent) and the Northwest Territories (33 per cent) are the highest in Canada.

Cohabitation is selective. Census data provide unequivocal evidence that cohabitation is particularly popular among young Canadians. In 1996, more than one-half of all cohabitors (52 per cent) were under age 35. Cohabitation is also a preferred family form among separated/divorced people. The 1996 census shows that nearly one-third of cohabiting relationships (32 per cent) involved at least one separated/divorced partner. Cohabitation is also more common among men than women, and the gap has been widening over time.

Attitudes

The rapid increase in cohabitation may reflect changing attitudes towards premarital sexual behaviour, cohabitation, and marriage. Our national survey data demonstrated that these attitudes have shifted towards being less conventional and more permissive. The vast majority of Canadians, particularly young people, now accept premarital sex. Non-traditional attitudes towards cohabitation and marriage are widespread. Our cohort analysis indicated that attitudes towards marriage have fundamentally changed: Canadians place less importance on marriage in their life over time. Although most Canadians now accept non-marital cohabitation, the majority of Canadians, even young adults, also believe it is important to be married. Quebec clearly leads the country in the trends of family attitudes. For each measure of family attitudes examined,

Quebec is more liberal than the rest of the country, and the differences are by no means in small measure.

Formation

Our survey data provided further evidence that cohabitation is on the rise. By age 20, one-fifth of Canadian women and one-tenth of men have already formed their first cohabiting relationship. By age 25, these figures rise to one-half for women and one-third for men. For Canadians who have ended their first marriage, the entry into cohabitation is more rapid. One-tenth of these Canadians, women and men, have formed a cohabiting relationship within one year since marital breakdown. Within three years, these numbers rise to one-fifth for women and one-fourth for men. Similar to remarriage patterns, the rate of post-marital cohabitation is higher, and the tempo is faster, for men than for women.

Who cohabits? As far as premarital cohabitation is concerned, cohabitation particularly attracts Canadians who work outside the home, who are non-students, less educated (among women), non-religious, live in Quebec, are pregnant (or their partners are pregnant), are Canadian-born, and had an unhappy childhood, a working-class background, and grew up in a broken family (women only). For post-marital cohabitations, age and gender are the predominant factors determining the likelihood of cohabitation. Men, particularly younger men, stand considerably better chances of forming a cohabiting union than women do. Older women are in the least advantageous position in the cohabiting market.

Child-bearing

As the popularity of cohabitation increases, child-bearing within cohabitations also becomes commonplace. Our survey data indicated that nearly one-half of cohabitors say they want children. This figure rises to over 60 per cent for childless cohabitors. There is also considerable uncertainty involved in fertility plans, particularly among men. The desire for children increases with men's income, but decreases with women's income. Women's desire for children is high for those who are young, living with (considerably) older men, residing outside Quebec, had a happy childhood, and have better-educated fathers. Men's desire for children is high when they are cohabiting with women who share the same marital status and when they have a large number of siblings and better-educated fathers.

What people say may not always be translated into what they will do. Our survey data showed fewer women actually gave birth while cohabiting than their intentions suggested. For recent (cohabiting) cohorts, one in 10 women gave birth within five years of cohabiting. The rate is higher among the older cohorts. The chances of giving birth in cohabitations have been/are particularly high among cohabitations formed in early periods (prior to 1970), among the less educated, by people living in Quebec, by (more recent) immigrants, for those cohabiting with previously married men, and for women who began cohabiting at young ages.

Dissolution

While more people are now choosing cohabitation over marriage when they begin their first intimate sexual relationship (Wu, 1999a), most cohabiting relationships are dissolved after a short period of time. Only one-third of cohabitations survives for three years. About one out of 20 cohabitations lasts for 15 years. For the dissolved relationships, less than one-half end in separation and the remainder become marriages. Cohabitations have become less stable over time, with more recent cohabitations experiencing greater risks of disruption. The risk of union separation is especially high among women students, non-Quebecers, and women who began cohabiting at young ages. However, cohabitation stability increases substantially when the relationship involves a younger woman and a substantially (10+ years) older man. Stability also improves with the arrival of a child, although it suffers when children are brought into the relationship.

Do cohabitors actually want to marry? On the one hand, if cohabitation is truly some form of trial marriage, then all cohabiting couples would want to marry and will do so eventually. On the other hand, if cohabitation is in essence an alternative to formal marriage, then no cohabitors would want to marry or actually will. There is evidently some 'grey' area in between. Our survey data demonstrate that only about one-half of cohabitors want to marry. One-third have no intention of marrying at all, and one-sixth are uncertain about their marriage plans. The desire to marry is considerably weaker among cohabitors living in Quebec and those who have previously been married.

Desirability aside, how many cohabitors do actually marry? Our analysis shows that more than one-half of cohabiting couples eventually marry each other. Over one-third of the couples do so within three years of cohabiting. This figure rises to 40 per cent within five years. The marriage rate is elevated among cohabitors who have a Christian background, who began cohabiting at young ages, among cohabitations involving a younger woman and a substantially (10+ years) older man, and for cohabitations initiated before 1970. However, the marriage rate is reduced among student (women) cohabitors, Quebecers, if legal marital status differs between partners, and when children (who belong to either or both partners) are involved in the relationship.

Consequences

The recent increase in non-marital cohabitation has important life-course consequences for individuals living in the cohabiting family. This study has examined the role of cohabitation in three dimensions of family life: marriage timing, marital stability, and the division of household labour. Our survey data provide consistent evidence that premarital cohabitation has a delaying effect on marriage. It delays the timing of first marriage by 26 per cent for women and 19 per cent for men. The delaying effect remains substantial and significant even after the selectivity of cohabitation is taken into account. Our analysis also reveals evidence of self-selection into cohabitation, although the experience of cohabiting is a far more important factor than self-selection in the delay of marriage timing.

Are marriages preceded by cohabitation more stable than those that were not? The answer is 'no'. Our data show that the risks of marital disruption are approximately doubled for couples who cohabited premaritally compared to couples who did not. Indeed, regardless of whether couples cohabited together premaritally, any premarital cohabitational experiences may double the risks of subsequent marital disruption.

While cohabitational experiences delay marriage timing and impair marital stability, they have a minimal impact on the division of housework in the home. There is virtually no difference in the gender division of household labour between married and cohabiting families. In both types of family, women do more housework inside the house (e.g., cooking, cleaning, and laundry), while men do more outside the house (outside maintenance). Overall, women spend more time doing housework than men in all marital statuses. The gender inequality in the division of housework is more salient in married and cohabiting families than in other family types. There is no evidence that cohabiting families are more egalitarian in their division of household labour than married families.

Implications for Society

The re-emergence of non-marital cohabitation as a widespread social phenomenon has important implications beyond the individuals living in the cohabiting family. In Chapter 9, we expressly examined the role of cohabitation in three aspects of family life at the individual level and found that cohabitational experience contributes to delays in marriage and an increase in marital disruption, but has little impact on the division of household labour. In this section, we expand our discussion to consider the consequences of cohabitation for the institution of marriage, fertility change, and the definition of the family.

The Institution of Marriage

As noted in Chapter 1, cohabitation may pose a greater threat to the institution of marriage than the high incidence of divorce, because while both undermine the permanence of marriage, only cohabitation can provide an alternative to marriage (Schoen, 1989). Our data demonstrate that cohabitation is increasingly common among young and previously married Canadians. Canadians are now spending more time in cohabitations, and consequently marriages and remarriages are being delayed and sometimes avoided altogether. These findings are consistent with the notion that cohabitation is increasingly becoming an alternative form of family living, at least for a short period of time. Indeed, the recent surge in cohabitation has offset much of the decline in marriage in recent years (Wu, 1999a).

As Rindfuss and VandenHeuvel (1990: 722) noted, the ideology and transient nature of cohabitation also undermine the notion of permanence embedded in the institution of marriage. It is no wonder that most of the cohabiting relationships examined in this study were short-lived. Only about one-half of cohabitations are expected to survive for two years. Our data also suggest that the instability of cohabitation has been rising over time. While only a few more cohabitations are terminated through marriage than through union separation, marriages preceded by cohabitation have increased risks of subsequent marital breakdown. Taken together, the rise in cohabitation implies an increase in the instability of formal and informal unions. One reason that the rate of divorce has levelled off since the late 1980s (a trend that potentially contradicts this implication) is that many couples opt out of formal marriage, and the incidence of cohabiting union separation replaces what otherwise may have been divorces.[2]

Not everyone chooses to cohabit. Cohabitation is particularly selective of individuals who hold less conventional attitudes towards marriage and the family (Axinn and Thornton, 1992). Our analysis provides similar evidence of self-selection into cohabitation. People who reject the institution of marriage and, by implication, the roles and responsibilities married couples assume may select cohabitation (Holland, 1998: 1–7). For example, to some, marriage may be seen as 'an outdated institution embodying many offensive aspects—for example the notion of the wife as chattel to be passed from her father to her husband'. Thus, choosing cohabitation over marriage may imply greater enjoyment, flexibility, and freedom to experiment with alternative lifestyles.

Cohabitation may also select people who lack emotional and financial commitments to their partners. Our analysis suggests that cohabitation has become a popular union choice after marital disruption. One reason that cohabitation attracts previously married people is that many may be fearful of the emotional and financial consequences of divorce; few want to repeat the process of separating and divorcing. What some may not anticipate is that uncoupling is a traumatic event whether one is married or cohabiting. There 'may well be an element of self-deception in choosing cohabitation over marriage—a feeling that because of the "absence of commitment" there will be less of an emotional toll on breakdown' (ibid.). As mentioned briefly above, the selection of less-committed individuals into cohabitation may also contribute to the recent decline in the divorce rate for the very reason that these people may choose not to marry. Had these individuals married, rather than chosen to cohabit, it is likely that their marriages would be the most prone to breakdown and would thus inflate the divorce rate.

While there is little dispute that the rise in cohabitation has weakened the institution of marriage, marriage has not been abandoned by Canadians. Our data demonstrate that only about one-third of cohabitors have no marriage intentions, and (all else being equal) a much smaller proportion of single (never-married) people share this sentiment (the results are not shown).[3] There are many reasons why the institution persists. For one thing, there is still some social pressure to marry, particularly for young people. Despite the growth in cohabitation, marriage is still the norm in terms of establishing a long-term heterosexual relationship (Cherlin, 1992: 128–9). Also, married people have more legal rights and privileges than cohabiting people (see below for more discussion on legal issues).

In his seminal article on the meaning of remarriage, sociologist Andrew Cherlin (1978) described remarriage as an 'incomplete social institution' because there were no normative standards for remarriage as an institutional form in society. He argued that the lack of social norms and institutional controls contributed to the higher rate of dissolution for remarriages than for first marriages. Over the past two decades, the high rate of marital dissolution has been matched fairly well by the high rate of remarriage in Canada and the US. Surely in response to the needs of families of remarriages, the institution of the family has changed. Remarriage is now almost fully accepted as a social institution. As Steven Nock (1995) predicts, the same may well occur to the institution of cohabitation.

Fertility Implications

The survival of any society relies on whether its members can replace themselves. Population replacement, nurture, and socialization of the next generation are the most important functions of the family institution. As we have noted, one argument that the rise in cohabitation threatens the institution of marriage is that it also provides a family environment in which children are born, cared for, and raised. Our survey data have demonstrated that more children today are born in cohabitation relationships than ever before.

If marital fertility and marriage rates remained constant, the rise in fertility among cohabiting women may raise the total fertility. However, as has been known for some time now, Canadian fertility has been in decline since the early 1960s, although the change has not been monotonic (Balakrishnan and Wu, 1992; Ford and Nault, 1996). In fact, Canadian fertility has been below the replacement level (of approximately 2.1 births per woman) since the mid-1970s (Statistics Canada, 1986). Recent data from Statistics Canada show that the total fertility rate stood at 1.55 in 1997, which has fallen below the former record low of 1.58 in 1987 (Statistics Canada, 1999). While we cannot be certain about future trends, most observers appear to agree that there are no signs of a recovery in Canadian fertility to at- or above-replacement levels. To be sure, Canada is not alone. Below replacement-level fertility is now observed in virtually the entire Western world. If such trends continue, Western industrial societies, as we have known them, will not survive.

While the long-term decline in fertility is primarily attributed to the decline in marital fertility, the increase in cohabiting (non-marital) fertility may have offset some of the decline. If cohabiting fertility continues to rise, it may eventually compensate for the loss in marital fertility. This scenario could only come true if the trends in cohabitation continue and if cohabiting fertility exceeds

Figure 10.1: Mean Number of Children Born to Currently Married and Cohabiting Women

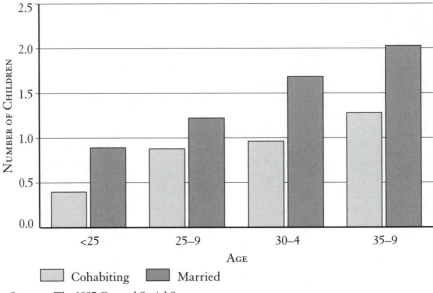

Source: The 1995 General Social Survey.

marital fertility. Although the cohabitation trend may continue for the time being, there is no good reason to believe that cohabiting fertility may surpass marital fertility any time soon. While scarce, studies have suggested that cohabiting couples desire fewer children than married couples and that cohabitation is much less fertile than marriage.[4] These results are not surprising because population replacement and the care of the next generation are traditionally monitored, regulated, and to a large extent monopolized as part of the institution of marriage (Davis, 1985b). However, the fertility differential between marriage and cohabitation has not yet been confirmed in Canada. It would be worthwhile to make a cursory comparison.

Using data from the GSS–95, Figure 10.1 shows the mean number of children ever born to women married and cohabiting in 1995. The difference in observed fertility is evident between married and cohabiting women: for each age group considered, the fertility level is higher for married women than for cohabiting women. For example, the average number of children for married women under age 25 is 0.9. The corresponding figure for cohabiting women is only 0.4. For ages 35–9, the comparable figures are respectively 2.0 and 1.3.[5]

These findings are consistent with the thesis that cohabitation is an incomplete social institution. They also suggest that the increase in cohabitation may have contributed indirectly to the decline in fertility over the past two decades or so. What will the future impact of cohabitation be on fertility? In the short term, as cohabitation becomes more widespread and more institutionalized, we should expect an increase in cohabiting fertility. However, the long-term impact on fertility remains undetermined. On the one hand, if the rising trend in cohabiting fertility persists, overall fertility may eventually stabilize or even increase. On the other hand, if cohabiting fertility remains lower than marital fertility, which is the most likely scenario, the rise in cohabitation may cause a further reduction in fertility. To be sure, the future state of Canadian fertility probably depends more on social and structural changes that may provide an incentive or a disincentive to become parents and, more important, for women to attain higher-order births.

Towards a New Definition of the Family

The declining trend in marital fertility is matched by a rising trend in non-marital fertility, as was noted in Chapter 7. I argued that the rise in cohabitation and the subsequent increase in cohabiting fertility might have contributed to much of the increase in non-marital fertility. I also called for a redefinition of non-marital fertility. Indeed, as cohabitation continues to rise, the definition of the family, as we have known it, should be expanded to include cohabiting families, which may or may not have children belonging to one or both partners.

The rise in cohabitation has implications for redefining other family types as well. For example, in a recent paper on American single-parent families, Bumpass and Raley (1995) demonstrated how a significant proportion of single-parent families are actually two-parent cohabiting families. Using data from the 1987–8 National Survey of Families and Households, they estimated the prevalence and duration of single-parent families using two definitions: a marital definition and a union definition that included both cohabitations and marriages. Their results suggested that when the marital definition is applied, the prevalence and duration of first single-parenthood have increased, but these have decreased substantially when the union definition is used. Indeed, from children's perspective, in the early 1980s as much as 20 per cent of the single-parent spell, as officially defined, was spent in cohabiting families.

In a related paper on American stepfamilies, Bumpass, Raley, and Sweet (1995) showed how the rise in cohabitation may also influence the way in which the stepfamily is routinely defined. Using the same data source, they estimated the prevalence and duration of stepfamily experiences from both mothers' and children's perspectives. Again, they used separately a marital definition and a union definition as the formation of a stepfamily. Their findings showed that, for example, when the stepfamily is defined at the formation of marriage, 32 per cent of mothers and 23 per cent of children are likely to spend some time in a stepfamily. However, when the stepfamily is defined at the formation of cohabitation, the comparable figures rise to 39 per cent and 30 per cent.

For centuries, the 'family' has been equated with 'marriage' both in the public eye and in our legal system (Ontario Law Reform Commission, 1993). The analyses presented in this book and other studies have demonstrated that the nature of the family has changed in significant ways. Recent trends in cohabitation have indicated that the traditional definition of the family must be expanded beyond marriage to include unmarried cohabitations. Disregarding cohabiting unions in defining the family seriously misrepresents the reality of Canadian family life. As Bumpass et al. (1995: 434) noted, we have come to the point that marriage can only 'be treated as an important *variable* rather than the *defining* characteristic of families: the social interactions that constitute co-residential family life are not created by civil registration.' While beyond the scope of this study, I believe that the same can be said for same-sex relationships.[6]

The Future of Cohabitation

What will the future be? In Chapter 4, we saw the increasing trends in cohabitation throughout almost all Canadian social strata. To the extent that more young Canadians think of living together as a natural and logical prelude to marriage and that more Canadians in general think of cohabitation as a rejection or an alternative to the traditional model of marriage, the rate of cohabitation will continue to rise. The growing number of cohabiting couples, which inevitably leads to a reduction in the married proportion of the population, may constitute a serious challenge to the survival of the Western family we have known.

However, could the rise in cohabitation come to an end, or might the trends be reversed in the near future? A more reasonable way to look into the future of cohabitation is to look to the main theories used to explain these trends and see what they suggest.[7] After all, the course of future trends is determined by social conditions that underlie the contemporary rise in cohabitation.

Implications of the Theories

In Chapter 2 we discussed three theoretical perspectives (economic, sociological, and demographic theories), which are briefly re-examined below.

The Economic Perspective

Becker's (1981) economic theory suggests that the single most important factor behind the decline in marriage is the rise in the earning power of women, which encourages women to invest more in formal education, spurs on their participation in the paid labour market, and reduces the mutual economic dependence between marital partners. A weakened sexual division of labour within the family reduces the gains from marriage, which in turn leads to a decline in marriage and a rise in marital instability.

The decline and delays in formal marriage make non-marital cohabitation an attractive alternative. Cohabitation implies less commitment while offering many of the advantages of marriage. It allows the couple to live in a family environment, provides the couple with the scale of economy, and, at the same time, offers them benefits of the single state. More important, it allows them to try out the relationship and see whether the relationship will work. In short, the decline in the gain from formal marriage gives rise to informal cohabitation. The key determinant of the future trends in cohabitation is the direction of women's employment patterns in the labour market.

Our analysis supports the thesis that women's employment outside the home encourages the entry into unmarried cohabitation (Chapter 6). Indeed, it has now become common knowledge that there has been a rapid increase in women's labour force participation and their relative wage rate in recent decades. The increase in labour force participation has been particularly dramatic for married women and women with young children at home. For example, in 1981, 51 per cent of married women were in the labour force. But this percentage rose to 62 per cent in 1996, which represents a 22 per cent increase (Statistics Canada, 1984, 1997d). During the same period, the percentage of women with preschool children at home who participated in the labour force increased from 48 per cent to 66 per cent, representing a 38 per cent increase (Statistics Canada, 1997d). Not only are more women involved in the labour market, their wage rate has also increased over time. For example, in 1967 the average earnings for women were only 58 per cent of men's. This earning ratio rose to 64 per cent in 1981 and 73 per cent in 1996 (Statistics Canada, 1990, 1998). While the gender gap in the wage rate remains substantial, a declining trend in this gap is unmistakable. At this point, we have no convincing reason to believe that the level of women's labour participation has reached its upper limit. The trends may continue, at least for the time being, as significant gender gaps remain in the participation rate and wage rate.

The Sociological Perspective

A sociological explanation of family change focuses on the impact of changing social norms, values, and attitudes on family behaviours. According to this perspective, there has been a *definitive* ideational change in the Western world since the turn of the century. The ideology of the Western family has shifted from more family-oriented interests to more individualistic pursuits (Aries, 1980; Lesthaeghe, 1980, 1983). The rise of individualism and the rejection of traditional gender roles (i.e., the husband as breadwinner and the wife as homemaker) are the key determinants of the recent changes in family life. As societal controls over sexual behaviour become less effective, the traditional family regulatory mechanisms upheld by parents and kinship groups gradually give way to the freedom of individual choice (Lesthaeghe, 1980). In short, changing family values and attitudes are believed to lie behind the weakening institution of marriage.[8]

Our analysis provides evidence that attitudes towards family issues have changed over the past decades (Chapter 5). We demonstrated that Canadians now place less value on marriage than in the past. Attitudes towards marriage and non-marital sexual behaviour have become more permissive. Other research has also been consistent in stating that there has been some fundamental change in our value system over the past several decades and that recent family change has been linked to the growth of individualism in industrial countries (e.g., Beaujot, 1991; Lesthaeghe and Surkyn, 1988; van de Kaa, 1987).

Research has shown that the spread of new norms and attitudes tends to diffuse more rapidly within (geographic) regions than across regions (Coale, 1973). Thus, one test of this sociological theory is to examine the regional patterns of cohabiting behaviour. In Canada, the English-French dualism has been the predominant feature of Canadian demographics throughout the nation's history (Beaujot and McQuillan, 1982; Le Bourdais and Marcil-Gratton, 1996; Pollard and Wu, 1998; Wu and Baer, 1996). Our analyses showed strong Quebec/non-Quebec patterns throughout the study. Quebecers hold more liberal attitudes towards family issues than other Canadians (Chapter 5); cohabitations are more widespread (Chapters 4 and 6), more stable (Chapter 8), and more fertile (Chapter 7) in Quebec than elsewhere in Canada. These findings provide evidence that Quebec has been leading the country in the institutionalization of cohabitation. They also lend support to a sociological explanation of family change.

What does the sociological theory have to say about the future? As changes in family values and attitudes are perpetuated by social change in the society, and we have seen no signs of reversal in the direction of social change (e.g., rising women's labour force participation and social status), the current trends in marriage and the family may well continue. The future, as demographer Charles Westoff (1978: 82) predicted, 'seems less and less compatible with long term traditional marriage'.

The Demographic Perspective
Cohabitational experience can be viewed as a demographic event over one's life course (a cohort perspective), or as an event within a time interval (a period perspective). This distinction is central in the analysis of demographic events, such as births, deaths, and unions (Hirschman, 1994: 205). As noted in Chapter 2, because period effects tend to be responsive to the influences of prevailing social and structural conditions within a specific time interval, they are proxies for periodic social and structural changes in the society. Changes in period effects do not necessarily signal a fundamental change in behaviour.

Cohort effects, on the other hand, are attributed to the long-term impact of important historical and social events that occurred in one's childhood (Ryder, 1965). Traditional cohort analysis compares the measures of a demographic event within one cohort (e.g., birth cohort) at two or more time intervals, or compares the measures of the same event between cohorts at one particular time interval. A change in the measurement is believed to indicate some fundamental change in behaviour. The cohort approach was thought to be superior to the period approach until recently because it captures the life experiences of a real group of people who live through a particular historical era together (Hirschman, 1994: 205; also see Ryder, 1965, 1983). However, recent studies of fertility trends have suggested that period effects tend to explain more fertility

Figure 10.2: Observed and Projected Cohabitation Rates

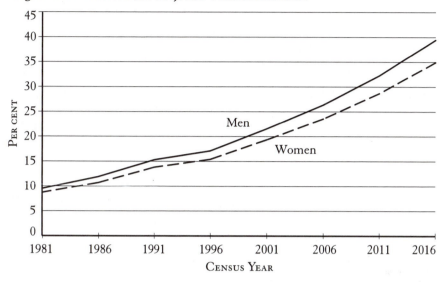

Note: The cohabitation rate is defined as the percentages for those living common-law among the single, separated, divorced, and widowed populations. The 1981–96 rates were computed using the census data. The 2001–16 rates are projected using the equations: $Rate_{women} = 1.232E–33 \times exp(0.03935 \times year)$, and $Rate_{men} = 2.092E–34 \times exp(0.04029 \times year)$. See text for details.

Source: Dumas and Péron, *Marriage and Conjugal Life in Canada*. Cat. no. 91–534E (Ottawa: Statistics Canada, 1992), 97. Calculations by author.

variations than do cohort effects (see Hirschman, 1994: 206, for citations of this literature).

Our analyses have demonstrated both period and cohort influences on cohabitational behaviour. Cohabitation has been on the rise from both cohort and period perspectives (Chapter 4), and attitudes to premarital sexual behaviour and marriage have shifted towards being less traditional between cohorts and across historical times (e.g., calendar periods) (see Chapter 5). Indeed, the transition into cohabitation has been accelerated in more recent birth cohorts and (marital) separation cohorts (Chapter 6), while the stability of cohabitation has deteriorated in more recent cohabitation cohorts (Chapter 8). These results indicate that union attitudes and behaviour have changed in some fundamental ways. They have not yet shown signs of reversal in the direction of change.

In sum, all three theories suggest that the trends in cohabitation are likely to continue. But what will the future trends look like? As an exercise, I extrapolated the trends in cohabitation from 1981 to 1996 into the next 20 years. Figure 10.2 projects the rate of cohabitation for women and men from 1996 to 2016 (the rate is defined as the percentage of cohabitors in the unmarried population). For the sake of continuity, the fitting curves based on the 1981–96 census data are also plotted in the figure.[9] In some sense, Figure 10.2 is an extension of Figure 4.3, under the assumption that the current trends would continue for the next 20 years. If this assumption were true, the future would be self-evident. Nearly two-fifths of the unmarried population would be living in cohabitations in 2016. The cohabitation rate would more than double in 20 years. Cohabitation might represent one-third of all unions in two decades.[10] Sounds familiar? Indeed, this is most likely what is happening in Swedish society today.[11] To better anticipate and prepare for the future, it would be useful to take a look at the Swedish experience.

The Swedish Experience

In Sweden, cohabitation has become a normal way of life, affecting virtually every member of the society. In past decades, cohabitation has been more prevalent in Sweden than elsewhere in the Western world, although Denmark and other Nordic countries are approaching a similar level (Bracher and Santow, 1998).[12]

As in many industrial countries, marriage in Sweden has declined since the late 1960s. This decline has been coupled with an increase in non-marital cohabitation. No national data on cohabitation were available prior to the 1960s (Trost, 1975). The information on the development of cohabitation in the 1960s and 1970s comes primarily from the 1981 Swedish Fertility Survey (Hoem and Hoem, 1988). The survey reveals that about one-third of women born in the 1930s cohabited premaritally. This proportion rose to over 80 per cent for women born in the early 1950s. The survey also suggests that premarital birth was a rare event in the late 1960s; a typical life-course path for Swedes was to cohabit first, then marry, and then have children. However, by the late 1970s, it became more common to have a first child born in cohabitation than in marriage.[13] As the incidence of cohabitation rose quickly in the 1970s, cohabitation has become more an alternative lifestyle choice than a prelude to legal marriage (Hoem and Hoem, 1988).

The most recent information on cohabitation comes from the 1992 Swedish Family Survey (Bracher and Santow, 1998). A rather striking finding of the survey was that cohabitation had already become prevalent in the late 1960s. For example, Bracher and Santow (1998: 278, Table 1) showed that 53 per cent of women born in 1949 had cohabited by age 22. The comparable figure for men was 34 per cent. While we did not construct cohort life tables of cohabitation, the analogous Canadian figures would be around 30 per cent and 20 per cent for women and men, respectively (see Figure 6.2). For Swedes born in 1964, the corresponding figures were 61 per cent and 40 per cent.

Another important finding from the survey was that while over 90 per cent of first unions formed in Sweden were cohabitations, the propensity to marry had declined among Swedish cohabitors. For example, 64 per cent of cohabiting women born in 1964 had married their (first) partner within five years. The comparable figure for cohabiting women born in 1969 was only 22 per cent (ibid.). Moreover, as with Canada (Wu, 1999a), the overall union rate in Sweden has changed little in recent decades.

In Sweden today, there are few distinctions between marriage and cohabitation. The choice between them is a private matter. Marriage increasingly serves as a ceremony publicly confirming the relationship rather than signifying the beginning of the relationship. Marriage not preceded by cohabitation is extremely rare and marriage following the arrival of a child (children) in a cohabitation is now a common practice.

While social and structural changes have played a pivotal role in the changing patterns of family formation in Sweden, the Swedish experience has two unique traits. One is the long-standing Scandinavian tradition of non-marital union formation, whereby engagement, rather than marriage, could signify the beginning of a union and receive public recognition. According to Bracher and Santow (ibid., 277; also see Kiernan and Estaugh, 1993: 63–4), there were two types of cohabitation in Sweden. One was known as 'conscience marriage', which was practised by a small but highly publicized group of intellectuals who chose to cohabit as a protest against church marriage, which had been the only form of sexual union allowed around the turn of the century. Their protest was instrumental in the introduction of civil marriage in 1909. The second type of cohabitation was called 'Stockholm marriage', practised primarily by poor people who could not afford to marry but who were unwilling to delay living together.[14] According to Trost (1975), cohabitation may well have been practised in many parts of the country in the last century. He suspects that, in historical times, some Swedes may have chosen to cohabit because they wanted to be sure that the woman was fertile, particularly as regarded her capacity for giving birth to a son.

A second unique reason for the rise in Swedish cohabitation has to do with the long-standing work ethic in the society. As Bracher and Santow (1998: 278) noted, working outside the home 'has a special place in the Swedish ethos'. People are expected to support themselves whether they are men or women, married or unmarried. There are no direct or indirect economic incentives to marry for either gender. In fact, there is probably more social pressure to become a parent than to get married (Benoit, 1999). The principle of self-sufficiency between marital (and non-marital) partners is built into the social and welfare system. For example, a universal maternity leave was institutionalized as early as 1955, providing benefits to new mothers for a three-month period. The entitlement period was subsequently extended to six months in 1963, nine months in 1978, and 12 months with 90 per cent of previous earnings in 1989 (Benoit, 1999). Spousal support after marital breakdown is now uncommon, available only when there is a special need and the other spouse can afford the support. Canadian- or American-style alimony was abandoned with the 1973 Marriage Code (Fawcett, 1990).

In response to the rapid rise in non-marital cohabitation, the Swedish government has made a series of legislative changes with the guiding principle of accommodating cohabiting couples without disturbing the position of marriage.[15]

The first major legislative change was the 1973 revision of the Swedish Marriage Code. The Code accommodated family change by introducing the 'neutrality principle' to family law. The tenets of the Code are stated as follows:

> The individual's freedom to shape his own life should be respected. Thus, choice of the form of cohabitation and choices of ethical norms should not be interfered with.... Marriage has a central place in family law, but the laws should not create unnecessary difficulties or inconveniences for those who have children and raise families without marrying. (Fawcett, 1990: 181)[16]

Subsequent legislative activity in this area was limited to solving practical problems, thereby developing laws that could be accepted by all citizens, regardless of their living arrangements. The legislation also strove to develop tax and social laws that could *not* influence an individual's decision to cohabit or marry, to leave a marriage, or to stay married. The 1973 law also granted limited marital-type property rights to cohabiting partners based on the existing law governing property settlement upon divorce.[17] The 1973 Marriage Code was a landmark in that for the first time it gave legal recognition to unmarried people living in marriage-like relationships.

The second major revision of the Swedish Marriage Code took place in 1987. The 1987 Act extended the limited marital-type property rights to cohabitors by including a much wider range of property. The new guiding principle in the legislation was that 'special rules for unmarried cohabitants ought to be made only to the extent that special reasons dictate' (ibid., 183–4). The special reasons that dictate the new law were a continuous rise in cohabitation and a growing need to resolve property disputes between partners upon union disruption. Under the new law, (union) property included items acquired during the period of cohabitation, provided that the property was acquired with the intent for mutual use. These property items include, for example, the mutual home, furniture, and appliances. The Act grants no rights to the (net) income of the other partner or alimony upon union disruption. Moreover, the acquisition of property rights is progressive over time, in the sense that the claim over the other partner's property rights increases with the duration of cohabitation. In brief, the 1987 Act was essentially an extension of family law (governing marital rights and obligations) to cohabitation, even though the government did not expressly state it in the legislation.

The crux of the 1987 legislation is the definition of a 'marriage-like relationship'.[18] While the law does not prescribe the elements of a qualifying relationship, it stipulates that the relationship must be judged as a whole based on several criteria. One such criterion is having a common child, which is seen as almost sufficient evidence of such a relationship. Another element is the duration of the relationship, with a minimum of six months being required, and five or more years being considered as a mature relationship. Other essential requirements include having a mutual house and mutual housekeeping and a normal sex life.

In a review article on cohabitation in industrial countries, Trost (1980) described the development of cohabitation in three distinctive stages. In stage one, cohabitation is generally viewed as deviant behaviour. In stage two, there is some recognition of the rights and obligations of cohabitors in the legal system. In stage three, there is full recognition of cohabitation as a social institution. Trost believed that countries like Sweden and Denmark had advanced to the second stage of the development by the mid-1970s. Of course, Trost was writing before the 1987 Swedish legislation. But our discussion of the Swedish experience leaves us with little doubt that heterosexual cohabitation in Sweden is coming to the end of the final stage of its development. It has been almost completely accepted as a social institution by the law and the public. Now one may ask: what is the legal status of cohabitation in Canada? This is the topic we now turn to.

Policy Issues

This section reviews the rights and responsibilities of cohabitors in Canada and makes policy recommendations.[19] Using Trost's transition model, I believe that Canadian cohabitation is now approaching the final stage of development. Heterosexual cohabitation has now been generally accepted and recognized by the public and the law. In the coming decades, there will be a greater acceptance of cohabiting relationships and a greater reduction in the legal distinction between marriage and cohabitation.

The Rights and Responsibilities of Cohabitors

Since the early 1960s, the rise in cohabitation has been paralleled by an increase in litigation involving cohabiting couples, which has spurred the development of the rights and obligations of cohabitors. Since laws dealing with non-marital cohabitation are part of family law, they fall under provincial jurisdiction. Consequently, the legal status of cohabitors varies by province. Some provinces (e.g., New Brunswick and Ontario) have acted quickly to narrow the gap between marriage and cohabitation, while others (e.g., Alberta) have resisted the change. Although some provinces have almost equated cohabitation with marriage, no Canadian province has completely removed the distinction between the two family forms.

The development of the rights of cohabitors has focused on five domains: property rights, spousal support, occupation rights in the family home, intestacy, and cohabitation agreements. More recently, the courts have begun to address a number of other issues, such as social security benefits, pension rights, workers' compensation, health insurance, and tax benefits (Holland, 1998).

Property Rights

Property includes everything from the family home to household items. Legislation protecting the property rights of cohabitors is scarce. Indeed, at present no province grants the statutory rights to share in family property that are available to married persons.[20] However, a cohabiting partner 'who has contributed, directly or indirectly, to the acquisition, maintenance, or preservation of an asset held in the name of the other spouse may seek restitution of her efforts, according to the doctrine of unjust enrichment' (Ontario Law Reform Commission, 1993: 10).

The doctrine of unjust enrichment was introduced in the 1980 Supreme Court of Canada's landmark ruling in *Pettkus v. Becker*. The Supreme Court stipulated three requisite elements in the principle that have been adopted in all subsequent decisions: (1) an enrichment of the defendant; (2) a deprivation suffered by the plaintiff; and (3) the absence of a juristic reason for the enrichment (Holland, 1998: 1–10).[21]

There are fundamental differences in property right provisions between cohabitors and married persons. First, for cohabiting couples, the burden of proof is on the partner who seeks compensation (the plaintiff) to prove that the other partner (the defendant) has been unjustly enriched. However, for marital couples, both partners are assumed to have contributed equally to the marriage such that each is entitled an equal share of (net) family property. The burden of proof is on the spouse seeking an unequal division. Second, the range of assets covered is much wider for marriages than for cohabitations. For example, marital assets cover both family and business assets acquired during the marriage (including pension rights), as well as the increase in value of the assets acquired before the marriage. For cohabitors, family property is generally limited to the family home. Any claim to a division of business assets depends usually on his/her contribution, financial or otherwise, to the business.

Spousal Support

Although the term 'spouse' is generally reserved for married persons, unmarried heterosexual couples are sometimes treated as spouses in some parts of provincial matrimonial statute law (e.g., Ontario). In recognition of the economic dependencies that may arise in cohabitations, most provinces (except Alberta) have introduced laws to protect the dependent partner.[22] However, unlike marriage, a minimum period of cohabitation is required, and the period varies between the provinces, ranging from one year (e.g., Nova Scotia) to three years (e.g., Ontario).[23] The duration requirement is waived in several provinces when there is a mutual child in the family (e.g., Ontario). Overall, there is little difference in the provision of spousal support between marriage and cohabitation. The key issues in litigation frequently involve whether the union concerned is a cohabitation, how long it has lasted, and whether there is economic dependency within the relationship.

Occupation Rights in the Family Home

Occupation rights in the family home vary by province. In general, few provinces grant any occupation rights in the family home to cohabitors. However, these rights are available to married persons under provincial matrimonial statute. In Ontario, Part II of the Family Law Act states that both married spouses have a right to possession of the family home, regardless of who owns the property. However, this part of the Act does not cover unmarried cohabitors. It is generally agreed that cohabitors cannot access the family home using the spousal support provisions (Part III of the Act). While common law may grant unmarried spouses occupation rights in the family home, Canadian courts have not yet recognized such rights. The only other avenue for redress is through the doctrine of contractual licence, a method that has not been tested in Canadian courts.

A few provinces do grant occupation rights to cohabitors under certain conditions. For example, the Family Maintenance Act in Manitoba applies to cohabiting persons who have cohabited for at least a year and have a mutual child in the relationship, or otherwise if they have cohabited for five years. The Family Relations Act in British Columbia allows for temporary possession of the family home pending determination of the occupation rights of the property. A cohabiting partner can seek 'temporary relief' under the Act provided a property claim against the family home is being filed (ibid., 1–19).

Intestacy

Intestacy refers to the situation where a spouse dies without making a valid will. If a cohabiting partner dies with a will, the surviving partner may go through the usual legal procedures to probate the will, although the partner's debts will have to be met first. If the surviving partner is left out of the will, he or she may go to court to have it changed. However, only under very unusual circumstances does the court change a will to include the surviving partner.

If a cohabiting partner dies without a will, intestacy provisions available to married persons do not apply to unmarried cohabitors in any jurisdiction. However, as with spousal support, if economic dependency can be established, the court may make 'dependents' relief' types of provisions to the surviving partner (ibid.). For example, the 1992 Ontario Succession Law Reform Act contains provisions for family dependants who are not adequately provided for following the death of certain family member(s).

Cohabitation Agreements

A cohabitation agreement is a written contract outlining the rights and obligations of the cohabiting couple with respect to a variety of issues, such as property rights, spousal support, the provisions on death, and custody of children. While contracts promoting immoral sexuality (e.g., extramarital sex) were deemed illegal under common law, things have certainly changed over the years. Four provinces (New Brunswick, Newfoundland, Prince Edward Island, Quebec) and Yukon have introduced legislation making cohabitation contracts enforceable. While the other provinces do not have express provisions for cohabitation contracts, it is unlikely that contracts drawn up in these jurisdictions could be struck down in court. To be legally binding, requirements found in contract law must be followed. For example, a cohabitation agreement should spell out clearly what is covered and be signed by both partners and two witnesses.

Recent Developments

Several recent developments in state benefits also affect the life of Canadian cohabitors. For example, the Canada Pension Plan has now extended spousal benefits to cohabitors who have lived together for at least one year. Ontario's Pension Benefits Act has also extended benefits to cohabitors. The Canadian Income Tax Act has equated cohabitation with marriage for tax purposes since the 1993 tax year, provided that the couple has cohabited for at least one year or are natural or adoptive parents of a child. A large number of other statutes have been amended to include heterosexual cohabitors as well (e.g., Ontario's Equality Rights Amendments Act, 1986).

Policy Recommendations

Married heterosexual couples clearly have more rights and obligations than unmarried heterosexual couples.[24] Can this difference be justified in the matter of the law? This question has been vigorously debated in the legal community, provincial legislatures, and the media. The following is a synopsis of two opposing views.

One argument for maintaining the distinction between marriage and cohabitation is that marriage as a traditional model of heterosexual union should be promoted as the preferred family form because the regulation of marriage advances state interests by promoting public morality and ensuring family stability, support obligations, and protection of children in the family. Eliminating the distinction would undermine these goals and provide a disincentive to marry. A greater recognition of cohabitation would inevitably induce a further decline in marriage and encourage individuals to choose cohabitation over marriage. Consequently, cohabitation would continue to increase and become increasingly a substitute for legal marriage, further weakening marriage as one of the oldest social institutions. Traditional marriage as we have known it for centuries would be eventually replaced by unmarried cohabitation.

Another reason for maintaining the status quo is to promote individual autonomy. The argument here is that marriage and cohabitation are two distinctive lifestyle choices. Individuals make rational decisions to choose one over the other and the state should respect individual choices. Individuals are generally aware of the rights and obligations that each union choice entails when they make union decisions. The state should not impose married status on cohabiting couples who may choose not to marry for the very reason of avoiding these responsibilities. In Chapter 8, we demonstrated that cohabitors are a select group of people who differ from married people (also see Rindfuss and Vanden-Heuvel, 1990). We also know that cohabitors are less committed to long-term relationships and their partners than married people are (see Chapter 8, and also see Axinn and Thornton, 1993). Indeed, Ruth Deech (1980, cited in Holland, 1998: 1–22) has gone so far as to say that to 'allow claims by female cohabitants is in effect to treat cohabitation as long-term prostitution with delayed payment subject to arbitration.'

For these reasons, some observers have suggested that cohabitors should be encouraged to resort to the contractual route to regulate their relationships (see ibid.). The contract option would attract cohabitors who value individual autonomy and reject accepting married status, but who, at the same time, wish to have some protection if the union is dissolved through either separation or the death of one partner. Rather than being subject to the same set of matrimonial obligations, cohabitors can devise their own 'tailor-made' contracts that address their individual needs and concerns. These contracts are flexible and enforceable under contract law. Disagreements about the scope of the contract can be settled through negotiation, and disputes over the respective rights and responsibilities of the cohabiting partners can be resolved through a dispute resolution mechanism stipulated in the contract.

There are also good reasons for equating marriage and cohabitation. First and foremost, treating married couples and cohabiting couples differently may be inconsistent with human rights legislation and violate the Canadian Charter of Rights and Freedoms. Human rights legislation varies by province. For example, in Ontario the Human Rights Code protects all citizens against any form of discrimination in the provision of goods, services, and facilities. The Code has primacy over all other provincial legislation. While it may not have a direct impact on the core issues in family law, the Code is relevant in the discussion 'as a legislative expression of fundamental values of our society' (Ontario Law Reform Commission, 1993: 12–13). The preamble to the Code states:

> recognition of the inherent dignity and the equal and inalienable rights of all members of the human family is the foundation of freedom, justice and peace in the world and is in accord with the Universal Declaration of Human Rights as proclaimed by the United Nations; it is public policy in Ontario to recognize the dignity and worth of every person and to provide for equal rights and opportunities without discrimination that is contrary to law, and having as its aim the creation of a climate of understanding and mutual respect for the dignity and worth of each person so that each person feels a part of the community and able to contribute fully to the development and well-being of the community and the Province. (Ibid., 13)

Human rights jurisprudence is important also because of its cross-pollinating relationship between the interpretation of human rights legislation and Charter rights. The Charter, embedded in the constitution, grants a constitutional right of equality to all Canadians, and the constitution 'is the supreme law of Canada, and any law that is inconsistent with the provisions of the Constitution is, to the extent of the inconsistency, of no force or effect' (Constitution Act, 1982). Clearly, family law and human rights legislation are subject to the Charter.

Unmarried heterosexual cohabitors are protected in the human rights legislation and the Charter. It can be argued that the exclusion of unmarried cohabitors from certain statutory rights and privileges conferred only to married people violates Charter rights and constitutes legal discrimination prohibited by human rights legislation in all Canadian jurisdictions. If this argument were valid, the possible violation of Charter rights and human rights legislation alone would warrant the need for law reform.[25]

A second reason for treating marriage and cohabitation the same under the law focuses on the functional similarity between the two union types. As noted in Chapter 1, there are many similarities between marriage and cohabitation. Like married couples, cohabiting couples pool their resources, give each other financial and emotional support, and provide a safe family environment for the care of the next generation. To the extent that family law is designed to provide protection against the economic consequences of marriage (upon marital break-down), it should apply to unmarried cohabiting couples who perform similar functions valued by society. While it was argued earlier that some cohabiting couples choose to cohabit for the reasons of maintaining individual autonomy and avoiding the obligations of matrimony, it is believed that family law should provide 'a fundamentally fair regime for dealing with the economic conse-quences of marriages and similar relationships' (ibid., 27–8). It should also allow unmarried couples to contract out of some (all) of its provisions, preserving indi-vidual autonomy.

Third, eliminating the distinction may also remove some public confusion about the difference between marriage and cohabitation. As Holland (1998: 1–9) noted, a common misconception about cohabitation is that couples who cohabit for a certain time period are actually married as far as the law is concerned (e.g., property rights). The term 'common-law marriage' compounds this confusion.

Fourth, equating cohabitation with marriage may also reduce the risk that the contribution of one cohabiting partner may not be adequately compensated if the union is dissolved. As with married-couple families, the traditional division of labour in and outside the home is prevalent among many cohabiting-couple fam-ilies. Such a division may particularly favour men working outside the home and women working inside the home. Becker (1981) believed that this distinct sexual division of labour prevailed throughout modern history. Indeed, according to Becker, households with only women or only men would be less efficient than those with both because they would not be able to gain from their comparative biological differences (see Chapter 2). In Chapter 9, we saw that there is virtually no difference in the division of household labour between cohabitors and married people. It can be argued that the possible economic and career sacrifices on the part of women should be compensated once the union is dissolved. Of course, the same reasoning applies to male partners who choose to stay at home. While it is argued that people choose to cohabit for the reason of avoiding matrimonial obli-gations, it would be dangerous to assume that this motivation applies to both partners. In addition, the reason for cohabiting may also change with the passage of time. The initial motivation may become irrelevant as time elapses.

It is also argued that maintaining the status quo advances state interests and promotes public morality. Marriage should be the preferred family form on the grounds of safeguarding family stability, mutual obligations, and the care of children. While we have shown that cohabitation is indeed less stable than marriage (Chapter 8), extending the same rights and obligations to cohabitors would ensure the (economic) security of the members of the family, particularly the children. As far as public morality is concerned, cohabitation is no longer perceived as 'immoral' or 'living in sin'. This negative view may also be inconsistent with the Charter, in which freedom of conscience and religion is guaranteed. Cohabitation has been generally recognized as a valid and viable family form and has partially been included in provincial legislation.

The above analysis provides convincing arguments for family law reform in all provincial jurisdictions. In recognition of the changing patterns of non-marital cohabitation, the rights and responsibilities imposed on matrimonial couples should be extended to cohabiting couples in all provinces provided that some permanence of the relationship is established. The threshold level of permanence can be achieved through (1) cohabiting continuously for at least one year, (2) becoming the natural or adoptive parents of a child, or (3) registering as 'Domestic Partners' (as recommended by the Ontario Law Reform Commission, 1993). In short, cohabiting individuals should have the same rights and obligations as married persons.

For centuries and perhaps millennia, the Western family has centred on the institution of marriage. There has been little room for other relationship forms that may also encompass the core elements that constitute what we call the *family*: sexual intimacy, common residence, mutual dependency (division of labour), anticipated children, assumed permanence, and public approval and recognition (Davis, 1985b: 4–9; Ontario Law Reform Commission, 1993: 1). Surely, marriage meets all six criteria. While other family forms may share some of these traits, as Davis (1985b) wrote 15 years ago, it is only the last trait— public approval and recognition—that distinguishes marriage as a unique family form. Canadian cohabitation has come a long way to where it is today. It has not yet been fully approved, recognized, or supported as a family form. Yet, with the arrival of the new century and the new millennium, there is little doubt that the cohabiting-couple family will soon be accepted as a full-fledged Canadian institution.

Appendix: Census Questions on Cohabitation

Question 2 in the 1981 and 1986 Canadian Census Questionnaires

Question 2: Relationship to Person 1

For each person in this household, mark [X] **one box only** to describe his or her relationship to Person 1. If you mark the box 'Other relative' or 'Other non-relative', print in the relationship to Person 1. Some examples of the 'Other' relationships are: grandmother, uncle, roommate's daughter, employee's husband, common-law partner of son or daughter.

01 [X] Person 1

02 [ ] Husband or wife of Person 1
03 [ ] Common-law partner of Person 1
04 [ ] Son or daughter of Person 1
05 [ ] Father or mother of Person 1
06 [ ] Brother or sister of Person 1
07 [ ] Son-in-law or daughter-in-law of Person 1
08 [ ] Father-in-law or mother-in-law of Person 1
09 [ ] Brother-in-law or sister-in-law of Person 1
10 [ ] Grandchild of Person 1

11 [ ] Nephew or niece of Person 1
    [ ] Other relative of Person 1
        (*print below*)
12 [ ] Lodger
13 [ ] Lodger's husband or wife
14 [ ] Lodger's son or daughter
15 [ ] Roommate
16 [ ] Employee
    [ ] Other non-relative
        (*print below*)
17 [ ] [_____]

Source: Statistics Canada, *User's Guide to 1986 Census Data on Families*. Cat. no. 99–113E. (Ottawa: Statistics Canada, 1989), 16.

Notes

Chapter 1 Introduction

1. The participation rate data are obtained at Statistics Canada's official Web site, accessed 15 March 1999: <http://www.statcan.ca/english/Pgdb/People/Labour/labor05.htm>. The participation rate by parental status is from Statistics Canada (1995a: 72).

2. For example, the 1995 General Social Survey (GSS–95) found that less than 0.2 per cent of the respondents aged 15 and over lived in a same-sex relationship. The 1994–5 National Population Health Survey (NPHS) found that less than 0.5 per cent of the respondents aged 20–64 chose 'living with a partner' when asked about their marital status, although 'living common-law' was also an available response.

3. See a detailed discussion on the definition of cohabitation from different data sources in Chapter 3.

Chapter 2 Theoretical Perspectives

1. Becker (1993: 385) makes a clear distinction between the economic approach and Marxian analysis. He maintains that the economic approach is 'a *method* of analysis', not simply an assumption about particular human motivations, such as the Marxian approach makes. Further, unlike Marxian analysis, the economic approach assumes that individuals are not solely motivated by self-interest or material gains, but rather by a much richer host of values and preferences.

2. In acknowledgement of his contributions, Gary Becker received the 1992 Nobel Prize for Economics for extending the domain of microeconomic analysis to a wide range of non-market human behaviour and interaction, such as marriage, child-bearing, educational attainment, and crime and deviant behaviour. Among his other honours, in 1997 he also received the biennial Irene Taeuber Award for Excellence in Demographic Research from the Population Association of America to acknowledge his contributions to human population studies.

3. In the broadest sense, as Becker (1981: 20) noted, the benefit from trade arises from international differences in a host of factors such as endowments of labour, human and physical capital, and natural resources. However, the comparative advantage of specialized investment in different countries, as in households, constitutes the primary gain from trade.

4. Besides economic gains, the existence of a sexual division of labour in families is also attributable to intrinsic differences between the sexes (Becker, 1981: 21). Compared to men, who make their biological contribution to the reproduction of children when women's eggs are fertilized, women have a much heavier biological commitment to reproduction (e.g., carrying to term and breast-feeding their children).

5. These social forces may include, for example, the decline in religious authority, the growth of individualism, the rise in mass education, the demand for gender equality, and the growth of consumerism (Westoff, 1983: 101).

6. Indeed, modern economies have changed in ways that have reduced the demand for workers in heavy industries but increased demand for workers in rapidly expanded educational systems, high technology, and trade and service industries (McQuillan, 1988). Clerical and secretarial, service, teaching, and nursing jobs, which are traditionally dominated by women, continue to be defined as women's work (Cherlin, 1992), and improved educational systems allow educated women to compete for professional jobs with men (Grindstaff, 1991). Consequently, the job market for women has been greatly expanded, and more women, particularly married women, are employed in paid work and become economically independent.

7. Becker makes a clear distinction between non-marital and marital-specific capital (Becker et al., 1977: 1152). The former includes assets such as houses, automobiles, major appliances, and market and non-market skills. The major source of the latter is children born within the marriage. Other examples of this latter type include marital adjustment to one's spouse and skills that are more relevant while being married. The key distinction between the two is that the latter assets are worth considerably less than the former once the marriage is dissolved. This is because the former types of assets are generally transferable to a new relationship, whereas the latter are not.

8. This is a fairly strong assumption. I suspect that perhaps because humans are social animals, and social contact and interactions are essential to our physical and mental well-being, most people would rather live with someone than live alone. It is not just economic need, as Becker correctly claims, but also psychological and emotional needs that motivate people to marry, cohabit, or share a household. Thus, apart from economic reasons, this also explains why households, historically, always had both sexes.

9. One original purpose of the project was to assess the proposition that the modern fertility decline, which started in Western Europe during the second half of the nineteenth century, was largely a response to economic development, the so-called demographic transition theory (e.g., Notestein, 1945). The basic argument of transition theory is that when a country is developed and the standard of living improved, child mortality will decline, which will result in a surge of excess children. Reduced child mortality means fewer children are needed to achieve and maintain a desired family size. This gives rise to conscious control of fertility. The project's findings clearly cast doubt on transition theory as there was little evidence that the decline in fertility timing had much to do with the levels of industrialization.

10. The World Fertility Survey (WFS) is a collection of internationally comparable surveys of human fertility carried out in 41 developing countries during the late 1970s and early 1980s. The International Statistical Institute in the Netherlands conducted this project with funding from the United States Agency for International Development (USAID) and the United Nations Population Fund (UNFPA).

11. This idea originates from Easterlin's (1971, 1987) relative cohort size hypothesis. The basic argument is that when persons are born during periods of low birth rates (e.g., the 1930s), they tend to be reared with low material aspirations owing to the tough economic conditions their parents are experiencing. However, when they become young adults and enter into the labour market, they find that they are in scarce supply relative to older workers. Jobs are easier to come by and life is better relative to what their parents experienced. Consequently, they marry young and raise large families. (The opposite scenario applies when persons are born into a large cohort.) This is what may have happened to the baby-boom cohort. Their parents were born during the 1930s when birth rates were low. When they became young adults, they were able to take advantage of a favourable labour market, married at younger ages, and had more children than their parents did. Easterlin's hypothesis is a cyclical explanation of family change, in which marriage and fertility rates are believed to oscillate in response to changes in relative cohort size and subsequent material aspirations. See Pampel and Peters (1995) for a critical review of Easterlin's hypothesis and other applications of the hypothesis.

12. Canada is comprised of six geographic regions: Atlantic Canada (Newfoundland, Prince Edward Island, Nova Scotia, and New Brunswick), Quebec, Ontario, the Prairie (Manitoba and Saskatchewan), western Canada (Alberta and British Columbia), and the northern territories (Yukon, Northwest Territories, Nunavut). However, some would define region by province (Brym, 1986b). The population distribution of the country is extremely uneven, with, for example, 37.7 per cent of the population residing in Ontario and less than 0.4 per cent living in the northern territories.

13. On 5 July 1979, the Canadian government created a Task Force on Canadian Unity. This task force consisted of a number of prominent Canadian political scientists, economists, and other academics. Its mandate included collecting and publicizing the views of Canadians about the state of the country and providing ideas and initiatives regarding the question of Canadian unity (Pepin, Robarts, et al., 1979: 3).

14. There are also other explanations of Canadian regional diversity. For example, staples theory focuses on the 'human factor' *rather than* geographic factors as the root cause of these disparities. The basic argument of this theory is that, historically, federal politicians and the powerful economic interests centred in Ontario and English Montreal have drained the wealth from the weak peripheral or hinterland regions, which has created regional economic and other structural disparities (Brym, 1986b).

15. Canada has two official languages: French and English. Today French is the mother tongue of over a quarter of Canadians. Most Francophone Canadians now live in Quebec. In addition to its official bilingualism, Canada has gradually moved towards multiculturalism, partly through the Multicultural Act of 1971, which designated Canada as a country that is multicultural in a bilingual framework. The Constitution Act of 1982 further provides for minority-language educational rights throughout Canada. Now the constitution provides that every

ethnocultural group in Canadian society has the right to preserve and develop its own cultures and values.

16. The 1996 census did not collect information on religion. However, there is no reason to suspect that Canadian religious composition has changed drastically over the past five years.

17. Not long ago, exposure to the risk of child-bearing was assumed to be confined to married women, as non-marital fertility was numerically negligible and was routinely not included in fertility analysis (Coale, Anderson, and Harm, 1979). Even today, marital fertility in Canada still constitutes over two-thirds of total fertility (Ford and Nault, 1996).

18. Fertility, mortality, and migration are the three main areas of demography because of their centrality in determining the size of the population and its age structure.

19. Traditionally, virtually all demographic data were collected through the census and vital statistics registration systems. Neither method collected data on marital histories (i.e., the timings of marital transitions), which are crucial to the understanding of the dynamics of marital changes. Not until the 1980s were national demographic surveys carried out in Canada to collect these vital data. For example, the first Canadian Family History Survey (FHS) was conducted by Statistics Canada in 1984.

20. The term 'age cohort' is sometimes used erroneously as a synonym for 'birth cohort' because a birth cohort does not necessarily mean an age level (Glenn, 1977: 8). However, the word 'cohort' shares the same meaning as 'generation'. The latter term generally refers to a group of individuals born and living about the same time, and presumably having common values and attitudes (e.g., the television generation).

21. For more discussions on age-period-cohort effects, see Glenn (1977), Hobcraft et al. (1982), and Knoke and Burke (1980).

22. Throughout the study, 'sex' and 'gender' are used interchangeably, although some researchers prefer to use 'sex' and 'gender' to reflect biological and social aspects (meanings) of individuals.

Chapter 3   Data Sources

1. The quotation comes from Ralph Waldo Emerson (1803–82), an American writer and philosopher.

2. Censuses are carried out for other purposes as well. For example, in Canada, the Census of Agriculture is taken every five years, at the same time as the Census of Population, and collects information about Canadian agricultural operations, such as the number of farms, crops, land use, livestock and poultry, and farm machinery. It also enumerates farm operators and collects basic information regarding them, such as their age, sex, residence status, farm work, non-farm work, and injuries.

3. The discussion on the history of the Canadian census is based on Statistics Canada (1995b, 1997b) and McVey and Kalbach (1995).

4. The discussion on cohabitation data prior to the 1991 census draws from Statistics Canada (1989: ch. 10).

5. There was an indirect, albeit ambiguous, reference to common-law relationships in Question 2 of the 1976 census form, where 'partner' appeared in the pre-coded response set. The 1976 Census Guide defined 'partner' as 'a person who is unrelated to the head of the household, who has equal access to dwelling facilities and/or shares responsibility for the maintenance of the household (e.g., a roommate)' (Statistics Canada, 1989: 41).

6. Scientific sampling procedures are based on sampling theory that allows research scientists to determine the appropriate sample size and methods of sample selection, to estimate sampling errors (the differences between sample and population characteristics), and to make inferences about the population on the basis of sample characteristics (see, e.g., Cochran, 1977).

7. The Labour Force Survey (LFS) is a national household survey, conducted monthly by Statistics Canada, to monitor changes in the labour market, such as numbers of people employed, not employed, and not in the labour force. The first LFS was conducted in 1945.

8. This section draws on materials from Chapter 2 in Balakrishnan, Lapierre-Adamcyk, and Krótki (1993) and the introductory chapter in the User's Guide for the Canadian Fertility Survey (Population Studies Centre, 1988). See Balakrishnan et al. (1993: ch. 2) for details.

9. The discussion on the GSS is based on Norris (1990) and the User's Guide for the GSS–90 and the GSS–95 (Statistics Canada, 1991, 1997c). See GSS User's Guides for details.

10. In fact, the public-use microdata file for the GSS–95 only became available in the summer of 1997, when the present work was in its planning stages. In many respects, it has improved the core content of the 1990 cycle. For example, it has a section on family attitudes and values, a section on childhood experiences, and a section on contraceptive usage; none of these was available in the 1990 cycle.

11. However, it is worth noting that the CFS identifies a cohabitation relationship by asking the respondent, 'Have you ever lived with a partner without being married?' There is no reference to either 'common-law' or 'husband and wife' in the question. Also, the estimated rate of cohabitation was not much different from the one obtained from the Family History Survey, another national survey conducted at about same time (see Burch, 1985: 35–9). The FHS used the identical wording for the question on cohabitation as the GSS–90.

12. This figure is based on the post-censal estimate of the 1996 population (reported in Statistics Canada's official Web site: <http://www.statcan.ca/english/Pgdb/People/Population/demo23a.htm>, accessed 17 March 1999) and on the census finding of the number of common-law union families (reported in Statistics Canada's *Daily*, 14 Oct. 1997).

Chapter 4 Cohabitation Trends Since the 1980s

1. This statement is only true in the broadest sense—that is, when age variations for the adult population (aged 15 and over) are ignored. As will be shown later, when

the rate of cohabitation is compared between selected age groups, age-patterns of cohabitation emerge.

2. This is equivalent to the cohort-table analysis (see Glenn, 1977).

3. As the incidence of cohabitation is particularly common among young people, it is more sensible to follow younger age cohorts over time than older age cohorts. However, even for some older age groups, there is evidence of an increase in cohabitation.

4. The Canadian census did not ask the question on whether people ever cohabited.

5. The 1996 census recorded a little over 30,000 and 64,000 residents in Yukon and the Northwest Territories, respectively.

6. The issue of whether older widows are more likely to cohabit than women in other marital groups cannot be resolved using census data. I attempted to use the GSS–95 data to address this question. However, the GSS–95 shows that less than 10 women aged 60 and over in the sample (N = 10,749) were cohabiting at the time of the survey. The small sample size prevents further investigation of the relationship between cohabitation and marital status at older ages. For the same reason, the census figures on cohabitation at older ages should also be interpreted with caution.

7. The review of studies on cohabitation in other countries is intended to be suggestive and illustrative. No exhaustive review is attempted.

Chapter 5 Changing Attitudes towards Union Relationships

1. See Maddala (1984) and Long (1997) for technical details.

2. See Fox (1996) for technical details.

3. To conserve space, the definitions and descriptive statistics for the explanatory variables used in the analyses have not been included. This information is available from the author upon request.

4. As noted in Chapter 2, we cannot entirely separate the effects of age, period, and cohort. For example, in discussing age effects, while we are able to control for period effects, we cannot separate cohort effects from the age effects. Similarly, when we discuss period effects, while we can control for age effects, we cannot eliminate cohort effects from the period effects. Therefore, our discussion on possible age/period/cohort effects is only suggestive.

5. Because the GSS–95 has a wider age representation than the CFS, the marginal distributions (see the bottom of each panel in Table 5.2) are not directly comparable between the two surveys.

Chapter 6 The Transition to Cohabitation

1. Cohabitation and marriage markets can be quite distinct, and factors influencing one's search in one market can differ from those affecting a search in the other. Therefore, the use of individual-level marriage determinants in the analysis of the entry into cohabitation is only tentative.

2. It is estimated that less than 4 per cent of widowed respondents ever cohabited after the death of their spouses.

3. The reason that more women are represented in the sample is due to the low sex ratio of the original sample (i.e., the GSS–90) as well as to the mortality differentials between the sexes in later life.

4. The GSS–90 collected union history data on up to two marriages and two cohabitations. The GSS–95 increased the coverage to three marriages and four cohabitations.

5. In modelling the timing of premarital cohabitation, marriage was considered to be a competing 'risk' in the sense that those who had married were removed from the analysis at the time of marriage simply because they were no longer at 'risk' of cohabitation. Thus, exposure time for those who married without prior cohabitation was measured by age at marriage.

6. As with premarital cohabitation, in modelling the timing of post-marital cohabitation, remarriage was considered as a competing 'risk'. Exposure time for those who had remarried without prior cohabitation was measured from the date of separation (divorce) to the date of remarriage.

7. Survival model techniques are appropriate analytical tools because our data were collected from a cross-sectional, retrospective survey. The life histories of the respondents are complete up to the time of the survey (e.g., reaching a given age or duration), but are also censored at the point of survey. That is, they were unable to provide information of a given event at older ages or longer durations. The result is that exposure time varies between respondents. Survival model techniques are capable of making adjustments for the effects of censoring by incorporating both complete and censored segments of event (union) histories in the analysis. For technical discussion of these techniques, see, e.g., Lee (1992); Namboodiri and Suchindran (1987).

8. Among the explanatory variables, several were coded as time-varying (also known as time-dependent) indicators, in the sense that the value of the indicator may change with time (exposure). For example, employment status is a time-varying covariate, with a value of 1 indicating that the respondent was employed outside the home (0 otherwise) at the time interval in which the hazard rate of cohabitation was computed (one month). Put differently, we assume that the hazard of cohabitation at time t depends on the value of employment status at time t. The same principle applies to other time-varying covariates shown in the table. Variable definitions and their descriptive statistics are available from the author upon request.

9. A 'shotgun marriage' is a marriage precipitated due to a generally unplanned pregnancy.

10. Dissolution of cohabitation, including dissolution via marriage, is discussed in Chapter 8.

11. Another explanation is also plausible. The analysis of premarital cohabitation was based on the 1995 data, whereas the analysis of post-marital cohabitation used the 1990 data. Since widespread cohabitation is a relatively recent event, the lower rate of post-marital cohabitation could reflect the different 'eras' (periods) during which the surveys were conducted. This 'period' effect is augmented particularly when retrospective survival data were analysed and different age groups were

selected. Recall that respondents of all age groups were included in the analysis of post-marital cohabitation, whereas respondents under 35 years of age were used in the analysis of premarital cohabitation. The implication here is that we could trace back several decades to reconstruct union histories of separated/divorced individuals (depending on their current age and age at marital disruption), when non-marital cohabitation was an extremely rare event.

Chapter 7   Child-bearing in Cohabitational Relationships

1. If the respondent was unclear about the question, the interviewer was allowed to explain that intended children do not include step- and adopted children.
2. The primary reason for excluding pregnant respondents (and respondents with pregnant partners) is that for these respondents, a first child is almost a certainty. Since our focus is on child-bearing intentions (not the decision to terminate a pregnancy), including these respondents would introduce biases in our estimates of intentions. Surgically sterilized respondents were excluded because our focus is on intentions, not the decision to undergo a surgical sterilization procedure. As the GSS–95 does not have information on the date of surgical operations or the timing of sterilization, the key explanatory variables could not be considered to be causally prior to sterilization and would therefore have to be excluded from the analysis.
3. It is important to note here that a 'yes' response to the intention question does not necessarily mean that respondents intended to have a child born into their *current* relationship.
4. This does not preclude women who gave birth prior to the start of cohabitation.
5. The transformation for categorical variables takes a different form because the design matrix of categorical (explanatory) variables was constructed in such a way that the estimates of all categories for a given variable sum to zero (i.e., $\Sigma_{\alpha i} = 0$, where α_i = parameter estimate for category i); and α_i indicates the difference between ith category mean and the grand mean.
6. There are two possible explanations for this discrepancy. One is that intention measures may not be good predictors of actual fertility after all, as many critics of intention studies have claimed (see earlier discussion). Second, our *intention* and *experience* studies address two different populations: the former includes currently childless cohabitors; the latter is comprised of the population of first premarital cohabitors.
7. This is because age at start of cohabitation is associated with age at initiation of sexual activity, which, in turn, is related to premarital child-bearing (e.g., Jones et al., 1986). The implication is that age at cohabitation may not have much net effect on the hazard rate when age at sexual activity is added to the model. However, we do not have data on initiation of sexual activity to test this possibility.
8. This hypothesis comes from Becker's (1960) economic theory of fertility. The theory views children as essentially a consumer's 'durable good', which yields income to parents, primarily through 'psychological income'. It follows that a rise in income and a decline in price should increase parents' demand for more *and* higher-quality children (Becker, 1960: 231).

9. See Friedman et al. (1994) for a detailed discussion of uncertainty reduction theory of parenthood, and Wu (1996) for applying this theory to first births in cohabitations.

Chapter 8 The Transition out of Cohabitation

1. However, the parameters for the hazard of widowhood were not estimated, in part, because the analysis of the risk of widowhood is beyond the scope of this study. Moreover, the mechanism of transition to union separation or marriage is also fundamentally different from that of widowhood because, unlike the former, the latter event is usually outside personal control.

2. There are two reasons for using eight-month intervals: (a) to be consistent with prior research (e.g., Morgan, Lye, and Condran, 1988), and (b) to reduce the computational burden.

3. In the analysis of transition to union separation, we treated marriage as a competing risk, removing the individuals who married without prior separation from the risk of experiencing a subsequent separation at the time of marriage. Similarly, in the examination of termination by marriage, we treated separation as a competing risk, removing those who broke up the cohabitation relationship prior to marriage from the risk of experiencing a subsequent marriage at the time of separation. Widowhood was also a competing risk, and a similar procedure was followed to eliminate widowed cases from the analyses of separation and marriage.

4. Despite high rates of divorce, Canadian marriages are much more stable than, for example, their American counterparts. Adams and Nagnur (1990) estimated that about one-third of Canadian first marriages are likely to end in divorce (the data from the GSS–90 and GSS–95 are generally supportive of this estimate). American divorce rates are considerably higher. According to one estimate (Castro-Martin and Bumpass, 1989), as many as two-thirds of current marriages are likely to end in divorce.

5. The estimates for the rates of separation and marriage (see Figures 8.3 and 8.4) are generated from the same life table.

6. In the analysis of marital disruption, exposure to the 'risk' of disruption is measured from the date of first marriage until the date of marital separation, divorce (if divorced without a separation or the date of separation is unavailable), or the death of one's spouse. Again, widowhood was treated as a competing risk, and widowed cases are censored at the time of widowhood.

7. It is also worth noting that women and men are about equally likely to terminate a cohabitation relationship.

8. While the GSS–95 collected data on up to four cohabitations, only 18 respondents (0.17 per cent) experienced four or more cohabitations. A sample of 18 is simply too small for any meaningful analysis.

9. In measuring the marital status of respondents' partners, it is noted that about 9 per cent of the cohabitors (for both genders) failed to provide information on their partner's marital status. It is possible that the reluctance of some respondents to reveal their partner's marital status may reflect that their partners were married at

the time of the survey. In keeping with this possibility, and to avoid substantial sample size reduction, partner's marital status was measured in four levels: single, separated/divorced, widowed, and not stated. Indeed, consistent with this hypothesis, we observe that the individuals in the category of 'not stated' are much less likely to terminate a cohabitation relationship than those whose partners are single (see Table 8.1). Also recall that all respondents in the study were never married and many may see themselves as being single.

10. As noted, respondents were not asked whether they intend to marry their current partners but if they would ever marry.

11. As we have noted, investing in children is different from investing in other durable goods. Unlike other investments, children constitute what is known as a *union-specific* investment, which is worth considerably less in several respects in the event of union disruption, whether it is marital or non-marital union. See Becker et al. (1977) for more discussion.

Chapter 9   Consequences of Cohabitation

1. The selected dimensions of cohabitation by no means constitute an exhaustive list of all the important implications of cohabitation. My goal is rather modest. I wish to point out some short-term and long-term implications of non-marital cohabitation. Other aspects of interest include, for example, the short-term and long-term effects of cohabitation on children born either in or outside cohabitations, women's employment, health benefits, and completed fertility.

2. Roelants (1998: 24) calls this the 'taken for granted hypothesis', partly because both partners take it for granted that they do not need to try as hard to keep their marriage together once they are married.

3. In the analysis, widowhood was modelled as a competing risk in a similar fashion as in the union disruption study (see Chapter 8).

4. See the data and methods section in Chapter 6 for explanations of using the date of separation as the timing of marital breakdown.

5. When the respondent was unclear about the question, the interviewer was allowed to give some examples of housework, such as preparing meals, doing laundry, household planning, shopping, and mowing the lawn.

6. The Weibull distribution was selected as the functional form for the baseline hazard function partly because there are good theoretical and empirical reasons to assume that the hazard rate of first marriage is an increasing function of age for young adults, particularly in their late teens and early twenties (e.g., Coale, 1971).

7. A caveat is in order here. Although we may be able to establish a causal relationship at the individual level, one cannot simply infer that a similar relationship exists at the aggregate level (which, otherwise, is known as the ecological fallacy).

8. Heckman's method is a two-stage estimation procedure. In stage one, I estimated a probit model to estimate the propensity to cohabit, separately for women and men. The probit model considers several explanatory variables (e.g., age, gender, race, religion, and education) known to be important (see Chapter 6, and Bumpass and Sweet, 1989; Wu and Balakrishnan, 1994). Using the probit estimates, a correction

factor, known as the hazard rate or the inverse Mills ratio, is computed for each observation. In stage two, the hazard rate is entered as an explanatory variable in the failure time models of marriage timing. See Greene (1993), Little and Rubin (1987), Nelson (1984), and Stolzenberg and Relles (1990, 1997) for technical details and empirical assessments of this approach.

9. The relationship between premarital cohabitation and marital stability has been examined in two Canadian studies. Using the CFS data, Balakrishnan and his colleagues (1987) reported a positive effect of premarital cohabitation on subsequent marital disruption. A similar finding was reported using the GSS–90 (Hall and Zhao, 1995). There are several reasons for re-examining this relationship. First, an empirical assessment of the relationship is simply too important to ignore. Second, the analysis reported in this section updates the two prior studies through the use of more recent data. Third, the current analysis uses substantially more controls than before, including an array of time-varying covariates, measuring employment status, school enrolment, and fertility variables that were not considered in most of the earlier studies in Canada or abroad.

10. The difference between the two estimates is statistically significant.

11. In analyses not shown here, I also tested the *marital duration* hypothesis, which suggests that an elevated risk of marital disruption among cohabitors can be explained by the duration of the relationship rather than by cohabitation itself (e.g., Bennett et al., 1988; DeMaris and Rao, 1992; Teachman and Polonko, 1990). In other words, because the risk of disruption generally increases (though not monotonically) with the duration of marriage, the increased risk of marital disruption for cohabitors (as a direct consequence of cohabitation) should be reduced and even eliminated when exposure to the risk of marital disruption is measured from the date of premarital cohabitation initiation rather than the date of marriage. I tested this model specification using the GSS–95 data. The results provide strong evidence against this hypothesis. The parameter estimates for premarital cohabitation are positive and highly significant; and the sizes of estimates are even greater than (but not significantly different from) the ones reported in Table 9.2.

12. I am not aware of any other national surveys in, or perhaps even outside, Canada that have ever collected information of this sort.

13. There are a few notable exceptions (e.g., Roelants, 1998; Shelton and John, 1993; South and Spitze, 1994; Stafford, Backman, and Dibona, 1976).

14. It is theoretically possible that the observed differences are *suppressed* by other variables such that the differences emerge when the effects of these other variables are held constant.

15. This regional difference cannot be attributed to the lower rate of home ownership in Quebec (Balakrishnan and Wu, 1992), as home ownership is held constant in the models. However, it could reflect the differences in gender role attitudes and other cultural factors (e.g., Presser, 1994). For example, a reduced time spent on housework for Quebec women may reflect the less traditional gender role attitudes held by Quebecers (e.g., Wu and Baer, 1996). However, the reason for a reduction in Quebec men's time spent on housework remains unclear.

16. Rindfuss and VandenHeuvel (1990) used data from the fifth (1986) follow-up of the US National Longitudinal Study of the High School Class of 1972 (NLS72).

Chapter 10 The Future of Cohabitation

1. Marriages in Scotland or contracted overseas were not covered under this Act. Thus, common-law marriage continued to be lawful in Scotland long after it was abolished in England, and it remained valid in the US until it was abolished by local legislation. The situation in Canada remains unknown (see Holland, 1998: 1–2, n. 7).

2. The Canadian divorce rate peaked in the late 1980s after the liberalization of divorce laws in 1986.

3. As we have noted, what people say does not imply what they will do. Sociologist Kingsley Davis (1985a) cautioned us that strong approval and satisfaction of marriage reported in surveys may reflect more the ideal side of marriage than the contemporary social and demographic situation about marriage. People place high value on marriage because they tend to see it as an end in itself, rather than as a means to achieve something else. The same can be said for child-bearing intentions.

4. See, for example, Newcomb (1979), Macklin (1983), and Tanfer (1987) for reviews of this literature.

5. Caution must be exercised when interpreting these data. Because current union status is used to group the fertility data, some children reported by cohabiting women may have been born in previous marriages and/or out of wedlock. The same can be said in regard to married (remarried) women. Thus, these data can only be suggestive rather than definitive.

6. The familial status of same-sex partnerships is more complicated and more intensely debated, in part because there is much diversity in the form and practice of gay and lesbian relationships (Ontario Law Reform Commission, 1993).

7. Espenshade (1985) used a similar strategy when he speculated about the future trends in American marriage.

8. However, a rejection of marriage does not imply a rejection of sexually intimate relationships. Recent studies have shown that the onset of sexual relationships begins at increasingly younger ages (e.g., Brewster et al., 1998; Zelnik and Kantner, 1980; Thomas, DiCenso, and Griffith, 1998). With less social pressure to marry, young people may choose cohabitation over marriage to begin a sexually intimate relationship. Indeed, these developments have led Sweet and Bumpass (1987) to conclude that the recent rise in cohabitation could well be a direct consequence of the growth of premarital sexual intimacy.

9. The projected rates were computed using a two-stage generalized least squares (GLS) procedure. In stage one, two exponential models were computed using the observed census data (1981–96). The two fitted models are given by:

$$Y_w = 1.232 \times 10^{-33} \times \exp(0.03935x) \quad (1)$$

$$Y_m = 2.092 \times 10^{-34} \times \exp(0.04029x) \quad (2)$$

Where Y_w and Y_m are vectors of observed rates for women and men, respectively; x is a vector of four census years (i.e., 1981, 1986, 1991, and 1996). In stage two, equations (1) and (2) were used to compute the projected rates.

10. Of course, there are no strong theoretical reasons for extrapolating the trends too far into the future. As predictions cannot be reliably based on simple mechanistic views of secular change and a single cause (Rindfuss, Morgan, and Swicegood, 1988: 236), caution must be exercised when speculating trends too far from the present.

11. The current prevalence rate of cohabitation in Sweden is unavailable. The most recent data are from the 1990 census, which suggests that cohabiting couples comprised 23 per cent of all couples in Sweden (personal communication with the Swedish Bureau of Central Statistics). I thank Mikael Jansson for assistance in the communication. However, extrapolating the Swedish trends suggests that the 30 per cent rate would be a reasonable estimate.

12. The materials from this section draw primarily from Bracher and Santow (1998), Hoem (1986), Hoem and Hoem (1988), Hoem and Rennermalm (1985), Kiernan and Estaugh (1993), and Trost (1975).

13. According to Trost (1978: 307), 33 per cent of children were born out of wedlock in 1976, up from 11.3 per cent in 1960. It is also worth noting that there had been virtually no change in the illegitimate birth rate between the turn of the century and the early 1960s, with the rate standing at 11.4 per cent in 1900.

14. The situation where people cohabit because they are too poor to marry may exist in other societies as well.

15. The discussion of the legal aspect of Swedish cohabitation draws primarily from Fawcett (1990).

16. The principles are clearly in conflict. One cannot devise laws that support the centrality of marriage in family law and at the same time sustain societal neutrality to the form of the family. This *laissez-faire* approach to cohabitation was later abandoned in the 1987 legislation.

17. The new law guaranteed a more needy partner or child a home in the event of union disruption, irrespective of who owned the property.

18. In Sweden, cohabitors are known as *sambor* (*sambo* in singular). According to Fawcett (1990: 185), the term *sambor* carries a sense of dignity to the relationship, which has no equivalent word(s) in the English language.

19. The materials in this discussion draw heavily from Holland (1998), Holland and Stalbecker-Pountney (1998), Ontario Law Reform Commission (1993), and Fels (1981: ch. 5).

20. In 1979 the New Brunswick government introduced legislation to grant property rights to unmarried heterosexual couples who have cohabited for three or more years. This section of the bill was later dropped in anticipation of strong opposition.

21. The concepts of enrichment and deprivation are flexible: 'the defendant is said to be enriched when he or she obtains some benefit, and the benefit can be financial or be derived from unremunerated labour relating to either business or domestic

situations. . . . Deprivation . . . refers to any loss of money or money's worth through unremunerated contributions' (Holland, 1998: 1–12).

22. Although the Alberta Law Reform Institute has recommended the introduction of a limited spousal support obligation between cohabiting partners, the government of Alberta has not yet acted on this recommendation.

23. In Yukon, there is no minimum time requirement for cohabitors to be eligible for spousal support, although the partner seeking the support must prove that they have lived in a cohabiting relationship of some permanence.

24. This section draws materials primarily from Holland (1998) and Ontario Law Reform Commission (1993).

25. See Holland (1998: 1–26–45) and Ontario Law Reform Commission (1993: 11–27) for detailed analyses and discussion.

References

Adams, Owen, and Dhruva Nagnur. 1990. 'Marrying and divorcing: A status report for Canada', in Craig McKie and Keith Thompson, eds, *Canadian Social Trends*. Toronto: Thompson Educational Publishing, 142–5.

Antill, John K., and Sandra Cotton. 1988. 'Factors affecting the division of labor in households', *Sex Roles* 18: 531–53.

Aries, Philippe. 1980. 'Two successive motivations for the declining birth rate in the West', *Population and Development Review* 6: 645–50.

Axinn, William G., and Arland Thornton. 1992. 'The relationship between cohabitation and divorce: Selectivity or causal influence?', *Demography* 29: 357–74.

———— and ————. 1993. 'Mothers, children, and cohabitation: The intergenerational effects of attitudes and behavior', *American Sociological Review* 58: 233–46.

————, Marin E. Clarkberg, and Arland Thornton. 1994. 'Family influences on family size preferences', *Demography* 31: 65–79.

Bachrach, Christine A. 1987. 'Cohabitation and reproductive behaviour in the U.S.', *Demography* 24: 623–37.

Baer, Douglas E., Edward Grabb, and William A. Johnston. 1990. 'The values of Canadians and Americans', *Social Forces* 68: 693–713.

Balakrishnan, T.R., and Jiajian Chen. 1990. 'Religiosity, nuptiality and reproduction in Canada', *Canadian Review of Sociology and Anthropology* 27: 316–40.

————, Evelyne Lapierre-Adamcyk, and Karol J. Kròtki. 1993. *Family and Childbearing in Canada: A Demographic Analysis*. Toronto: University of Toronto Press.

————, K. Vaninadha Rao, Evelyne Lapierre-Adamcyk, and Karol J. Kròtki. 1987. 'A hazard model analysis of the covariates of marriage dissolution in Canada', *Demography* 24: 395–406.

———— and Zheng Wu. 1992. 'Regional patterns of nuptiality and fertility in Canada: 1921–1986', *Genus* 48: 151–71.

Beaujot, Roderic. 1991. *Population Change in Canada: The Challenges of Policy Adaptation*. Toronto: McClelland & Stewart.

———— and Kevin McQuillan. 1982. *Growth and Dualism: The Demographic Development of Canadian Society*. Toronto: Gage.

Becker, Gary S. 1960. 'An economic analysis of fertility', in National Bureau of Economic Research, *Demographic and Economic Change in Developed Countries*. Princeton, NJ: Princeton University Press, 209–31.

————. 1973. 'A theory of marriage: Part I', *Journal of Political Economy* 81: 813–46.

————. 1981. *A Treatise on the Family*. Cambridge, Mass.: Harvard University Press.

————. 1993. 'Nobel lecture: The economic way of looking at behavior', *Journal of Political Economy* 101: 385–409.

————, Elisabeth M. Landes, and Robert T. Michael. 1977. 'An economic analysis of marital instability', *Journal of Political Economy* 85: 1141–87.

Belanger, A., and J. Dumas. 1998. *Report on the Demographic Situation in Canada, 1997.* Catalogue no. 91–209. Ottawa: Minister of Industry.

Bennett, Neil G., Ann K. Blanc, and David E. Bloom. 1988. 'Commitment and the modern union: Assessing the link between premarital cohabitation and subsequent marital stability', *American Sociological Review* 53: 127–38.

Benoit, Cecilia M. 1999. *Women, Work, and Social Rights: Canada in Historical and Comparative Perspective.* Toronto: Prentice-Hall.

Bergen, Elizabeth. 1991. 'The economic context of labor allocation', *Journal of Family Issues* 12: 140–57.

Bernard, Jessie. 1956. *Remarriage: A Study of Marriage.* New York: Dryden Press.

Bibby, Reginald W. 1982. *Project Can80: A Second Look at Deviance, Diversity, and Devotion in Canada.* Codebook. Lethbridge, Alta: University of Lethbridge.

————. 1983. 'Religionless Christianity', *Social Indicator Research* 13: 1–16.

Blair, Sampson-Lee, and Daniel T. Lichter. 1991. 'Measuring the division of household labor: gender segregation of housework among American couples', *Journal of Family Issues* 12: 91–113.

Blanc, Ann K. 1987. 'The formation and dissolution of second unions: Marriage and cohabitation in Sweden and Norway', *Journal of Marriage and the Family* 49: 391–400.

Bongaarts, John. 1990. 'The projection of family composition over the life course with family status life tables', in Bongaarts et al. (1990: 189–212).

————. 1992. 'Do reproductive intentions matter?', *International Family Planning Perspectives* 18: 102–8.

————, Thomas Burch, and Kenneth Wachter, eds. 1990. *Family Demography: Methods and Applications.* New York: Oxford University Press.

Booth, Alan, and David R. Johnson. 1988. 'Premarital Cohabitation and Marital Success', *Journal of Family Issues* 9: 255–72.

Bracher, Michael, and Gigi Santow. 1998. 'Economic independence and union formation in Sweden', *Population Studies* 52: 275–94.

Brewster, Karin L., Elizabeth C. Cooksey, David K. Guilkey, and Ronald R. Rindfuss. 1998. 'The changing impact of religion on the sexual and contraceptive behavior of adolescent women in the United States', *Journal of Marriage and the Family* 60: 493–504.

Brym, Robert J., ed. 1986a. *Regionalism in Canada.* Toronto: Irwin Publishing.

————. 1986b. 'Introduction', in Brym (1986a: 2–45).

Bumpass, Larry L., and R. Kelly Raley. 1995. 'Redefining single-parent families: Cohabitation and changing family reality', *Demography* 32: 97–109.

————, ————, and James A. Sweet. 1995. 'The changing character of stepfamilies: Implications of cohabitation and nonmarital childbearing', *Demography* 32: 425–36.

———— and James A. Sweet. 1989. 'National estimates of cohabitation', *Demography* 26: 615–25.

———, ———, and Teresa Castro-Martin. 1990. 'Changing patterns of remarriage', *Journal of Marriage and the Family* 52: 747–56.

———, ———, and Andrew Cherlin. 1991. 'The role of cohabitation in declining rates of marriage', *Journal of Marriage and the Family* 53: 913–27.

Burch, Thomas K. 1985. *Family History Survey: Preliminary Findings*. Catalogue no. 99–955. Ottawa: Statistics Canada.

———. 1996. 'Icons, straw men and precision: Reflections on demographic theories of fertility decline', *Sociological Quarterly* 37: 59–81.

——— and Ashok K. Madan. 1986. *Union Formation and Dissolution: Results from the 1984 Family History Surveys*. Catalogue no. 99–963. Ottawa: Statistics Canada.

——— and Beverly J. Matthews. 1987. 'Household formation in developed societies', *Population and Development Review* 13: 459–511.

Carlson, Elwood D. 1985. 'Couples without children: Premarital cohabitation in France', in Davis (1985a: 113–30).

Carmichael, Gordon A. 1990. 'A cohort analysis of marriage and informal cohabitation among Australian men', *Australian and New Zealand Journal of Sociology* 27: 53–72.

Castro-Martin, Teresa, and Larry L. Bumpass. 1989. 'Recent trends in marital disruption', *Demography* 26: 37–51.

Chiang, Chin Long. 1984. *The Life Table and Its Applications*. Malabar, Fla: Robert E. Krieger.

Cherlin, Andrew. 1978. 'Remarriage as an incomplete institution', *American Journal of Sociology* 84: 634–50.

———. 1992. *Marriage, Divorce, Remarriage*, rev. edn. Cambridge, Mass.: Harvard University Press.

——— and Pamela Barnhouse Walters. 1981. 'Trends in United States men's and women's sex role attitudes: 1972 to 1978', *American Sociological Review* 46: 453–60.

Clarkberg, Marin E. 1997. 'Income and the entrance into nonmarital cohabitation', paper presented to the annual meeting of the Population Association of America, Washington, Apr.

Cleland, John, and Christopher Wilson. 1987. 'Demand theories of the fertility transition: An iconoclastic view', *Population Studies* 41: 5–30.

Coale, Ansley J. 1971. 'Age patterns of marriage', *Population Studies* 25: 193–214.

———. 1973. 'The demographic transition', in *International Population Conference Proceedings*, vol. 1. Liege: International Union of Scientific Study of Population, 53–72.

———, Barbara A. Anderson, and Erna Harm. 1979. *Human Fertility in Russia Since the Nineteenth Century*. Princeton, NJ: Princeton University Press.

——— and D.R. McNeil. 1972. 'The distribution by age of the frequency of first marriage in a female cohort', *Journal of the American Statistical Association* 67: 743–9.

——— and James T. Trussell. 1974. 'Model fertility schedules: Variations in the age structure of childbearing in human populations', *Population Index* 40: 185–258.

——— and Susan C. Watkins, eds. 1986. *The Decline of Fertility in Europe*. Princeton, NJ.: Princeton University Press.

Cochran, William G. 1977. *Sampling Techniques*, 3rd edn. New York: Wiley.

Cox, D.R. 1972. 'Regression models and life tables (with discussion)', *Journal of the Royal Statistical Society* Series B34: 187–220.

Davis, Kingsley. 1963. 'The theory of change and response in modern demographic history', *Population Index* 29: 345–66.

———, ed. 1985a. *Contemporary Marriage: Comparative Perspectives on a Changing Institution*. New York: Russell Sage.

———. 1985b. 'Introduction: The meaning and significance of marriage in contemporary society', in Davis (1985a: 1–21).

———. 1985c. 'The future of marriage', in Davis (1985a: 25–52).

———, M.S. Bernstam, and R. Ricardo-Campbell, eds. 1986. 'Below-replacement fertility in industrial societies: causes, consequences, and policies', *Population and Development Review* 12 (supplement).

DeMaris, Alfred, and Gerald R. Leslie. 1984. 'Cohabitation with the future spouse: Its influence upon marital satisfaction and communication', *Journal of Marriage and the Family* 46: 77–84.

——— and K. Vaninadha Rao. 1992. 'Premarital cohabitation and subsequent marital stability in the United States: A reassessment', *Journal of Marriage and the Family* 54: 178–90.

Durkheim, Emile. 1984. *The Division of Labor in Society*. New York: Free Press.

Easterlin, Richard A. 1971. 'Does human fertility adjust to the environment?', *American Economic Review* 61: 399–407.

———. 1987. *Birth and Fortune: The Impact of Numbers on Personal Welfare*. Chicago: University of Chicago Press.

Elder, Glen H., Jr, ed. 1985. *Life Course Dynamics: Trajectories and Transitions, 1968–1980*. Ithaca, NY: Cornell University Press.

Espenshade, Thomas J. 1985. 'Marriage trends in America: Estimates, implications, and underlying causes', *Population and Development Review* 11: 193–245.

Fawcett, Matthew. 1990. 'Taking the middle path: Recent Swedish legislation grants minimal property rights to unmarried cohabitants', *Family Law Quarterly* 24: 179–202.

Fels, Lynn. 1981. *Living Together: Unmarried Couples in Canada*. Toronto: Personal Library.

Ford, David, and François Nault. 1996. 'Changing fertility patterns, 1974 to 1994', *Health Report* 8: 39–46.

Fox, John. 1997. *Applied Regression Analysis, Linear Models, and Related Methods*. Thousand Oaks, Calif.: Sage.

Freedman, Deborah, Arland Thornton, Donald Camburn, Duane Alwin, and Linda Young-DeMarco. 1988. 'The life history calendar: A technique for collecting retrospective data', *Sociological Methodology* 18: 37–68.

Freedman, Ronald. 1963. 'Norms for family size in underdeveloped areas', *Proceedings of the Royal Society* 159: 220–40.

Fricke, Tom. 1997. 'The uses of culture in demographic research: A continuing place for community studies', *Population Development Review* 23: 825–32.

Friedman, Debra, Michael Hechter, and Satoshi Kanazawa. 1994. 'A theory of the value of children', *Demography* 31: 375–401.

Fuchs, Victor R. 1983. *How We Live*. Cambridge, Mass.: Harvard University Press.

George, Linda K. 1993. 'Sociological perspectives on life transitions', *Annual Review of Sociology* 18: 353–73.

Gillis, John R. 1985. *For Better, For Worse: English Marriages, from 1960 to the Present*. New York: Oxford University Press.

Glenn, Norval D. 1977. *Cohort Analysis*. Beverly Hills, Calif.: Sage.

Goldscheider, Frances K., and Linda J. Waite. 1986. 'Sex differences in the entry into marriage', *American Journal of Sociology* 92: 91–109.

———— and ————. 1991. *New Families, No Families? The Transformation of the American Home*. Berkeley: University of California Press.

Goode, William J. 1976. 'Family disorganization', in Robert K. Merton and Robert Nisbet, eds, *Contemporary Social Problems*, 4th edn. New York: Harcourt Brace Jovanovich, 513–54.

Greene, William H. 1993. *Econometric Analysis*, 2nd edn. New York: Macmillan.

Grindstaff, Carl F. 1991. 'The Canadian family in transition', working paper, Population Studies Centre, University of Western Ontario.

Guindon, Hubert. 1988. *Quebec Society: Tradition, Modernity and Nationhood*. Toronto: University of Toronto Press.

Hall, David R., and John Z. Zhao. 1995. 'Cohabitation and divorce in Canada: Testing the selectivity hypothesis', *Journal of Marriage and the Family* 57: 421–7.

Heckman, James. 1976. 'The common structure of statistical models of truncation, sample selection and limited dependent variable and a simple estimator for such models', *Annals of Economic and Social Measurement* 5: 475–92.

————. 1979. 'Sample selection bias as specification error', *Econometrica* 47: 153–61.

Hendershot, Gerry E., and Paul J. Placek, eds. 1981. *Predicting Fertility: Demographic Studies of Birth Expectations*. Toronto: Lexington Books.

Henripin, Jacques. 1972. *Trends and Factors of Fertility in Canada*. 1961 Census Monograph. Ottawa: Statistics Canada.

Henry, Louis. 1961. 'Some data on natural fertility', *Eugenics Quarterly* 8: 81–91.

Hernes, Gudmund. 1972. 'The process of entry into first marriage', *American Sociological Review* 37: 173–82.

Hirschman, Charles. 1994. 'Why fertility changes', *Annual Review of Sociology* 20: 203–33.

Hobart, Charles W. 1984. 'Changing profession and practice of sexual standards: A study of young anglophone and francophone Canadians', *Journal of Comparative Family Studies* 15: 231–55.

Hobcraft, John, Jane Menken, and Samuel Preston. 1982. 'Age, period, and cohort effects in demography: A review', *Population Index* 48: 4–43.

Hoem, Britta, and Jan M. Hoem. 1988. 'The Swedish family: Aspects of contemporary developments', *Journal of Family Issues* 9: 397–424.

Hoem, Jan M. 1986. 'The impact of education on modern family-union initiation', *European Journal of Population* 2: 11–33.

—— and Bo Rennermalm. 1985. 'Modern family initiation in Sweden: Experience of women born between 1936 and 1960', *European Journal of Population* 1: 81–112.

Hogan, Dennis P., and Evelyn M. Kitagawa. 1985. 'The impact of social status, family structure, and neighborhood on the fertility of black adolescents', *American Journal of Sociology* 90: 825–55.

Holden, Karen C., and Pamela J. Smock. 1991. 'The economic costs of marital dissolution: Why do women bear a disproportionate cost?', *Annual Review of Sociology* 17: 51–78.

Holland, Winifred H. 1998. 'Introduction', in Holland and Stalbecker-Pountney (1998: 1–62).

—— and Barbro E. Stalbecker-Pountney, eds. 1998. *Cohabitation: The Law in Canada*. Toronto: Carswell.

Hutchens, Robert M. 1979. 'Welfare, remarriage, and marital search', *American Economic Review* 69: 369–79.

Jones, E.F., J.D. Forrest, N. Goldman, S. Henshaw, R. Lincoln, J.I. Roseoff, C.F. Westoff, and D. Wulf. 1986. *Teenage Pregnancy in Industrialized Countries*. New Haven: Yale University Press.

Kalbfleisch, John P., and Ross L. Prentice. 1980. *The Statistical Analysis of Failure Time Data*. New York: Wiley.

Kiernan, Kathleen E., and Valerie Estaugh. 1993. *Cohabitation: Extra-marital Childbearing and Social Policy*. London: Family Policy Studies Centre.

Knoke, David, and Peter J. Burke. 1980. *Log-linear Models*. Beverly Hills, Calif.: Sage.

Kottak, Conrad P. 1987. *Anthropology: The Exploration of Human Diversity*, 4th edn. New York: Random House.

Kuo, Wen H., and Yung-Mei Tsai. 1986. 'Social networking, hardiness and immigrants' mental health', *Journal of Health and Social Behavior* 27: 133–49.

Landale, Nancy S., and Renata Forste. 1991. 'Patterns of entry into cohabitation and marriage among mainland Puerto Rican women', *Demography* 28: 587–607.

Lasch, Christopher. 1975. 'What the doctor ordered', *New York Review of Books*, 11 Dec., 50–4.

Laumon, B., N. Mamelle, F. Munoz, and A. Measson. 1988. 'Sociodemographic characteristics and intentions for further births in France', *Journal of Biosocial Science* 20: 31–6.

Le Bourdais, Celine, and Nicole Marcil-Gratton. 1996. 'Family transformation across the Canadian/American border: When the laggard becomes the leader', *Journal of Comparative Family Studies* 27: 415–36.

Lee, Elisa T. 1992. *Statistical Methods for Survival Data Analysis*. New York: Wiley.

Leridon, Henri. 1990. 'Cohabitation, marriage, separation: An analysis of life histories of French cohorts from 1968 to 1985', *Population Studies* 44: 127–44.

Lesthaeghe, Ron. 1980. 'On the social control of human reproduction', *Population and Development Review* 6: 527–48.

——. 1983. 'A century of demographic and cultural change in Western Europe: An explanation of underlying dimensions', *Population and Development Review* 9: 411–35.

———. 1998. 'On theory development: Applications to the study of family formation', *Population and Development Review* 24: 1–14.

——— and Johan Surkyn. 1988. 'Cultural dynamics and economic theories of fertility change', *Population and Development Review* 14: 1–45.

Levinger, George. 1976. 'A social psychological perspective on marital dissolution', *Journal of Social Issues* 32: 21–47.

Lichter, Daniel T., Diane K. McLaughlin, George Kephart, and David J. Landry. 1992. 'Race and the retreat from marriage: A shortage of marriageable men?', *American Sociological Review* 57: 781–99.

Liefbroer, Aart C. 1991. 'The choice between a married or unmarried first union by young adults', *European Journal of Population* 7: 273–98.

Lillard, Lee A., Michael J. Brien, and Linda J. Waite, 1995. 'Premarital cohabitation and subsequent marital dissolution: A matter of self-selection?', *Demography* 32: 437–57.

——— and Linda J. Waite. 1993. 'Joint model of marital childbearing and marital disruption', *Demography* 30: 653–81.

Lipset, Seymour M. 1990. *Continental Divide: The Values and Institutions of the United States and Canada*. New York: Routledge.

Little, Roderick J.A., and Donald B. Rubin. 1987. *Statistical Analysis with Missing Data*. New York: Wiley.

Long, J. Scott. 1997. *Regression Models for Categorical and Limited Dependent Variables*. Thousand Oaks, Calif.: Sage.

Macklin, Eleanor D. 1983. 'Nonmarital heterosexual cohabitation: An overview', in Eleanor D. Macklin and Roger H. Rubin, eds, *Contemporary Families and Alternative Lifestyles*. Beverly Hills, Calif.: Sage.

McLanahan, Sara, and Gary Sandefur. 1994. *Growing Up with a Single Parent: What Hurts, What Helps*. Cambridge, Mass.: Harvard University Press.

McLaren, Angus. 1978. 'Birth control and abortion in Canada, 1870–1920', *Canadian Historical Review* 59: 319–40.

McLaughlin, Steven D., et al. 1988. *The Changing Lives of American Women*. Chapel Hill: University of North Carolina Press.

McQuillan, Kevin. 1988. 'Family change and family income in Canada', Working Paper for Canadian Demographic Review Project, University of Western Ontario.

McVey, Wayne E., Jr, and Warren E. Kalbach. 1995. *Canadian Population*. Toronto: Nelson Canada.

Maddala, G.S. 1983. *Limited Dependent and Qualitative Variables in Econometrics*. Cambridge: Cambridge University Press.

Marini, Margaret M. 1978. 'The transition to adulthood: Sex differences in educational attainment and age at marriage', *American Sociological Review* 43: 483–507.

———. 1985. 'Determinants of the timing of adult role entry', *Social Science Research* 14: 309–50.

Marshall, Alfred. 1898. *Principles of Economics*, vol. 1. London: Macmillan.

Mason, Karen Oppenheim, John L. Czajka, and Sara Arber. 1976. 'Change in U.S. women's sex role attitudes, 1964–1974', *American Sociological Review* 41: 573–96.

———— and Anju Malhotra Taj. 1987. 'Differences between women's and men's reproductive goals in developing countries', *Population and Development Review* 3: 611–38.

Menken, Jane. 1985. 'Age and fertility: How late can you wait?', *Demography* 23: 469–83.

Miller, Warren B. 1992. 'Personality traits and developmental experiences as antecedents of childbearing motivation', *Demography* 29: 265–85.

———— and David J. Pasta. 1995. 'Behavioral intentions: Which ones predict fertility behavior in married couples?', *Journal of Applied Social Psychology* 25: 530–55.

Modell, John. 1989. *Into One's Own: From Youth to Adulthood in the United States, 1920–1975.* Berkeley: University of California Press.

Morgan, S. Philip. 1981. 'Intention and uncertainty at later stages of childbearing: The United States, 1965 and 1970', *Demography* 18: 267–85.

————. 1982. 'Parity-specific fertility intention and uncertainty: The United States, 1970 and 1976', *Demography* 19: 315–24.

————, Diane N. Lye, and Gretchen A. Condran. 1988. 'Sons, daughters, and the risk of marital disruption', *American Journal of Sociology* 94: 110–29.

———— and Ronald R. Rindfuss. 1985. 'Marital disruption: Structural and temporal dimensions', *American Journal of Sociology* 90: 1055–77.

———— and Linda J. Waite. 1987. 'Parenthood and the attitudes of young adults', *American Sociological Review* 52: 541–7.

Nam, Charles B. 1994. *Understanding Population Change.* Itasca, Ill.: F.E. Peacock.

Namboodiri, Krishnan, and C.M. Suchindran. 1987. *Life Table Techniques and Their Applications.* San Diego: Academic Press.

Nelson, Forrest D. 1984. 'Efficiency of the two-step estimator for models with endogenous sample selection', *Journal of Econometrics* 24: 181–96.

Nemeth, M. 1994. 'The family', *Maclean's*, 14 June, 30–8.

Newcomb, Paul R. 1979. 'Cohabitation in America: An assessment of consequences', *Journal of Marriage and the Family* 41: 597–603.

Newell, Colin. 1988. *Methods and Models in Demography.* New York: Guilford.

Nock, Steven L. 1995. 'A comparison of marriages and cohabiting relationships', *Journal of Family Issues* 16: 53–76.

Norris, Douglas A. 1990. 'Statistics Canada's General Social Survey', *Society* (Newsletter of the Canadian Sociology and Anthropology Association) 14: 34–5.

Notestein, F.W. 1945. 'Population: In long view', in Theodore W. Schultz, ed., *Food for the World.* Chicago: University of Chicago Press, 36–57.

Ontario Law Reform Commission. 1993. *Report on the Rights and Responsibilities of Cohabitants under the Family Law Act.* Toronto: Ontario Law Reform Commission.

Oppenheimer, Valerie K. 1988. 'A theory of marriage timing', *American Journal of Sociology* 94: 563–91.

————. 1994. 'Women's rising employment and the future of the family in industrial societies', *Population and Development Review* 20: 293–342.

————. 1997. 'Women's employment and the gain to marriage: The specialization and trading model', *Annual Review of Sociology* 23: 431–53.

————, Matthijs Kalmijn, and Nelson Lim. 1997. 'Men's career development and marriage timing during a period of rising inequality', *Demography* 34: 311–30.

Ornstein, Michael D. 1986. 'Regionalism and Canadian political ideology', in Brym (1986a: 47–87).

Pampel, Fred C., and Elizabeth H. Peters. 1995. 'The Easterlin effect', *Annual Review of Sociology* 21: 163–94.

Parsons, Talcott. 1951. *The Social System*. New York: Free Press.

Pepin, Jean-Luc, John P. Robarts, et al. 1979. *A Future Together: Observations and Recommendations*. Vol. 1 of the Report of the Task Force on Canadian Unity. Hull: Ministry of Supply and Services.

Pina, Darlene L., and Vern L. Bengtson. 1993. 'The division of household labour and wives' happiness: Ideology, employment, and perceptions of support', *Journal of Marriage and the Family* 55: 901–12.

Plotnick, Robert. 1992. 'The effects of attitudes on teenage premarital pregnancy and its resolution', *American Sociological Review* 57: 800–11.

Pollard, Michael S., and Zheng Wu. 1998. 'Divergence of marriage patterns in Quebec and elsewhere in Canada', *Population and Development Review* 24: 329–56.

Population Studies Centre. 1988. *Canadian Fertility Survey 1984*. London, Ont.: Population Studies Centre, University of Western Ontario.

Presser, Harriet B. 1994. 'Employment schedules among dual-earner spouses and the division of household labor by gender', *American Sociological Review* 59: 348–64.

Preston, Samuel H. 1986. 'Changing values and falling birth rates', *Population and Development Review* 12 (supplement): 176–95.

Raley, R. Kelly. 1995. 'Why cohabit? Why marry? Some determinants of first union type', paper presented to the annual meeting of the Population Association of America, San Francisco, Apr.

Ramsøy, Natalie R. 1994. 'Non-marital cohabitation and change in norms: The case of Norway', *Acta Sociologica* 37: 23–37.

Rao, K. Vaninadha. 1990. 'Marriage risks, cohabitation and premarital births in Canada', *European Journal of Population* 6: 27–49.

Rindfuss, Ronald R., S. Philip Morgan, and Gray Swicegood. 1988. *First Births in America: Changes in the Timing of Parenthood*. Berkeley: University of California Press.

——— and Audrey VandenHeuvel. 1990. 'Cohabitation: A precursor to marriage or an alternative to being single', *Population and Development Review* 16: 703–26.

Rocher, Guy. 1987. 'A half-century of cultural evolution in Quebec', in Michael Behiels, ed., *Quebec Since 1945: Selected Readings*. Toronto: Copp Clark Pitman, 289–99.

Roelants, Dominique. 1998. 'Cohabitation and Domestic Labour', Master's thesis, University of Victoria.

Rogers, Stacy J., and Paul R. Amato. 1997. 'Is marital quality declining? The evidence from two generations', *Social Forces* 75: 1089–100.

Ross, Catherine E. 1987. 'The division of labor at home', *Social Forces* 65: 816–33.

Ryder, Norman B. 1965. 'The cohort as a concept in the study of social change', *American Sociological Review* 30: 843–61.

———. 1969. 'The emergence of a modern fertility pattern: United States, 1917–66', in Samuel J. Behrman, Leslie Corsa, Jr, and Ronald Freedman, eds, *Fertility and Family Planning: A World View*. Ann Arbor: University of Michigan Press, 99–123.

———. 1980. 'Where do babies come from?', in Hubert M. Blalock, ed., *Sociological Theory and Research: A Critical Appraisal*. New York: Free Press, 189–202.

———. 1983. 'Cohort and period measures of changing fertility', in Rodolfo A. Bulatao and Ronald D. Lee, eds, *Determinants of Fertility in Developing Countries*. New York: Academic Press, 737–56.

Sander, William. 1993. 'Catholicism and marriage in the United States', *Demography* 30: 373–84.

Sarantakos, S. 1984. *Living Together in Australia*. Melbourne: Longman Cheshire.

Schoen, Robert. 1989. 'Whither the family', *Contemporary Sociology* 18: 618–20.

———, Young J. Kim, Constance A. Nathanson, Jason M. Fields, and Nan M. Astone. 1997. 'Why do Americans want children', *Population and Development Review* 23: 333–58.

Seltzer, Judith A. 1994. 'Consequences of marital dissolution for children', *Annual Review of Sociology* 20: 235–66.

Shelton, Beth Ann, and Daphne John. 1993. 'Does marital status make a difference? Housework among married and cohabiting men and women', *Journal of Family Issues* 14: 401–20.

Shorter, Edward. 1975. *The Making of the Modern Family*. New York: Basic Books.

Shryock, Henry S., Jacob Siegel, et al. 1971. *The Methods and Materials of Demography*. Washington: US Bureau of the Census.

Sloane, Douglas M., and Che-Fu Lee. 1983. 'Sex of previous children and intentions for further births in the United States, 1965–1976', *Demography* 20: 353–67.

Smith, Ken R., Cathleen D. Zick, and Greg J. Duncan. 'Remarriage patterns among recent widows and widowers', *Demography* 28: 361–74.

South, Scott J., and Glenna Spitze. 1986. 'Determinants of divorce over the marital life course', *American Sociological Review* 51: 583–90.

——— and ———. 1994. 'Housework in marital and nonmarital households', *American Sociological Review* 59: 327–47.

Spanier, Graham B. 1985. 'Cohabitation in the 1980s', in Davis (1985a: 91–111).

Spitze, Glenna. 1988. 'Women's employment and family relations: A review', *Journal of Marriage and the Family* 50: 595–618.

Stafford, Rebecca, Elaine Backman, and Pamela Dibona. 1976. 'The division of labor among cohabiting and married couples', *Journal of Marriage and the Family* 39: 43–57.

Statistics Canada. 1976. *Canada's Religious Composition*. Catalogue no. 999–710. Ottawa: Statistics Canada.

———. 1986. *Births and Deaths, 1986*. Catalogue no. 84–204. Ottawa: Statistics Canada.

———. 1989. *User's Guide to 1986 Census Data on Families*. Catalogue no. 99–113E. Ottawa: Statistics Canada.

———. 1990. *Earnings of Men and Women, 1989*. Catalogue no. 13–217. Ottawa: Statistics Canada.

———. 1991. *1990 General Social Survey—Cycle 5: Family and Friends: Public Use Microdata File Documentation and User's Guide*. Ottawa: Statistics Canada.

———. 1995a. *Women in Canada: A Statistical Report*, 3rd edn. Catalogue no. 89–503E. Ottawa: Statistics Canada.

————. 1995b. *Focus for the Future—Census 1996* 10, 1 (Summer). Ottawa: Statistics Canada.

————. 1997a. *Household Facilities and Equipment, 1997*. Catalogue no. 64–202–XPB. Ottawa: Statistics Canada.

————. 1997b. *1996 Census Handbook*. Catalogue no. 92–352–XPE. Ottawa: Statistics Canada.

————. 1997c. *1995 General Social Survey, Cycle 10: The Family: Public Use Microdata File Documentation and User's Guide*. Catalogue no. 12–M0010–GPE. Ottawa: Statistics Canada.

————. 1997d. *Annual Labour Force Averages 1996*. Catalogue no. 71–220. Ottawa: Statistics Canada.

————. 1998. *Earnings of Men and Women, 1996*. Catalogue no. 13–217. Ottawa: Statistics Canada.

————. 1999. 'Births', *The Daily*, 16 June.

Stolzenberg, Ross M., and Daniel A. Relles. 1990. 'Theory testing in a world of constrained research design: The significance of Heckman's censored sampling bias correction for nonexperimental research', *Sociological Methods and Research* 18: 395–415.

———— and ————. 1997. 'Tools for intuition about sample selection bias and its correction', *American Sociological Review* 62: 494–507.

Suitor, J. Jill. 1991. 'Marital quality and satisfaction with the division of domestic labour across the family life cycle', *Journal of Marriage and the Family* 49: 483–97.

Sweet, James A., and Larry L. Bumpass. 1987. *American Families and Households*. New York: Russell Sage.

———— and ————. 1990. 'Young adults' views of marriage, cohabitation, and family', paper prepared for conference on Demographic Perspectives on the American Family: Patterns and Prospects, Department of Sociology, State University of New York at Albany, 6–7 Apr.

Tan, Poo Chang, and Nai Peng Tey. 1994. 'Do fertility intentions predict subsequent behavior? Evidence from Peninsular Malaysia', *Studies in Family Planning* 25: 222–31.

Tanfer, Koray. 1987. 'Patterns of premarital cohabitation among never-married women in the United States', *Journal of Marriage and the Family* 49: 484–97.

Taylor, Charles. 1985. *Philosophy and the Human Societies*. Cambridge: Cambridge University Press.

Teachman, Jay D., and Karen A. Polonko. 1990. 'Cohabitation and marital stability in the United States', *Social Forces* 69: 207–20.

Thomas, B. Helen, Alba DiCenso, and Lauren Griffith. 1998. 'Adolescent sexual behaviour: Results from an Ontario sample. Part I: Adolescent sexual activity', *Canadian Journal of Public Health* 89: 90–3.

Thomson, Elizabeth. 1997. 'Couple childbearing desires, intentions, and births', *Demography* 34: 343–54.

———— and Ugo Colella. 1992. 'Cohabitation and marital stability: Quality or commitment?', *Journal of Marriage and the Family* 54: 259–67.

Thornton, Arland. 1985. 'Changing attitudes toward separation and divorce: Causes and consequences', *American Journal of Sociology* 90: 856–72.

————. 1988. 'Cohabitation and marriage in the 1980s', *Demography* 25: 497–508.

————. 1991. 'Influence of the marital history of parents on the marital and cohabitational experiences of children', *American Journal of Sociology* 96: 868–94.

————, Duane F. Alwin, and Donald Camburn. 1983. 'Causes and consequences of sex-role attitudes and attitude change', *American Sociological Review* 48: 211–27.

————, William G. Axinn, and Daniel H. Hill. 1992. 'Reciprocal effects of religiosity, cohabitation, and marriage', *American Journal of Sociology* 98: 628–51.

————, ————, and Jay D. Teachman. 1995. 'The influence of school enrollment and accumulation on cohabitation and marriage in early adulthood', *American Sociological Review* 60: 762–74.

———— and Donald Camburn. 1989. 'Religious participation and adolescent sexual behavior and attitudes', *Journal of Marriage and the Family* 51: 641–53.

———— and Deborah Freedman. 1979. 'Changes in the sex role attitudes of women, 1962–1977: Evidence from a panel study', *American Sociological Review* 44: 831–42.

———— and ————. 1982. 'Changing attitudes toward marriage and single life', *Family Planning Perspectives* 14: 297–303.

Trost, Jan. 1975. 'Married and unmarried cohabitation: The case of Sweden, with some comparisons', *Journal of Marriage and the Family* 37: 677–82.

————. 1978. 'A renewed social institution: Non-marital cohabitation', *Acta Sociologica* 21: 303–15.

————. 1980. 'Cohabitation without marriage in Sweden', in John M. Eekelaar and Sanford N. Katz, eds, *Marriage and Cohabitation in Contemporary Societies: Areas of Legal, Social and Ethical Change*. Toronto: Butterworths, 16–22.

Turcotte, Pierre, and Frances K. Goldscheider. 1998. 'Evolution of factors influencing first union formation in Canada', *Canadian Studies in Population* 25: 145–73.

Udry, J. Richard. 1974. *Social Context of Marriage*, 3rd edn. Philadelphia: J.B. Lippincott.

Uhlenberg, Peter. 1989. 'Remarriage: A life-cycle perspective', in E. Grebenik, C. Hohn, and R. Mackensen, eds, *Later Phases of the Family Cycle*. Oxford: Oxford University Press, 66–82.

United Nations. 1963. *Determinants and Consequences of Population Trends*. New York: UN.

————. 1982. *Model Life Tables for Developing Countries*. New York: UN.

van de Kaa, Dirk J. 1987. 'Europe's second demographic transition', *Population Bulletin* 42: 3–17.

Vander Zanden, James W. 1985. *Human Development*, 3rd edn. New York: Knopf.

Veevers, Jean E. 1979. 'Voluntary childlessness: A review of issues and evidence', *Marriage and the Family Review* 2: 3–26.

Waite, Linda J., Frances K. Goldscheider, and Christina Witsberger. 1986. 'Nonfamily living and the erosion of traditional family orientations among young adults', *American Sociological Review* 51: 541–54.

———— and Lee A. Lillard. 1991. 'Children and marital disruption', *American Journal of Sociology* 96: 930–53.

Wallerstein, Judith S., and Joan B. Kelly. 1980. *Surviving the Breakup: How Children and Parents Cope with Divorce*. New York: Basic Books.

Watkins, Susan C. 1986. 'Regional patterns of nuptiality in Western Europe', in Coale and Watkins (1986: 314–36).

Weeks, John R. 1996. *Population: An Introduction to Concepts and Issues*, 6th edn. Belmont, Calif.: Wadsworth.

Westoff, Charles F. 1978. 'Some speculations on the future of marriage and fertility', *Family Planning Perspectives* 10: 79–83.

———. 1983. 'Fertility decline in the West: Causes and prospects', *Population and Development Review* 9: 99–104.

———. 1990. 'Reproductive intentions and fertility rates', *International Family Planning Perspectives* 16: 84–96.

——— and Norman B. Ryder. 1977. 'The predictive validity of reproductive intentions', *Demography* 14: 431–53.

Wu, Lawrence L., and Brian C. Martinson. 1993. 'Family structure and the risk of a premarital birth', *American Sociological Review* 58: 210–32.

Wu, Zheng. 1992. 'A social psychological analysis of remarriage', Ph.D. dissertation, University of Western Ontario.

———. 1994. 'Remarriage in Canada: A social exchange perspective', *Journal of Divorce and Remarriage* 21: 191–224.

———. 1995. 'Remarriage after widowhood: A marital history study of older Canadians', *Canadian Journal on Aging* 14: 719–36.

———. 1996. 'Childbearing in cohabitation relationships', *Journal of Marriage and the Family* 58: 281–92.

———. 1999a. *Fertility and Family Surveys in Countries of the ECE Region: Standard Country Report—Canada*. New York and Geneva: United Nations.

———. 1999b. 'Premarital cohabitation and the timing of first marriage', *Canadian Review of Sociology and Anthropology* 36: 109–27.

——— and Douglas E. Baer. 1996. 'Attitudes toward family life and gender roles: A comparison of English and French Canadian women', *Journal of Comparative Family Studies* 27: 437–52.

——— and T.R. Balakrishnan. 1994. 'Cohabitation after marital dissolution in Canada', *Journal of Marriage and the Family* 56: 723–34.

——— and ———. 1995. 'Dissolution of premarital cohabitation in Canada', *Demography* 32: 521–32.

——— and Hui Wang. 1998. 'Third birth intentions and uncertainty in Canada', *Social Biology* 45: 96–112.

Wunsch, Guillaume J., and Marc G. Termote. 1978. *Introduction to Demographic Analysis: Principles and Methods*. New York: Plenum.

Zelnik, M., and J.F. Kantner. 1980. 'Sexual activity, contraceptive use and pregnancy among metropolitan area teenagers: 1971–1979', *Family Planning Perspectives* 12: 229–33.

Index

The *Studies in Canadian Population* Series

Ellen M. Gee and
Gloria Gutman (EDITORS)
The Overselling of Population Aging:
Apocalyptic Demography, Intergenerational
Challenges, and Social Policy, 2000
ISBN 0-19-541465-9

Zheng Wu
Cohabitation: An Alternative Form of
Family Living, 2000
ISBN 0-19-541378-4